MW01194412

The
Divided
North

A Volume in the Series

BLACK NEW ENGLAND

Edited by
Kabria Baumgartner, Kerri Greenidge,
Jared Ross Hardesty, and Nicole Maskiell

The Divided North

BLACK *and* WHITE FAMILIES *in the* AGE *of* SLAVERY

CAROL GARDNER

University of Massachusetts Press

AMHERST AND BOSTON

Copyright © 2025 by University of Massachusetts Press
All rights reserved
Printed in the United States of America

ISBN 978-1-62534-874-6 (paper); 875-3 (hardcover)

Designed by Sally Nichols
Set in Adobe Caslon Pro
Printed and bound by Books International, Inc.

Cover design by adam b. bohannon
Cover art by William Bache, *Silhouettes of unidentified
Black and White men and women*, c. 1804–1806.
—National Portrait Gallery, Smithsonian Institution;
partial gift of Sarah Bache Bloise. cco

Library of Congress Cataloging-in-Publication Data
A catalog record for this book is available from the Library of Congress.

British Library Cataloguing-in-Publication Data
A catalog record for this book is available from the British Library.

For Portland

Contents

Illustrations

A Note on Language

I've capitalized *Black* and *White* throughout the text where it refers to race. When referring to persons, *Black* conveys a unique ethnic, social and historical identity. Both the Associated Press (AP) and *The New York Times* capitalize it for those reasons. They do not capitalize *white* because, as the AP says, "capitalizing the term white, as is done by white supremacists, risks subtly conveying legitimacy to such beliefs."[1] *The New York Times* has argued that "white doesn't represent a shared culture and history the way Black does, and also has long been capitalized by hate groups."[2]

There are very good reasons to try to overcome hate groups' influence over language, and many organizations seem to agree. The National Association of Black Journalists, for example, "recommends that whenever a color is used to appropriately describe race, then it should be capitalized within the proper context, including White and Brown."[3] As Kristen Mack and John Palfry of the MacArthur Foundation have written, "choosing to not capitalize White while capitalizing other racial and ethnic identifiers would implicitly affirm Whiteness as the standard and norm."[4] Similarly, the Center for the Study of Social Policy contends that "the detachment of 'White' as a proper noun allows White people to sit out of conversations about race and removes accountability from White people's and White institutions' involvement in racism."[5]

I agree with these arguments. In American society especially, lowercasing *White* casts whiteness as the norm and helps to conceal White persons' responsibility for the social divisions caused by race. That's why I've chosen to capitalize both *Black* and *White* when they refer to individuals, their culture, or their institutions. I sometimes use the term *African American*, particularly when I'm sure that the individuals were born in or were citizens of the United States. I also use it as an adjective to describe certain institutions founded by and for Black Americans.

To acknowledge the humanity of individuals in bondage, I've tried to avoid using *slave* as a noun. I do, however, frequently use it as an adjective (as in *slave captain*, *slaveowner*, *slave state*, and *slave ship*) because I believe it graphically conveys the many ways in which people of all backgrounds and walks of life were complicit in what Frederick Douglass called "the bloody traffic."

Acknowledgments

I thank Bob Greene, native Mainer, journalist, historian, and descendent of the Rubys for his generosity in sharing all sorts of information about Maine's Black history and the Ruby family.

I also thank Michael Daicy, retired Portland firefighter and department historian and archivist at the Portland Fire Museum, for clarifying details about Portland's Great Fire of 1866 and William Ruby's firefighting career.

Abraham Schecter of the Portland Public Library was very helpful during my multiple visits to the Portland Room and Special Collections. By archiving historic photos, he has done Portland a tremendous service.

I also thank the staff at the Brown Research Library of the Maine Historical Society.

Special thanks go to Xavier Comas for his patience, his many incisive comments on multiple drafts, and his moral support throughout the writing of the book.

I'm grateful to Andreu Comas for designing the maps that illuminate the narrative, and his incisive comments on the text and the title.

Alex Comas's graphic renderings of the Ruby and Gordon family trees and his input on the title were tremendously helpful, as were his comments on parts of the text.

Joann Gardner provided particularly helpful comments on early drafts of the opening chapters.

Ruby Family

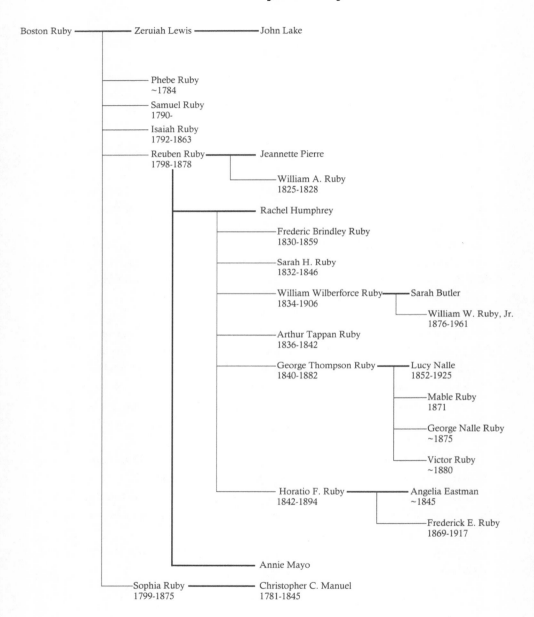

FIGURE I. The Ruby family tree.

Gordon Family

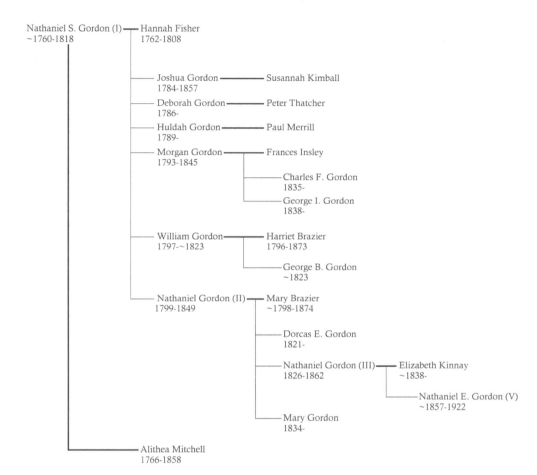

FIGURE 2. The Gordon family tree.

The
Divided
North

Family Portraits in Black and White

To understand the issues that divided nineteenth-century America—
and, in many ways, still divide the nation—few have looked to
the far North. In racial terms, northern New England has always been
among the Whitest sections of the country. Even today, that Whiteness
serves as a barrier: a reason for writing off its African American communities as too small to be significant, a reason for underestimating the
region's role in slavery. But the size of communities has little to do with
their significance or influence. And the "Free North" was in fact a critical proving ground for American notions of freedom and equality: as
telling as any town, plantation, state capital, or battlefield in the South.
To fully grasp the dynamics and magnitude of any powerful storm, one
must look beyond the eye.

During the 1800s, members of the Ruby family of Portland, Maine,
were prominent antislavery activists and operatives on the Underground
Railroad. Their neighbors, the Gordons, were well-to-do shipmasters
and owners: among them, the most notorious American slave captain of
the century. Although these two families were absent from history books
for nearly a century, their lives and accomplishments offer a detailed portrait of life in the Free North when slavery enthralled the nation.

Born eleven months apart in 1798 and 1799, Reuben Ruby and Nathaniel Gordon II spent much of their boyhoods roaming Portland's cobbled
streets and noisy, bustling waterfront. They lived just blocks from one
another, likely attended school together, and attended the same church
with their families. But they were worlds apart, separated by family culture and race: Reuben Ruby was Black, and Nathaniel Gordon was White.

At church, the Rubys were required to sit in the balcony, while the Gordons occupied the more coveted pews below. At school, masters directed their attention to White boys, who were expected to make something of themselves. Nathaniel was free to pursue any profession; Reuben's prospects were largely limited to unskilled manual labor. Both could go to sea as mariners, but only Nathaniel could expect to become master of a ship.

When the two were in their early twenties, Maine won its battle for statehood and embarked on a struggle to define its identity. Despite declaring itself a free state, it could not escape the contentious political and social environment caused by slavery. The Missouri Compromise of 1820, which admitted Maine and Missouri as free and slave states, stitched together the union's fraying fabric for another forty years. Yet the Compromise embodied the deep divisions among Americans everywhere: the push and pull of Black and White, freedom and slavery, ethics and economics, of a nation founded on equality that sought to preserve a perennial underclass.

Before the Civil War, the fault lines dividing the nation also divided communities. In Portland, those fault lines ran between houses and down the middle of streets. The town was home to a small group of committed abolitionists; their neighbors considered them radical extremists. The town's half-dozen newspapers took a variety of stances on abolition and civil rights for Blacks. Though virtually no enslaved persons labored in Maine after 1783, the district's maritime industry, among the most lucrative in the nation, benefited handsomely from building ships to bring captive Africans to the Americas and from trading in goods produced by enslaved laborers. And Portland would have the dubious distinction of producing the only U.S. citizen to be convicted and hanged for transporting Africans into slavery: Nathaniel Gordon III.*

History has a double edge. It can be a tool for reanimating and reexperiencing the past—or for burying it. And sometimes our collective memory fails us. We remember General Joshua Chamberlain for his heroics at Gettysburg. We forget that, as governor of Maine, he signed only one death warrant—for Clifton Harris, a young African American man convicted of murder—while commuting the sentences of thirty-five White criminals convicted of similar offenses.[1] We remember General

---

* The family produced numerous generations of Nathaniel Gordons, so in documenting four generations, I've avoided the confusion of *Jr.* and *Sr.*, using instead *I* for the Revolutionary veteran, *II* for his sea-captain son, *III* for the slave trader and sea captain, and *IV* for the diver.

O. O. Howard as a committed abolitionist who led the Freedmen's Bureau and established the illustrious historically Black university in Washington, D.C., that bears his name. We forget that he ordered the Nez Perce off their lands and onto reservations: that he and his army pursued Native men, women, and children for months as they fled over the Rockies toward Canada. Before the Civil War, Maine's abolitionists were verbally and physically attacked in newspapers, meeting halls, and streets. After the war, they were remembered as leaders of a unified North. "Those who had been classed as fanatics," wrote W. E. B. Du Bois in 1935, "who had been left out of the society of the respected, and mobbed, North, East, and West, suddenly became the moral justification by which the North marched onto victory."[2]

Many thousands of individuals, obscure and otherwise, drive society in one direction or another through collective action, complicity, acquiescence, and defiance, and society makes conscious choices to remember some but not others. This book seeks to recover some of what has been forgotten: in particular, what it was like to live in the North throughout the turbulent nineteenth century. It tells that story through the lenses of two families who played important but opposing roles: abetting and advocating against slavery. Their lives—as activists, traders, agents on the Underground Railroad, soldiers, slave captains, blockade runners, prospectors, and politicians—took them to New York, California, Texas, Louisiana, Africa, Cuba, Haiti, Colombia, and Brazil.

The Rubys and Gordons were neither typical nor symbolic of their races, their culture, or their times. In some ways, both families were outliers. Their passions drew them into dangerous and life-threatening situations that most other people assiduously avoided. They were real individuals who had real impacts on society: characters who were well known among their contemporaries but whose prominence quickly faded. Their lives recalled a period of upheaval, conflict, and shame that Americans were anxious to forget.

Family occupies a prominent place in this narrative. It is, after all, the key building block of culture. Like clans, religious and political groups, movements, and militias, families form small but powerful forces in society. What they celebrate and promote, tolerate or forbid influences their neighbors, communities, and sometimes, the nation. Rhode Island's DeWolf and Brown families made New England a powerful player in the slave trade of the late eighteenth and early nineteenth centuries. Thomas Jefferson no doubt had them in mind when he wrote that "our northern brethren . . . have very few slaves themselves yet they ha[ve] been pretty considerable carriers of them to others."[3] In contrast, the Adams family of Massachusetts and the Fessendens of Maine created political dynasties based on a strong belief in democracy and a strong distaste for the institution of slavery—though they did not go so far as to advocate for full racial equality. In Portland, the Dow, Winslow, Thomas, and Hussey families produced committed abolitionists over several generations.

The Gordons and Rubys were no different. Slave captain Nathaniel Gordon was born into a family of Yankee merchant sailors who valued risk, independence, and monetary gain and knowingly flouted the law. Reuben Ruby's antislavery activism and political engagement were no doubt inspired by his parents' enslavement, and his drive for equality was reflected in his sons: all who survived to adulthood were voters, party members, politicians, and equal rights activists.

Hailing from a free state meant that, despite race, both the Gordons and Rubys had choices. But both were products of their era. Neither they, nor their community, nor the North as a whole were free from the conflicts and contradictions of their times. These families—neighbors throughout much of the century—followed contradictory paths. But like all Americans, they were chained together like captives on the same tumultuous voyage.

INVENTED IN 1838, THE stereoscope was a popular device for viewing landmarks, vistas, and domestic scenes. With two lenses and two images offering right- and left-eye views, it allowed the viewer to see a three-dimensional image with enhanced depth and perspective. Similarly, *The Divided North* seeks to offer an in-depth portrayal of time and place. By following the actions and experiences of two families—how they were shaped by and responded to the events, trends, and society around them—the narrative seeks to sharpen, enhance, and adjust popular notions of the Free North. As families and individuals, the Rubys and Gordons help us to explore issues of slavery and freedom, racism and equality in America—topics that seem endlessly compelling, but never sufficiently understood. They help reveal what it meant to live in a free state, with all the promise, disappointment, irony, and hope that the notion entailed.

CHAPTER I

Free State

Nobody can tell the thousand ways in which by trade, by family affinity, or by political expediency, the free part of our country is constantly tempted to complicity with the slaveholding part.

—Harriet Beecher Stowe, letter to Lord Carlisle, 1852[†]

In the wake of the American Revolution, two former enslaved persons in the far north of the new nation experienced their first taste of freedom. In late 1783, Boston Ruby and Zeruiah Lewis married. Recently released from servitude, they had plenty to celebrate: no longer the property of others, they could control their own futures, and their children would be among the first generation of African Americans to be born free in the Massachusetts District of Maine.

That same year, Nathaniel Gordon, a White resident of Maine, married Hannah Fisher, and the two began a family of their own. Nathaniel had served as a private in the Continental Army.[1] He and some 230,000 soldiers across thirteen colonies had risked their property, lives, and livelihoods to launch a new nation, governed not by a monarch, but by the people. The patriots had succeeded against very long odds.

Yet for all their achievements, every generation leaves unfinished business behind. The new American states, proclaiming themselves united, responded in markedly different ways to advancing the values of freedom and equality that had birthed their independence. The inability of citizens and state and federal governments to resolve those differences, particularly on matters of slavery and race, would launch a new century of upheaval and strife. The descendants of Boston and Zeruiah Ruby and Nathaniel and Hannah Gordon would play important—and opposing—roles in this looming conflict.

FEW RECORDS SURVIVE TO tell us where Boston Ruby and Zeruiah
Lewis came from, who had owned them, or what they had done for
work while enslaved. We know little about the privations they suffered,
only that they were considered chattel and were at others' disposal every
waking moment of their lives. But their marriage on December 6, 1783,
in New Gloucester, Maine, marked a new beginning for the couple. That
year also marked a watershed in American history.[2] In April, a Massachusetts court declared that slavery was inconsistent with the commonwealth's constitution. As a district of Massachusetts, Maine, too, fell
under the ruling. In September, the Treaty of Paris certified the end of
colonial rule: the United States was a free and independent nation in the
eyes of the world. No matter how humble the ceremony, Boston's and
Zeruiah's marriage must have been a moment of great joy, brimming
with promise. Suddenly, the couple were free to marry, to work for themselves or for others, to earn wages, to own property, and to have children
who were neither property of a master nor subjects of a king.

New Gloucester lies twenty-five miles inland from present-day Portland. In the late eighteenth century, it was a rural settlement with roll-
ing hills, rich farmland, woods, fast-running streams, and a lake that
the newly established Shaker community called Sabbath Day Lake. The
Shakers were attracted to the remote, rural character of New Gloucester;
there, they meant to create a self-contained, self-sufficient community
with little outside interference.

But what were Blacks doing in this remote Maine town in 1783?
They or their forebears had been brought by force from Africa or the
Caribbean and deposited thousands of miles from their homes in the
midst of a wholly unfamiliar landscape with dense evergreen forests,
deep winter snows, and lakes and rivers that froze solid from October
to April. Throughout most of the seventeenth and eighteenth centuries,
involuntary immigrants of African descent could be found in dozens of
rural Maine communities. Like most of the thirteen original colonies,
Massachusetts—and thus Maine—had sanctioned slavery before the
Revolution. Many influential and wealthy White families in the North
held people in bondage: the Faneuils and Hancocks of Massachusetts;
Rhode Island's Brown brothers; and the Pepperell, Pendleton, and Shap-
leigh families in the District of Maine. Middle-class families enslaved

others, too. While enslaved, Boston and Zeruiah may have helped with farm labor and lumbering; assisted tradespeople; helped to cook, clean, spin, weave, and run the household; planted gardens; brewed beer and cider; and cared for small children. Though most Black individuals had been brought to the district in bondage, by 1800, 818 free people of African heritage were living in ninety-two towns and rural areas across Maine.[3]

Freedom for northern Blacks was a disjointed affair. Some men had earned their freedom by taking their masters' places in the Continental Army. And during and after the Revolution, northern states and jurisdictions began to question, litigate, and overturn laws regarding human bondage. Vermont outlawed slavery in 1777, before becoming a state. Pennsylvania followed in 1780; Massachusetts and New Hampshire in 1783; and Connecticut in 1784. Rhode Island and New Jersey passed gradual emancipation laws in 1784 and 1804.[4] New York, whose booming port relied heavily on cotton traffic between the American South and England, enacted a series of tentative, tortuous emancipation laws. A 1799 law freed Black children born after July 4, 1799, but forced them into indentures until they were young adults. In 1817, a new law established that enslaved people born before 1799 would be free, but not until 1827.[5]

In Massachusetts and the District of Maine, slavery didn't end as a result of a vote or decree by well-meaning lawmakers. Instead, several intrepid enslaved individuals demanded their freedom in court and won. In *Brom and Bett v. John Ashley, Esq.* (1781), Elizabeth "Mumbet" Freeman and Brom, with no known last name, sued their master, John Ashley, of Sheffield, Massachusetts. Freeman had overheard Ashley discussing the new Massachusetts Constitution, written by John Adams, and immediately understood its potential. In court, Freeman's attorney argued that slavery was contrary to the intent of the document, which stated, "All men are born free and equal, and have certain natural, essential, and unalienable rights; among which may be reckoned the right of enjoying and defending their lives and liberties; that of acquiring, possessing, and protecting property; in fine, that of seeking and obtaining their safety and happiness."[6]

In the North, at least, the words of the Declaration of Independence reverberated throughout the new state constitutions, forcing each state to grapple with the meaning of phrases like "all men are born free and equal." Freeman was convinced that the phrase included her, and a Massachusetts court agreed. Ashley, her former master, had intended to appeal, but a series of new trials involving another enslaved individual, Quock Walker, convinced him that it was pointless.

Quock Walker lived in Barre, Massachusetts, and was the property of Isabell Caldwell. Although she and her late husband, James Caldwell, had promised to free Walker when he turned twenty-five, her new husband, Nathaniel Jennison, refused to honor that promise. So Walker ran away to the Caldwell sons' home nearby, where he began working for wages. Jennison brought him back and beat him severely for leaving. But Walker wasn't deterred; he sued Jennison for assault and battery, stating that he was a free man. The court agreed. Jennison, in turn, sued the Caldwell brothers for sheltering Walker, saying they had enticed "his servant" to abscond. In that case, Jennison won a settlement for £25.

In yet a third trial, the state attorney general prosecuted Jennison for assault and battery of Walker. In that case, Chief Justice William Cushing of the Massachusetts Supreme Judicial Court declared that slavery was incompatible with the new state constitution: "Perpetual servitude can no longer be tolerated in our government," wrote Cushing, "and liberty can only be forfeited by some criminal conduct or relinquished by personal consent or contract." Jennison was convicted of assault and forced to pay forty shillings in damages. Quock Walker was declared free.[7]

None of these trials ended slavery in Massachusetts overnight. But Black individuals began to sue for freedom or simply walk away from their enslavers, and enslavers understood that winning them back through the courts was unlikely. According to the 1790 federal census taken nine years after the trials, 6,001 Blacks were living in Massachusetts and Maine; none were enslaved. Other records show that a few enslaved persons could still be found after this time in Maine and Massachusetts, but their numbers had practically disappeared.[8]

THE MASSACHUSETTS COURT RULINGS meant that Boston and Zeruiah Ruby owned themselves, their children, and their labor. But they and other northern Blacks still faced segregation and discrimination in housing, schools, churches, ships, stagecoaches, public houses, and inns. They had only limited freedom of movement. Settling in many states was forbidden, and even Massachusetts prohibited Blacks who were not citizens from staying longer than two months; in 1800, Boston selectmen warned 239 free Blacks that they must leave.[9]

Discrimination wasn't their only worry. Free Black individuals were being kidnapped and re-enthralled in states where slavery remained legal. In 1788, five years after slavery had virtually ended in Massachusetts, the legislature found it necessary to pass a law that prevented those of African heritage from being "privately carried off by force, or decoyed away under various pretences, by evil minded persons, and with probable intent of being sold as slaves."[10]

Even in the far North, free Blacks could still be bonded out as servants and apprentices, and if they ran away, they could be pursued, jailed, or forcibly returned to their masters. In 1802, John Goodwin of Portland placed this advertisement in a local paper:

> THIRTY DOLLARS REWARD. Ran away from the house of John Goodwin, of this town, on the night of the 2nd inst. a *Negro Servant Girl*, coal black, with large eyes, wears large ear rings, with a tear under one of her ears, about 17 years old, short thick made, and was dressed in either striped Holland or spotted Calico.—The above reward will be given for apprehending her, & lodging her in Prison, or bringing her to the house above named.[11]

The advertisement echoed runaway notices throughout the South and border states. It offered money for the young woman's return, gave a very detailed description of her appearance, but didn't bother with her name.

EARLY CENSUS REPORTS FROM rural Cumberland County, Maine, reveal a growing Ruby family, a fledgling Black community in the neighboring towns of Gray and New Gloucester, and the disappearance of outright slavery. The first U.S. census of 1790 records "Boston Black" as a head of household in New Gloucester, living with four "other free persons"—the phrase used for free non-White individuals.[12] They were the only Black residents in town. Census takers were notorious for taking poetic license with names, so "Boston Black" was most likely Boston Ruby, who was elsewhere recorded as "Boston Ruben." The "other free persons" would have been his wife Zeruiah, their six-year-old daughter Phebe, and two unnamed family members or housemates.[13]

The birth of Boston and Zeruiah's third son, Reuben, on December 28, 1798, places the family in the neighboring town of Gray.[14] The 1800 census notes that "Boston Ruby" was living there with eight "other free persons." These included Zeruiah, their five children—Reuben, Samuel, Isaiah, Phebe, and Sophia—and two others. Two other Black families lived nearby, one headed by Michael Frazer, with five additional family members; the other, by James Boaz, an African American landowner and Revolutionary War veteran, with seven.[15]

What brought these free Black families to Gray? Even today, the town is rural, so it's possible that all were involved in farm labor. But Gray also supported lumbermills and granite quarries, and seven years before Reuben Ruby was born, the Englishman Samuel Mayall established North America's first water-powered woolen mill on Collyer Brook, helping to launch America's Industrial Revolution.

Mayall had left England with the plans for building such an operation, but his countrymen were jealous of anyone who might try to steal the

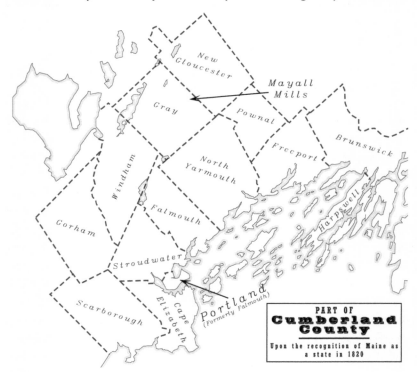

FIGURE 3. Gray and New Gloucester, Maine, where the Ruby family lived through 1800, are located some twenty-five miles from Portland. Mayall Mills (1791–1902), was located near the border of the two towns. Map by Andreu Comas. Used with permission.

technology, take it abroad, and compete with them on the woven goods markets. After he settled in Gray, Mayall received two packages from England: one contained a brand-new hat with pins laced with poison, and another held pistols rigged to fire when the box was opened. But Mayall survived and succeeded, and his mill ultimately employed twenty hands. The Rubys, Frazers, and Boazes may have helped to build its two original wooden structures or worked in scouring, carding, or spinning the wool; they may have even helped raise sheep to provide wool for processing.[16]

MARRIAGE RECORDS TELL US that Zeruiah Ruby was from Falmouth, Maine—now known as Portland—and that her family name was Lewis. But that's all we know of her background. Here's what we do know: after twenty years of marriage to Boston Ruby, Zeruiah became a widow. The prospects for any widow at the time were extremely challenging: particularly so for a woman of color with five children, four of whom were between the ages of five and thirteen. Zeruiah was likely illiterate and owned no property. So on December 1, 1804, she did the only thing she could to secure a future for herself and her children: she married again. Her second husband was John Lake. Like Zeruiah, John was widowed with small children and was a former resident of New Gloucester. By the date of their marriage, John and Zeruiah were living in Portland; with 4,000 residents, it was Maine's largest town.[17]

There is no telling what Reuben Ruby, who was nearly six years old when his mother remarried, thought of his new stepfather. But Reuben knew that, unlike him, John Lake was White.[18] Massachusetts had banned interracial marriages in 1705 and had reaffirmed the law in 1786, but that didn't prevent such unions from happening.[19] In fact, John and Zeruiah were married by a prominent White citizen: Samuel Freeman, a delegate to the Massachusetts Provincial Congress, justice of the peace, and postmaster in Portland.[20]

In 1821, seventeen years after the couple married, Maine, as a newly independent state, outlawed interracial marriages and nullified such marriages already existing. Whether John and Zeruiah lived to see this happen or not, we don't know; both disappeared from the records after their marriage.[21] But the Ruby children didn't disappear. Eldest daughter Phebe married Peter Green, and later, James Murray, and lived in

Portland. Son Samuel became a farmer in New Gloucester, and his younger brother Isaiah worked as a mariner and laborer in Portland. Daughter Sophia married a successful barber, Christopher Manuel, and the two made their home in Portland. Third son Reuben would become well known in Portland and beyond as a hack driver, entrepreneur, forty-niner, antislavery activist, and operative on the Underground Railroad. Their parents' experiences as enslaved laborers surely influenced all the Ruby children, but particularly Reuben. He would spend his life working to abolish slavery and secure equal rights for African Americans.

REUBEN AND HIS SIBLINGS spent much of their childhoods in Portland, a hilly peninsula jutting into the Atlantic with onshore breezes wafting salt and fish. Portland's busy waterfront was crowded with wharves and warehouses; its cobbled streets and dirt lanes were lined with towering elms, houses, more than a dozen churches, and several large public buildings and hotels. An eighty-six-foot-tall marine signal tower known as Moody's Observatory looked down from Mount-Joy, now Munjoy Hill, where, in clear weather, Captain Lemuel Moody could spy vessels thirty miles out to sea with his telescope.

At the turn of the nineteenth century, all Portland boys between the ages of six and seventeen who weren't otherwise employed had to attend school, and classes comprised a blend of ages and races. At the time, boys from the town's Black community in the East End attended the North School with White boys.[22] Reuben Ruby very likely attended this school with two White boys of similar ages, William and Nathaniel Gordon, who lived just a block away. [23]

Yet not all boys received the same treatment. John Brown Russwurm, a founder of the nation's first Black-run newspaper, *Freedom's Journal*, was a contemporary of Reuben Ruby and the Gordon brothers and briefly attended school in Portland. His White stepmother, Susan, said that in Portland around 1815 "it was rather difficult . . . to get a colored boy into a good school where he would receive an equal share of attention with white boys, and this I was very particular should be the case."[24]

Susan Russwurm was extraordinary. The prevailing attitude among Portland's White citizens was more in line with the city's earliest school historian: "In the early part of the present [nineteenth] century Portland had a considerable colored population. . . . These people were not likely to appreciate the advantages of education, but we find a few of their children attending the North School."[25] While Reuben wasn't expected to "appreciate the advantages of education," his future, and his children's, would prove otherwise: all were ambitious, well spoken, and literate. As for John Brown Russwurm, he went on to become the first Black graduate of Bowdoin College and among the first three African Americans to graduate from college in the United States.[26]

A large proportion of Portland's Black residents were connected with the waterfront, working as stevedores or mariners, as Reuben's older brother Isaiah did.[27] In his early twenties, Reuben worked as a "laborer"—perhaps on the docks or in some other capacity. He lived on Hampshire Street, next door to his sister Sophia and brother-in-law Christopher Manuel, just two blocks from the waterfront.[28]

Reuben was intelligent and enterprising. By age twenty-six he had saved enough money to buy a house, and he eventually saved or borrowed enough to purchase a horse and carriage that he used as a hack, or taxi, the first of its kind in Portland.[29] In this capacity, he became well known around town and to out-of-towners and fugitives from slavery who passed through Portland on their way to Canada or Europe.[30] Reuben operated his hack out of the Elm Tavern, a stop for stagecoaches serving inland towns. Advertisements for his hack service indicated that riders could find him at his home "at any time in the night." Being a hack driver could be lucrative, so much so that cities like Baltimore prohibited Blacks from the business altogether. In New York, Black hack drivers were said to be "as rare as a black swan."[31] Living in Portland did offer some advantages; Ruby's business appears to have thrived.

REUBEN'S WHITE SCHOOLMATES, NATHANIEL and William Gordon, were the youngest of Hannah and Nathaniel Gordon I's six children.[32] After serving in the Revolution, the elder Gordon became a joiner and housewright in Portland. During young Nathaniel II's childhood, his father bought and sold several lots on the Portland peninsula. The family eventually settled into a house on Smith Street, just two blocks from the neighborhood where most Black families lived.

In June 1808, when young Nathaniel was ten, he, too, lost a parent. His mother Hannah died "after a painful sickness of about nine months."[33] Her death was undoubtedly a traumatic event for the family,

FIGURE 4. Advertisement for Reuben Ruby's hack stand in the *Portland City Directory* for 1834. Courtesy of Portland Public Library, Special Collections and Archives.

and seven months later his father married again, this time to a woman named Althea Mitchell.[34] Then, in 1816, when Nathaniel II was nineteen, his father sailed to the Caribbean. On his return trip, the ship was caught in a violent storm and blown off course. It ended up in Saint Barthélemy in the Leeward Islands. Eldest son Joshua, a sea captain, went to St. Bart's to bring his father home. But Nathaniel I had died as a result of the traumatic voyage.[35]

Despite their father's death, the risks of going to sea didn't deter the next generation of Gordons. Three of Nathaniel I's children—Joshua,

Morgan, and Nathaniel II—became mariners, while William became a shipowner and merchant who traded in West Indian goods. Daughter Huldah married sea captain Paul Merrill. Daughter Deborah's family was the only one to work outside the profession; she married Peter Thatcher, a well-respected local lawyer.

Nathaniel II had set his sights on seafaring, so he probably left school by fifteen or sixteen years old. Typically, a young man would sign on as boy or seaman at that age—or even younger—often with family members or family friends. With experience, he would move up to second mate, mate, and then captain. The process was more rapid for those whose fathers, older brothers, or in-laws were sea captains. Nathaniel had at least four such connections in his family, including older brothers Joshua and Morgan. As a result, he advanced quickly, becoming a ship-master at age twenty-two.[36]

WHILE NATHANIEL AND REUBEN were growing into their own, the District of Maine was seeking to separate from Massachusetts and become a state in its own right. After the Revolution, Massachusetts had begun selling unsettled lands in Maine to pay off its war debts. Many families were anxious to leave the increasingly crowded Boston area, and they seized the chance to acquire this readily available farmland. In just thirty years, Maine's population more than trebled, from 96,000 in 1790 to nearly 300,000 in 1820.[37]

Some Mainers had begun to advocate for separation from Massachusetts immediately after the Revolution. Three decades later, on July 26, 1819, residents finally voted decisively to separate from the Bay State: 17,000 for separation and 7,000 against.[38] But gaining statehood would take more than a referendum. The U.S. Congress had to approve Maine's independence by March 4, 1820, or Massachusetts would retain it as a district.

Missouri had petitioned for statehood as a slave state in early 1818, but its admission threatened the balance of ten free and ten slave states.[39] Southern politicians pressed the issue while northerners established roadblocks. In February 1819, Representative James Tallmadge of New York proposed that Missouri be admitted as a free state, that no more enslaved individuals be allowed to enter once it achieved statehood, and that enslaved children born in Missouri after its admission be freed at age twenty-five. This bill passed the U.S. House narrowly. The Senate passed the statehood bill, but only after stripping away Tallmadge's restrictions. In turn, the House refused to accept the Senate's version. Nothing was accomplished, and each side blamed the other.

Missouri's statehood was still an open question when Maine petitioned for statehood in December 1819. As a compromise, Senator Jesse B. Thomas of Illinois added an amendment that would ban slavery in the rest of the Louisiana Purchase north of the 36°30' parallel. But the House rejected that bill, too, spurred on by those intent upon a free Missouri. It devolved into a bitter debate.

Undeterred, Speaker of the House Henry Clay insisted that representatives vote on the Senate bill with Thomas's amendment and he lobbied those on both sides to compromise. Maine's congressional contingent played key roles. Five Maine congressmen voted against the Missouri Compromise and Maine's independence, not because they didn't support statehood, but because they opposed the expansion of slavery into Missouri.[40] Two of Maine's seven representatives, John Holmes and Mark Langdon Hill, voted for the Compromise, putting the bill just over the top at ninety for and eighty-seven against.

Few could appreciate what this vote meant. But one senior statesman saw it clearly, writing to Holmes, "This momentous question, like a fire bell in the night, awakened and filled me with terror. I considered it at once as the knell of the Union. It is hushed indeed for the moment. But this is a reprieve only, not a final sentence." The statesman was seventy-seven-year-old Thomas Jefferson, who believed that the nation he'd helped to found had come mere inches from splitting apart.[41]

Portland's newspapers, like her citizens, were sharply divided on the outcome. "The labour is over. The mother is delivered," declared the *Portland Gazette* on March 14, 1820. "Maine is come into the world with a twin sister, black as erebus, deformed as sin, and ugly as Satan!" The *Gazette* cast blame on Holmes and Hill, who had "leagued themselves with southern slave drivers." Another local paper, the *Eastern Argus*, celebrated the Compromise, finding Holmes's and Hill's position reasonable:

> Maine has now the essential attribute of a Free State, the power to manage her own affairs . . . Perhaps we are not disposed to examine so critically as we ought into the means by which this glorious

and happy result has been effected. At least we will not affect to regret that Missouri is admitted with precisely the same rights, as we have always claimed, . . . the right of managing her own concerns in her own way.[42]

The irony, of course, was that Maine's becoming a free state had enabled the expansion of slavery, showing how pervasive the influence of slavery was, even in the North. And Maine itself was divided: while the Compromise was too much for some citizens to swallow, others felt it was the only practicable means of ending their oppression at the hands of their Massachusetts masters.[43]

On March 23, 1820, Maine became a state. Missouri followed on August 10, 1821. Despite Maine's free status, African Americans like Reuben Ruby lived in limbo. They had gained some freedoms in the wake of the Revolution, including the right to vote in a few states, but in the early nineteenth century, northern states had begun to restrict or remove Blacks' right to vote altogether. New Jersey rescinded suffrage for Black men in 1807; Connecticut did so in 1818; Rhode Island and Pennsylvania would follow suit in 1822 and 1838; and in 1821, New York would introduce property ownership requirements for Black male voters that were stricter than those for Whites.[44]

As Mainers began writing their new constitution, pondering the sort of state they hoped to create, one delegate to the constitutional convention suggested that African Americans should be denied the right to vote. John Holmes, the congressman who had cast a deciding vote on the Missouri Compromise, was a member of that convention. He declared, "I know of no difference between the rights of the negro and the white man—God Almighty has made none. Our Declaration of Rights has made none." The Declaration, he continued, stated "that 'all men' (without regard to colours) 'are born equally free and independent.'"[45]

Perhaps Holmes felt compelled to redeem his earlier vote; perhaps he saw his compromise on statehood as a means to a greater good. The convention ultimately agreed, and Maine became one of only four states—along with Massachusetts, New Hampshire, and Vermont—to permit Black men's suffrage without barriers from the start.[46] The decision was critical for Reuben Ruby, who became politically active, joining the Whig Party and serving in town government.[47]

Missouri's new constitution was a different affair. It prevented the state legislature from ever outlawing slavery. And Blacks could not vote, regardless of status. In fact, the Missouri Constitution banned free Blacks from entering the state altogether.[48]

Still, there was a shaft of light for Missouri's African Americans and the 1.7 million enslaved and 233,000 free Black individuals in the United States. In 1820, Congress amended the 1819 Act to Protect the Commerce of the United States and Punish the Crime of Piracy by imposing the toughest penalty for slave trading to date. The Act of 1820 declared that kidnapping Africans and bringing them into the ports of the United States or elsewhere aboard U.S. vessels was "piracy." The penalty for doing so was death.[49]

Bringing individuals into the United States to be enslaved was already forbidden under the 1808 Act to Prohibit the Importation of Slaves into Any Port or Place within the Jurisdiction of the United States. While that law had cut deeply into the trade between Africa and the United States, it had not prohibited the domestic slave trade between states and had imposed only monetary fines for convicted slave captains. Nor was the federal government capable of strictly enforcing the law along the nation's expanding coastline. As a result, many kidnapped Africans were being smuggled into the United States through remote areas of Texas, Louisiana, and Spanish Florida. In addition, many slave captains continued to ply the trade between Africa and the Americas, landing their captives in Cuba and Brazil rather than the United States.[50]

The 1819 law had provided for squadrons of armed U.S. Navy ships to patrol both the American and African coasts to thwart the trade. Though few in number, some of these warships did intercept slave ships before they could land their human cargos in the Americas.

The Act of 1820 took these efforts a step further, stipulating that those convicted of trafficking in humans would be sentenced to death. Yet it would prove a disappointment, too, since Americans' participation in the slave trade continued to grow until the eve of the Civil War. Not until 1861 would Abraham Lincoln become the first president to implement the full measure of the 1820 law. He would do so against a native son of Portland, Maine, from a respected and prominent seafaring family.

CHAPTER 2

Free Trade

I think all the world would gain by setting commerce at perfect liberty.

—Thomas Jefferson, letter to John Adams, 1785

There was money to be made in following the sea. The sprawling antique homes that line the New England coast bear witness to the profitability of its maritime trade during the nineteenth century. But not all shipmasters, merchants, and shipbuilders were wealthy; the trade was fraught with unpredictability and risk, and storms and rough seas were the least of their worries. Embargoes, pirates, shipwrecks, lawsuits, and seizures were part of the price of doing business. Such hazards produced a generation of merchant sailors who were opportunistic, independent, wary of government, and loosely observant of the law.

The Gordon brothers were in the thick of it. Joshua, Morgan, and Nathaniel II were all mariners, and East Coast newspapers tracked their movements during the 1820s and 1830s. The three often sailed back and forth to the Caribbean, carrying barrel parts, lumber, fish, flour, pork, and produce. They also traveled farther afield—to Cadiz, Barcelona, Gibraltar, Trieste, Amsterdam, Rio, and Montevideo. Portland newspapers printed regular advertisements for brother William Gordon's store on the city's busy waterfront, which sold "West Indian goods and groceries," including molasses, sugar, coffee, rum, and cigars directly from his own schooner, the *Enterprize*, and from ships captained by his brothers, his brother-in-law Paul Merrill, and others.

The West India trade was lucrative for the Gordons and for Portland. In the first half of the century, the town where Prohibition was born had seven distilleries, with others in towns nearby. The Gordons often captained "molasses brigs," bringing rum's essential ingredient to Maine from Havana, Cárdenas, and Matanzas in Cuba and San Juan

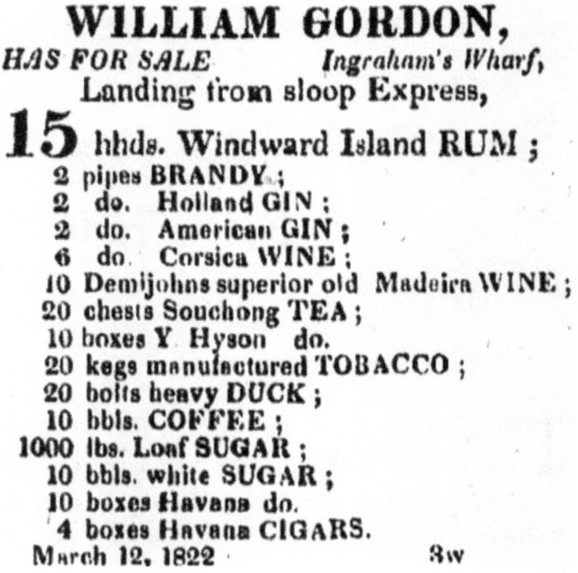

FIGURE 5. Advertisement for William Gordon's store in the *Weekly Eastern Argus*, March 12, 1822, http://www.genealogybank.com.

WILLIAM GORDON,

HAS FOR SALE   *Ingraham's Wharf,*
Landing from sloop Express,

15 hhds. Windward Island RUM ;
2 pipes BRANDY ;
2 do. Holland GIN ;
2 do. American GIN ;
6 do. Corsica WINE ;
10 Demijohns superior old Madeira WINE ;
20 chests Souchong TEA ;
10 boxes Y. Hyson do.
20 kegs manufactured TOBACCO ;
20 bolts heavy DUCK ;
10 bbls. COFFEE ;
1000 lbs. Loaf SUGAR ;
10 bbls. white SUGAR ;
10 boxes Havana do.
4 boxes Havana CIGARS.
March 12, 1822   3w

and Guayama in Puerto Rico.[1] Portland carried on a brisk trade with Cuba, ultimately surpassing Boston and other East Coast ports as an importer of molasses and sugar.[2] But the trade had a dark side: those goods were produced by enslaved persons laboring in the searing heat of Caribbean plantations.

Free Black mariners and dock workers were also engaged in the maritime trade, and the Gordons worked with and among them daily. Black men comprised about one-fifth of all American merchant sailors in the early part of the century.[3] Of the seventy-three Black individuals and heads of families listed in *The Portland Directory* for 1830, thirty-four, or nearly half, were mariners, and Black stevedores dominated longshore work on Portland's docks at least until midcentury.[4] "The discharging and fitting away of West Indiamen . . . was the principal and almost the only trade of Portland," one resident recalled. And this was carried out by "the black crew who discharged all the molasses by hoisting it out by hand, keeping time to their amusing songs while at work."[5] No ships could enter or leave Portland without engaging with individuals of African heritage.

AS THE NINETEENTH CENTURY dawned, the maritime trade was booming. But that quickly changed. By 1803, France and Great Britain were at war, and although the United States tried to remain neutral, the warring parties repeatedly captured American merchant ships and cargo headed for European ports, seizing the goods for their own purposes. Britain went a step further, impressing some 6,500 captured American merchant sailors into the Royal Navy.[6] Apprentice shipwright John Diguo was seized on his very first voyage, from Portland to New York.[7] Shepard Bourne, a Black sailor from Kennebunkport, Maine, was also seized and wrote a desperate and moving letter to his mother: "Der mother, I am sory to inform you that I hav the misfortune to be empresed In the British service and am now on bord the san juan lying at the Rock of Gibralters I hope you will . . . yous your endevers to get mea discharged as sson as posebel as I am very antious to get hom to my wife and family."[8] These sailors' only hope was to attract the attention of U.S. politicians and naval officers who might negotiate for their release.

Intent on neutrality, President Thomas Jefferson sought to discourage ship seizures and impressment via "peaceable coercion." He persuaded Congress to pass the Embargo Act of 1807, believing that the loss of American trade would cripple Britain and France. For fourteen months, U.S. ships were prohibited from sailing to, and trading with, foreign countries.

Whatever its deterrent effect upon the warring nations, the embargo brought economic disaster to the Northeast. Eighty thousand New England families fell into poverty.[9] "Our wharves have now the stillness of the grave, indeed nothing flourishes on them but vegetation," declared a Massachusetts newspaper.[10] In Portland alone, thirty firms folded during the embargo's first year.[11] Commercial houses couldn't pay their debts, shipyards ceased building deep-sea ships, shipowners and merchants went bankrupt, and fully 60 percent of workers were unemployed.[12] "Our Commerce is extinct," one citizen wrote to the *Portland Gazette*: "our farmers impoverished, . . . our most useful and enterprising Merchants bankrupts," and "the destructive business of smuggling in full practice caused by those iniquitous laws."[13]

"The distress of the district of Maine was intolerable," recalled Samuel Fessenden, a prominent Portland attorney and politician who would become a mentor and close friend of Reuben Ruby. Nathaniel Gordon II and Reuben Ruby, who were nine and ten years old during the embargo, endured the leanest years of their lives. "The children were naked and barefoot and their families were deprived of bread for six weeks together," wrote Fessenden.[14] Portland's wealthy families opened a soup kitchen to ensure that their destitute neighbors had something to eat. The embargo devasted prospects for the eldest Gordon brother, Joshua, who was then a young mariner of twenty-three. And it cut deeply into the Black community, which relied heavily on the maritime trade for their livelihoods. As jobs grew scarce, Black crewmembers were last in line for hiring.[15]

Angry Portlanders demonstrated. Protestors got a decrepit longboat, rigged it like a ship, and set it stern-first on a wagon. On it they painted the name "O-grab-me"—*embargo* spelled backward. The town's truckmen hitched their horses to the wagon in a single, long line and paraded it through the town as a band followed playing dirges. Unemployed shipmasters, mates, seamen, stevedores, and others marched solemnly behind in a funeral procession commemorating the demise of their livelihoods.[16]

Mainers protested in another way, too: by breaking the law. Desperate to earn a living, merchants, shipmasters, and sailors began to smuggle goods in and out of Maine ports while local courts looked the other way.[17] Passamaquoddy Bay, with its western shore in the United States and eastern shore in Canada, was the site of intense trafficking. Hundreds of barrels of flour were smuggled into Canada nightly. To help customs agents enforce the law, President Jefferson ordered the warship *Wasp* to patrol the bay. On a single night in 1808, the *Wasp* seized fourteen boats in the act of smuggling goods to Canada.[18]

To the southwest, the town of Bath formed a committee to warn sailors and captains of customs vessels patrolling the Kennebec River. And in Portland, ships regularly departed under cover of night for Canada and the West Indies, both of which willingly accepted cargoes from the United States without official papers.[19] On one night in 1808, two hundred masked men took control of Portland wharves and loaded two vessels with freight, keeping watch until the ships had safely left the harbor.[20] Their desperation was extreme. "How can you expect men to respect the *laws* which *oblige them to perish?*" wrote one embittered mariner.[21]

As tensions rose, some turned to violence. In December 1808, a group of men pulled a suspected customs informant from a ship at Portland, poured hot tar and feathers over him, and left him on the dock overnight, exposed to the frigid weather.[22] "Peaceable coercion," wrote Henry Adams, the great-grandson of John Adams, made "many smugglers and traitors, but not a single hero."[23]

To try to rectify the disastrous situation, Congress repealed the Embargo Act in 1809, replacing it with the Nonintercourse Act, which forbade trade only with France and Britain. Macon's Bill, enacted the following year, promised to normalize relations with the first of the belligerents to seek trade with the United States. France's Emperor Napoleon seized the chance, and President James Madison was forced to prohibit trade with Britain in February 1811. This act, along with U.S. efforts to expand its territory to the north and west, led to a second disaster: the War of 1812, declared by President Madison in June.

"Free Trade and Sailors' Rights" became the slogan of the war. It appeared in newspaper headlines and on ship standards and was proclaimed in Congress as the goal of the conflict.[24] But New England's mariners and merchants were skeptical. One newspaper remarked, "The starving . . . American Shipmasters and Seamen, who are idling in the streets . . . for want of employment, feel, that the sort of Free trade and Sailor's Rights which this war was waged to protect, are the Free Trade enjoyed by the Swedes, Spaniards, Portuguese, Greeks and infidels at the expense of the 'American Trade.'"[25]

Maine was hit particularly hard by the war. By 1814, the British occupied nearly half of its coastline, from the Penobscot River to its eastern boundary with Canada.[26] At the time, Maine was still a district of Massachusetts, but when its citizens asked for help in defending themselves, the government in Boston responded by fortifying its own immediate coastline.[27] The message was clear: Mainers were on their own.

Jefferson's embargo and the War of 1812 played key roles in shaping Maine's identity and the maritime culture of the United States. They impelled Maine to separate from Massachusetts, and they nurtured a culture of lawlessness among merchants, shipmasters, and sailors, who willingly broke the law to feed their families. Fierce self-reliance and lack of respect for government authority would become part of Yankee sailors' culture for several generations. The Gordon brothers came of age in that culture.

The embargo and the war would also inspire American shipbuilders to adapt. They would design some of the fastest sailing vessels to be found anywhere: merchant ships that could outrun U.S. naval and customs vessels, British men-of-war, and, later, both countries' antislavery squadrons.

BY 1820, THE YEAR that Maine achieved statehood, New England's maritime trade was back on its feet. In January 1821, Nathaniel Gordon II, then twenty-two, married Mary Brazier, daughter of well-to-do sea captain Daniel Brazier, at Portland's Second Congregational Church. That same year, their daughter Huldah was born. By 1823, Nathaniel II was a shipmaster living on the waterfront with or near his merchant brother William. Brothers Morgan and Joshua were also shipmasters and lived nearby with their families.[28] By 1830, Nathaniel was the head of a household of ten that included at least two servants or boarders, his wife, daughter Huldah, and son Nathaniel III.[29]

The maritime trade was robust, but still rife with hazards, as the Gordons' experiences show. In 1822, Joshua contracted to carry a shipment of mahogany from Saint Domingo, as Americans then referred to the island of Hispaniola, to Saint Thomas in the Virgin Islands. He offered $2,000 insurance to Levy and Sons, the cargo's owner: well over $50,000 today. On April 17, Gordon set sail on the brig *Sam*, but soon after leaving port, Gordon, his vessel, and crew were captured by a Spanish privateer and brought to Puerto Rico for adjudication. There, the *Sam* was given up, and a local court, colluding with the privateers, condemned the cargo to the captors. Gordon lost the cargo, the vessel, and $200 of his own money to the pirates. He was arrested and jailed in Puerto Rico for failing to deliver on his promise to Levy and Sons. His brother Nathaniel II and his brother-in-law Paul Merrill were forced to sail to the island and post bond to release Joshua from jail.[30] It was a huge financial loss for the Gordon clan.

As Joshua's experience shows, trading between the United States and the Caribbean colonies was lucrative but perilous. Between 1820 and 1830, pirates in the Caribbean captured some 500 ships carrying $20 million in cargo. Cuban and Puerto Rican merchants often benefited from this piracy, and local courts facilitated such activities.[31] But money wasn't the only thing at stake. In 1825, pirates massacred the crew of the brig *Betsey*, of Wiscasset, Maine, somewhere between Florida and Havana; like Ishmael of *Moby Dick*, only a single seaman escaped to tell the tale.[32]

Pirates operated beyond the Caribbean, too. In 1824, Nathaniel Gordon II was at the helm of the *Orono* in the Gulf of Mexico when it and an accompanying ship, the *Catharine*, were chased by "a piratical schooner." The pirates boarded the *Catharine*, robbing both ship and crew of cargo and valuables, stripping the sails, and demolishing the cabin. Under cover of night, Gordon managed to sail the *Orono* safely into a port. Two days later, when he set out again, the pirates were lying in wait and pursued his ship. A newspaper account claimed that "the [pirate] captain swore he would have the Orono if he sailed after her a month, and would cut the crew to pieces." After a long chase, however, an armed brig intercepted the pirates, who were taken to court in Tabasco. Gordon and the *Orono* escaped. But the young captain, intent on making a name for himself, was the likely source for the dramatic description of the adventure, which ran in newspapers around the country.[33]

In August 1822, the Gordons' brother-in-law Paul Merrill was captain of the *Enterprize* when it ran aground during rough weather at Saint Domingo. While salvageable, the vessel was in bad shape. Believing that there were no materials to repair the brig on the island, Merrill sold it on the spot for $1,086. William Gordon, who owned the ship, sued the Massachusetts Fire and Marine Insurance Company, claiming a total loss. But to the Gordons' dismay, a repaired *Enterprize* showed up later in Boston as evidence against their claim.[34]

During that trial, William Gordon disappeared. His brother Morgan stepped in to pursue his lawsuit, and advertisements for his store stopped appearing in Portland newspapers. William vanished from records altogether after 1823, when his wife Harriet and two-year-old son George began shuttling between the homes of her brothers-in-law Morgan and Nathaniel, indicating that she had been widowed.[35]

In early 1825, Captain Morgan Gordon, the most adventurous of the brothers, was in the Southern Hemisphere waiting to enter the port of Callao, Peru, aboard the brig *Sarah George* of Portland. He wasn't alone; dozens of other U.S. merchant ships were waiting to land their cargo. Peru, a Spanish colony, was in the late stages of revolution, and while most of the country had been wrested from the royalists, the castles at Callao still held forces loyal to Spain. In response, General Simon Bolívar, head of the Peruvian independence forces, declared the port closed.

Given the dangers of war, the French, British, and United States navies all sent warships to protect their commercial interests. The U.S. naval frigate *United States* was on hand to defend the U.S. merchant fleet. "In the Bay of Chorillos," wrote Commodore Isaac Hull to Secretary of the Navy Samuel Southard, were "ten to thirty valuable American merchant ships, with valuable cargoes, lying in a situation where they had no protection."[36] The *Sarah George* was among them.

Although the frigate *United States* was there to protect the ships, American merchant captains "took offence" at being asked questions by the boarding naval officer, and "wanted to know what business I had to inquire about the cost of their cargoes," wrote Hull.[37] Some captains reluctantly listed the things they were carrying: flour, salt, and provisions. Morgan Gordon admitted only to carrying "general merchandise": a likely protest against naval officers' inquiries.[38]

But Gordon was carrying something of great value. On February 27, 1825, the *Sarah George* delivered guns and ammunition for General Bolívar. Gordon's "general merchandise" turned out to be weaponry for the army seeking to liberate Peru.[39] Given his response to naval officers' boarding his ship, it's probable that Morgan Gordon provided the weapons, not in some official capacity but as an enterprising capitalist.

Gordon made more than one trip to Peru on the *Sarah George*. And sailing into South American ports was dangerous, given the atmosphere of war, rebellion, and revolution. But with risks came potentially higher profits. In July 1826, he captained the brig from Callao on the Pacific coast around Cape Horn to Montevideo and Rio de Janeiro on the Atlantic coast.[40] Upon reaching the Rio de la Plata on September 23, the *Sarah George* was seized by a brig-of-war belonging to Brazil's navy and escorted to Montevideo, where Gordon and crew were forced to abandon ship, leaving behind their clothes, belongings, and the ship's log.[41]

The Uruguayan struggle for independence involved a contentious conflict over territorial rights between Brazil and what would soon become Argentina.[42] At the time, Montevideo was under Brazilian control, and the *Sarah George* had been captured for breaching a military blockade. Gordon appealed to the American consul there, but Brazilian authorities flatly refused to allow him to sail the brig back to the States. Dismasted and moored in the Rio de la Plata, with no crew to protect her, the *Sarah George* was all but destroyed by late September gales.

FIGURE 6. South America in 1825, showing the Rio de la Plata and the Bay of Chorrillos. Map by Andreu Comas. Used with permission.

The return voyage was a total loss for Gordon: he had lost both vessel and cargo and couldn't pay his crew. So he contacted Congressman John Anderson of Maine, who urged the U.S. government to exert diplomatic pressure on Brazil. Ultimately, Brazil did agree to compensate the United States, and Congress authorized a direct payment to Gordon so that he could pay his crew. It took a mere eight years for the crew to receive their compensation.[43]

Tellingly, the owner of the *Sarah George*, Eli Merrill, had no idea what Gordon had been up to in South America. He submitted a competing claim to Congress for the ship and the seamen's wages, stating that "Captain Gordon had not given him any account of his voyage in the Pacific."[44] Morgan Gordon, it seems, used Merrill's ship for purposes other than what he'd contracted for, and felt no need to share his plans. In addition to his penchant for secrecy, two other personality traits were evident: he was willing to take risks and to seize opportunities to make money, even if it meant sailing well out of his way, breaching blockades, or navigating the notoriously dangerous waters around Cape Horn.

IT'S IMPOSSIBLE TO DOCUMENT the many unremarkable voyages the Gordons conducted throughout the decade. They faced hazards at sea, conducted business together, supported one another in and out of court, and were a tight-knit family. As merchant seamen, they were independent: committed to looking out for themselves and each other amid a larger maritime culture of lawlessness, embargoes, war, and unpredictable dangers across wide expanses of ocean. But they weren't merely victims. As shipmasters, they held the ultimate authority at sea, taking risks and making decisions affecting all who sailed with them, voluntarily or otherwise.

CHAPTER 3

Towns Divided

The North was not Abolitionist. It was overwhelmingly in favor of Negro slavery, so long as this did not interfere with Northern moneymaking. But, on the other hand, there was a minority of the North who hated slavery with perfect hatred; who wanted no union with slaveholders; who fought for freedom and treated Negroes as men.

—W. E. B. Du Bois, *Black Reconstruction in America, 1860–1880*

During the 1820s and 1830s, when Reuben Ruby was a young adult, Blacks in free states faced northerners' ire for all manner of complaints. They were blamed for White unemployment, for being economic burdens on the towns where they lived, and for the widely held belief that they sought to "amalgamate," or intermarry, with Whites. And because they lived in mostly segregated neighborhoods, they were easy targets.

A series of violent riots shook American cities during this period, showing that northern towns and citizens were deeply divided over matters of race and equality. In Providence, Rhode Island, in 1824, a mob of forty to fifty White men pulled down or set fire to the homes of some twenty Black families, because a Black man had refused to yield the sidewalk to passing Whites. A thousand spectators, including the town's police, stood by and watched. "Colored people had little or no protection from the law at those times," wrote William Brown, a free Black from Providence who witnessed the chaos and destruction. "If you were well dressed they would insult you for that, and if you were ragged you would surely be insulted for being so; be as peaceable as you could there was no shield for you."[1]

The Providence riots were just the start. In 1829, in response to a surge of Black migration into Ohio, Cincinnati officials invoked the 1807 Black Act, requiring that Black residents post a $500 bond to remain in the city. Those who couldn't meet the obligation by June 30 would be forced to leave. Ostensibly, the act sought to reassure Whites that their Black neighbors were economically solvent. But because few Americans at the time, regardless of race, had $500 in cash, the real intent was obvious: to push Blacks out of town.

Cincinnati's Black leaders sent envoys to Ontario to purchase land for a settlement there. They planned to name it Wilberforce, after English abolitionist William Wilberforce, who had advocated against slavery and the slave trade for more than two decades. They encouraged migration and informed their White neighbors of their progress. But it wasn't enough. Between August 15 and August 22, White mobs invaded Cincinnati's predominantly Black fourth ward, destroying businesses and homes and injuring citizens. City police were late to respond. By the time the smoke cleared, nearly half of the city's Black population had left for Ontario and elsewhere.[2]

Like most northerners, Cincinnatians were sharply divided on the issue of slavery. Abolitionist newspapers sprang up, inflaming pro-slavery residents. As president of Lane Theological Seminary, Lyman Beecher presided over a fiery student debate on abolition in 1834. His daughter Harriet, who would go on to write *Uncle Tom's Cabin*, was present for the debate, during which the majority of students, under the leadership of student abolitionist Theodore Weld, argued for an immediate end to slavery. Rumors of violence against the seminary spread. Fearing the worst, school trustees discontinued the campus antislavery society and forbade further discussions of abolition. These measures stemmed violence for the moment but nearly caused the demise of the seminary. One hundred students, including Weld, left in protest; only seven remained enrolled.[3]

In 1836, a new antislavery newspaper in Cincinnati triggered a mob, and violence spilled over into Black neighborhoods. Irish dockworkers, fearing that Blacks posed a threat to their jobs, launched a campaign of violence that lasted much of the summer. They burned Black homes and attacked free Blacks and White abolitionists in the streets. Sporadic outbreaks continued with the mayor's blessing, until volunteers organized a private force to keep the peace.[4]

Cincinnati and Providence were not alone. In 1834, a mob in Philadelphia destroyed two Black churches and the homes of more than thirty free Black families.[5] And in 1838, a mob stoned and burned the city's Pennsylvania

Hall, just four days after it opened. Rumors of "amalgamation" spread when men and women, Black and White, were invited to attend the Anti-Slavery Convention of American Women held at the hall.[6]

In 1834, stirred by a hysterical press fearful of amalgamation, an angry White mob laid waste to lower Manhattan. Mayor Cornelius Lawrence, an anti-abolitionist, was slow to quell the riots, which continued for four nights. Finally, Lawrence called out New York's National Guard, but the damage was done. Two Black churches and more than twenty Black families' homes were destroyed. In addition, the home of White abolitionist Lewis Tappan was looted and burned, and his brother Arthur's store was vandalized. A mob had already burned Arthur Tappan's summer home in New Haven, Connecticut, in 1831—along with a Black family's home and a church—after he and others advocated that a college for Blacks be built in that city.[7]

In 1835, White citizens at a town meeting in Canaan, New Hampshire, declared Noyes Academy, which accepted both White and Black students, "a public nuisance" and voted to remove it. Some three hundred men with ninety to a hundred yoke of oxen dragged the academy building a half mile to a swamp, and residents forced the Black students out of town.[8] Northern New England, it seems, was no more tolerant than New York or border states such as Ohio and Pennsylvania.

Even when they weren't met with violence, free Blacks were ostracized. In Providence, "the [Black] people had no place of worship of their own, and were obliged to attend the white people's churches," wrote William Brown. "But many attended no church at all, because they said they were opposed to going to churches and sitting in pigeon holes, as all the churches at that time had some obscure place for the colored people to sit in."[9]

The same was true in Portland. Although Portland's waterfront, ships, and maritime trade were well integrated, the town and its institutions were another thing entirely. Its Black population, which at times numbered as many as seven hundred, was packed tightly into a few city blocks at the foot of Munjoy Hill.[10] And although Portland had avoided much of the street violence of other cities and towns, its institutions were less than welcoming for Blacks. Reverend Calvin C. Lane, an African American minister, recalled that "Portland was a center of a great trade between her port and the Islands of the West Indies, [and] the many colored people who came over with the cargoes were churchly men." These sailors sought to attend Portland churches, but "the prejudice of the [White] church people was so great," said Lane, "that much opposition was made against the negro people attending the houses of worship of most of the denominations."[11]

Local Blacks were scarcely more welcome. During the 1810s and 1820s, Reuben Ruby attended Portland's Second Congregational Church as did the Gordons. Just a few months after the Reverend Edward Payson had married Nathaniel and Mary Gordon in January 1821, he married Reuben Ruby and Jeannette Pierre, whose father, Peter Pierre, had migrated to Portland from the West Indies.[12] In 1816, Payson had also married Reuben's sister Sophia to Christopher Manuel. But despite their regular attendance at church, Reuben, his family, and the sizable Black contingent endured slights from other members of the congregation. They were not allowed to vote in church matters and were forced to sit in the church's balcony, typical practice among New England congregations at the time. Balconies were farther removed from the pulpit and they were less comfortable: they were more cramped and hotter in summer and colder in winter than the main floor pews, typically reserved for White families like the Gordons.

Black members of the Second Congregational found their treatment maddening. In September of 1826, Ruby, his brother-in-law Christopher Manuel, and four other Black citizens wrote a letter of protest to Portland's *Eastern Argus* newspaper. They spoke for their community of "about six hundred," arguing that they valued "moral instruction" and "piety and religion." Yet, they wrote, with smoldering frustration: "We have sometimes thought our attendance [at church] was not desired." While they were permitted in the far corners of some churches in Portland, "the privilege granted us is . . . calculated to repel rather than to invite our attendance." The letter was carefully worded, designed not to incite White citizens' anger. The petitioners "respectfully" addressed their neighbors; they asked readers to "pardon our misapprehensions if they be such" and hoped their petition "would not be thought obtrusive." Nonetheless, it's clear they'd had enough: these Black Portlanders wanted a spiritual home of their own—a sanctuary where they felt welcome and free to worship. Yet they were well aware that they could do nothing without the White community's blessing.[13]

The idea gained some traction. John Neal, a local writer, activist, and Quaker, urged well-to-do Portlanders to support a separate church: "Instead of sending . . . tens of thousands of dollars to build churches . . . along the shores of Africa, what if we look about here and see what may be done for our next-door neighbors?"[14]

Ruby and the small Black contingent were determined. In 1828, a committee comprised of Ruby, Ephraim Small, Titus Skillings, Clement Thompson, and John Sigs petitioned the state legislature for permission to assemble their own religious community. The legislature agreed, and the petitioners and seventeen other Black Portlanders formed the Abyssinian Religious Society.[15] Between 1828 and 1831, they built a meeting house on the southern portion of a lot that belonged to Reuben Ruby. He mortgaged the parcel to the Abyssinian Society in 1831 and provided substantial financial and in-kind support for the building's construction and upkeep, much of it coming from his successful hack business.

The Abyssinian Meeting House was erected on Sumner (now Newbury) Street, where it stands today. Built by African American carpenters to whom specialized training was denied, the meeting house nonetheless exhibits well-executed traditional timber-frame construction.[16] Today, it is the third-oldest still-standing African American meeting house in the United States; only those in Boston and Nantucket are older.

Portland's Abyssinian Meeting House was more than a church; it became a religious and cultural center for locals as well as sailors and lecturers who visited the town; a school for Portland's Black children, who were segregated from White children in 1836; and a nexus for the Underground Railroad. Among the Abyssinian's members were George Black, who sold used clothing, some of which he provided to runaways; barber Christopher Manuel, who could help change the appearance of fugitives; hack drivers Reuben Ruby and Charles Pierre, who could transport escapees at all hours of the night to safe houses; and mariner Abraham Niles, who could lead fugitives to vessels that would safely carry them to Canada or Europe.[17]

As the Abyssinian was being built, Reuben Ruby was coming into his own as an activist for equal rights, abolition, and temperance. In 1827, he became the Portland agent for *Freedom's Journal*, the first Black-owned and -edited newspaper in the United States. Published in New York City by Reverend Peter Williams, the paper was edited by Samuel Cornish, a

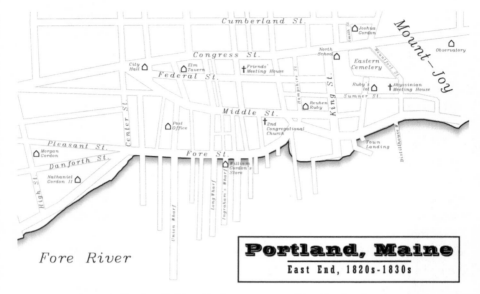

FIGURE 7. Portland's East End, 1820s–1830s. The Gordon brothers were raised on Smith Street, at or near the home of eldest brother Joshua. They attended the Second Congregational Church and the North School, as did Reuben Ruby. Ruby lived on Hampshire Street and purchased parcels on Sumner Street, on which his home and the Abyssinian Meeting House would later be built. He operated his hack out of the Elm Tavern. William Gordon operated a store on Ingraham's Wharf. Map by Andreu Comas. Used with permission.

Presbyterian minister, and John Brown Russwurm, a former resident of Portland and a contemporary of Ruby's who had graduated from Bowdoin College a year earlier. Ruby's work as an agent connected him to the thriving activist and abolitionist communities in New York, Boston, and Philadelphia.

But 1827 also brought tragedy. In October, Jeannette Ruby, Reuben's wife of six years, died at age twenty-two, leaving Reuben to care for their two-year-old son, William. Sadly, just a year after Jeannette died, William died, too.[18]

A year later, in November 1829, Reuben wed twenty-four-year-old Rachel Humphrey in Boston. Reuben's rapid remarriage was not unusual for the times. Nor was it unusual for him to find a bride so far from home: records show that New England's Black communities were well connected, no matter how small or distant from one another.[19] Reuben and Rachel moved to a home on Preble Street in Portland, and Reuben continued to operate his hack stand out of nearby Elm Tavern.[20] In 1831, the couple welcomed their first child, Frederic. In 1832, their daughter, Sarah, was born.

IN 1832, PORTLAND WAS both segregated and sharply divided on the matter of emancipation. But there was one issue that most citizens agreed upon: Andrew Jackson should not win a second term as president of the United States. A petition in the *Portland Weekly Advertiser*, signed by hundreds of Portlanders, explained why. Jackson had spent more federal dollars than "any of his six predecessors," and he behaved as an autocrat, "constituting himself the common superior of the Senate, the Judiciary, and the Congress of these United States." Among the signers were prominent Portlanders Samuel Fessenden and his son William Pitt Fessenden, then a state representative; Reuben Ruby; and Joshua, Morgan, and Nathaniel Gordon.[21]

In the election, Jackson, the Democratic incumbent, defeated Henry Clay, a National Republican, and William Wirt of the Anti-Masonic Party. He took the state of Maine by some ten percentage points.[22] But in Portland, the majority went for Henry Clay. The conservative *Weekly Eastern Argus* charged that "in this city the majority against the democratic party was made up entirely by the black voters, such as never before were known to be qualified voters." It accused Ruby's influential friend, Samuel Fessenden, of treating the city's Black voters to dinner and "grog" before they went to the polls and of frightening them into believing that a vote for Jackson was a vote to institute slavery throughout the United States.[23] But the petition that Ruby and the Gordons signed together demonstrates that Jackson was unpopular with many White Portlanders, too. What the *Argus* piece revealed—perhaps inadvertently—was that in Portland Black voters had clout. As Pastor Amos Gerry Beman of the Abyssinian Church would later write, "Any man that resides here and has been here three months, paid his tax, is entitled to vote and has the right of suffrage, a right of which a very large majority of the colored people avail themselves."[24]

Few states allowed Black men to vote or hold office, but, in Maine, Ruby and many of his neighbors actively participated in politics. When the Whig Party was founded in 1833, Ruby joined the Whig Citizens of Portland and became involved in town government as a "tythingman," a peace officer who brought accused citizens before grand juries and ensured that citizens didn't violate the Sabbath.[25] The Whig Party had been founded largely to oppose President Jackson's agenda. Although it took no formal stance on slavery, it attracted, at least in the North, many of the most outspoken abolitionists of the time: prominent Mainers like the Fessendens and national figures including Thaddeus Stevens, William Seward, and Horace Greeley. It was the obvious choice for a voter like Ruby.

IN SEPTEMBER 1832, William Lloyd Garrison, the nation's most prominent abolitionist and publisher of *The Liberator*, visited Portland and spoke at the Abyssinian Meeting House. Garrison and Arthur Tappan had founded the American Anti-Slavery Society, and Garrison traveled throughout New England to encourage the formation of local chapters. In Portland, Ruby served as Garrison's tour guide. "I was very highly indebted to my friend, Mr. Reuben Reuby, (a colored gentleman held in much esteem in this city,), for a protracted ride," wrote Garrison, "during which I obtained various and eminently beautiful views of Portland and the harbor." Garrison also attended a reception at the Rubys' home, where he "was gratified to meet about twenty colored gentlemen."[26] These were likely the town's Black elite: men who, although they had few financial resources, were politically engaged, voted, and had at least a modicum of education. The Rubys' home often served as a gathering place for those who sought to meet with the Black community, and Rachel Ruby no doubt played a critical behind-the-scenes role in planning and facilitating such meetings.

In October 1834, George Thompson, a good friend of Garrison's and a renowned English abolitionist, arrived in Maine for a speaking tour. A controversial figure at home and abroad, Thompson was welcomed with a volatile mixture of enthusiasm, animosity, and violence in most of the places he visited. On October 12, he addressed the congregation at the Abyssinian. "This was the first time I had ever worshipped in a place, exclusively appropriated to colored persons; nor had I ever, on any occasion, seen so many assembled together," he wrote, reflecting the vibrancy of Portland's Black congregation.

On the fifteenth, Thompson traveled north to Augusta to speak at the convention of Maine's newly formed chapter of the Anti-Slavery Society, which Reuben Ruby and Samuel Fessenden had helped to found.[27] While Thompson's remarks haven't survived, they "gave offence to a certain party in the town," and that evening as he slept, someone broke several windowpanes in the home of his host, Reverend Benjamin Tappan. Thompson returned to the convention the next day, leaving Tappan's house by a back window. At the convention, he was called out by a group of five men. "They said that they came from a meeting of citizens . . . to inform me, that my speech of the previous night, had given great offence—that I was regarded as a foreign emissary, an officious intermeddler & c. & c.—and that, therefore, I should not be permitted to attend the afternoon sitting of the Convention, but must leave town *immediately*."[28] Violence and intimidation weren't reserved exclusively for free Blacks; White abolitionists endured their share, too.

Despite his reception at Augusta, Thompson attended the afternoon session without incident. He then traveled downriver to Hallowell, a town which leaned abolitionist. There, he gave another lecture. "A number of my opponents from Augusta were present," wrote Thompson. But the large numbers of abolitionists kept the Augusta troublemakers from causing much of a disturbance.

Thompson was well received at Bowdoin College in Brunswick and then returned to Portland, where he met with a group of women who were anxious to start their own antislavery society. But his talk at the Friends Meeting House was interrupted by a mob. One person was arrested and jailed. Nonetheless, a group of Portland women soon formed the Ladies' Antislavery Sewing Society.[29] Later that day, Thompson again "met the colored people in the Abyssinian church," where "the attendance was exceedingly good."[30] Reuben Ruby was likely responsible for arranging many of these activities.[31]

Everywhere Thompson went, he spoke out forcefully against slavery. He also vigorously opposed colonization: the notion that encouraging free African Americans to emigrate to an all-Black settlement outside the United States would resolve the nation's racial woes. He was charismatic and eloquent. One young woman of fourteen recalled, "What enthusiasm I felt for him!"[32] Well-known abolitionist Lydia Maria Child waxed poetic about Thompson's speaking ability:

> I've heard thee when thy powerful words
> Were like a cataract's roar,
> Or like the ocean's mighty waves
> Resounding on the shore.[33]

She told a friend that "very large sums are offered for any one who will convey Mr. Thompson into the Slave States"—where, presumably, he'd receive retribution for stirring up antislavery zeal.[34]

Thompson's lectures also created a sensation in the press. The *New York Courier and Inquirer* referred to him as the "most impudent of itinerant mountebanks."[35] Even those who supported abolition were wary of a foreigner telling them what to do. "May the Lord send someone to awaken us, even if it be an Englishman," declared a Massachusetts paper.[36]

Others advocated outright violence. In Boston, a gallows inscribed with "Judge Lynch's Law" was erected outside Garrison's house where Thompson was staying, and a handbill circulated that promised $100 "to reward the individual who shall first lay violent hands on Thompson, so that he may be brought to the tar kettle before dark."[37] Garrison noted with delight that his friend Thompson "has shaken this land from side to side."[38]

In December 1834, another prominent abolitionist, Reverend Amos Phelps of Boston, visited Portland to promote immediate emancipation. His lecture attracted a large crowd. "The house was literally crammed," he wrote to his wife; "every seat, nook & corner being occupied & a great number standing in the aisles—the most perfect order & undivided attention." Phelps's visit to Portland caused no trouble. But in nearby Freeport, some residents threatened violence, forcing him to speak in a private home instead of the local meeting house.

Like Garrison, Phelps paid a visit to the Ruby home in Portland: "Tonight I took tea at Mr. Ruby's [a] colored man—and there were several colored persons there, and I did not see but the tea tasted as good, as if it had been prepared and served by some white lady." He also delivered two sermons at the Abyssinian Meeting House, where he found "more real religious enjoyment in one afternoon's worship . . . than I should in fifty of the good orthodox churches in this city." While there, he "baptized a little colored William Wilberforce," Reuben's and Rachel's infant son, named for the British abolitionist.[39] Although Portland and other northern towns were clearly divided on the matter of emancipation, the abolitionist community was well integrated: Whites and Blacks collaborated closely and felt comfortable in one another's presence.

IN LATE MAY OF 1835, Reuben Ruby and his neighbor George H. Black traveled as delegates to the fifth annual Convention of the Free People of Color in Philadelphia. Begun in 1831, the National Negro Convention movement brought together free Blacks from across the United States to protest discrimination, racial violence, and slavery and to organize politically and socially. Ruby and Black didn't travel together to the event, and while Ruby's trip was uneventful, Black's was humiliating. According to Black, when he tried to purchase a ticket on the steamship *Mac-Donough* for the multiday passage, he was "refused the liberty of the cabins on account of my color" and wasn't permitted on board unless he agreed to remain on the forward deck. Black refused to comply, "in respect to myself and my character," and was "obliged to postpone my trip at considerable inconvenience and disappointment."[40]

Ruby and six other men wrote to *The Liberator* protesting the behavior of the *MacDonough*'s captain. While the letter briefly criticized Black's treatment on the *MacDonough*, it proposed options for action: the same tactic used in the public letter urging creation of the Abyssinian Society. Ruby and his co-authors praised the steamship *Lexington* and its Captain Vanderbilt for his "kind treatment" and encouraged travelers to patronize Vanderbilt's *Lexington* "in preference to all others."[41]

A host of Black luminaries attended the 1835 convention in Philadelphia. They included Samuel Cornish, the editor of *Freedom's Journal*; Thomas L. Jennings, the first African American to hold a patent; Theodore S. Wright, a well-known abolitionist lecturer and the first Black to attend an American seminary; and Thomas Downing, a wealthy New York restauranteur and community leader. But Reuben Ruby was chosen to be president of the convention, an honor suggesting that his peers found him committed, capable, well spoken, and fair.

Attendees passed a series of key resolutions that shed light on race relations during the 1830s. But since few free African Americans could vote and had little if any influence in government, what was the point? Such resolutions proved to be much more than symbolic. The convention movement allowed African Americans to visualize and create roadmaps for equality and justice and to force dialogue on matters that White politicians sought to avoid. Like changing federal laws, changing the minds of White citizens was an arduous process. But the Black conventions and the discourse they fostered undeniably pushed matters forward.

At the 1835 convention, for example, attendees resolved to urge free Blacks throughout the United States to petition Congress and state legislatures "to be admitted to the rights and privileges of American citizens, and that we be protected in the same." At the time, nothing in the body of U.S. law protected African Americans as citizens, but in decades to come, the matter would prove to be contentious and divisive. Attendees unanimously urged the formation of temperance societies, "which we believe will facilitate the cause of immediate and universal emancipation." They agreed to "abstain from using the products of slave labour" and "to patronize . . . stages and steamboats, which make little or no distinction among their passengers," a resolution likely inspired in part by Black's experience and Ruby's protest letter. They unanimously approved a motion "to abandon the use of the word 'colored'" when speaking or writing about themselves, and the title "African" from their institutions. They expressed their disdain for the colonization movement and noted the harm that it was doing to the cause of abolition at home.[42] They were asserting themselves as Americans.

A new organization, the American Moral Reform Society, grew out of the 1835 convention's efforts to erase distinctions based on race. The society had ambitious aims: to uplift mankind through "education, temperance, economy and universal love." Ruby was named a vice president along with his friend Samuel Cornish.[43] But his connection with the society didn't last; he did not attend its first annual meeting in 1836.[44] Cornish did make an appearance but was disillusioned. He condemned the society's leaders as "vague, wild, indefinite, and confused in their views" and argued that they should focus on African Americans rather than all mankind.[45] Free Blacks in the antebellum North were not a unified bloc; they held diverse opinions and engaged in more than a little infighting. Still, although Ruby had lost interest in the Moral Reform Society, he remained engaged in issues of abolition and temperance. In the fall of 1837, he would attend a meeting of the New England Colored Temperance Convention in Boston and be elected to its executive committee.[46]

AT HOME, RUBY HAD developed a reputation as a radical: one who advocated immediate emancipation. Nonetheless, in 1835, he was selected as a delegate from Portland to the Whig convention at Augusta, a prominent and visible position for an African American. Portland's *Eastern Argus* called Ruby "the leading colored abolitionist of this city" but pointed out that, when he tried to organize abolitionist meetings, he was denied space in the churches, even by his friends in the Whig party.[47]

His stance on emancipation caused turmoil in town. In early August of 1835, ninety-two Portland citizens wrote to a local paper opposing the "immediate emancipation of slaves of the South." The petitioners "look[ed] with distrust and abhorrence upon all measures which may tend to instigate the blacks to insubordination and insurrection." They expressed support for "our countrymen of the South" and stated that they opposed "the placing in imminent peril the lives and property of the white population." Among the signatories was Reuben's White neighbor, shipmaster Morgan Gordon.[48]

The anti-emancipationists convened a large gathering on August 18, 1835. Attendees asserted that antislavery activism was pushing the nation toward civil war. They also denounced "intermeddling foreigners" like George Thompson.[49] Soon, Ruby was "placarded" in Portland by individuals who were alarmed by his call for an immediate end to slavery: an anonymous "scurrilous libel" against him was attached to the door of the post office. The content of the notice hasn't survived, but a letter to the *Portland Daily Advertiser* described it as an "outrageous and unjustifiable assault."[50]

As abolitionists like Ruby became more visible, violence against them increased. In September 1836, Henry B. Stanton lectured at the Friends Meeting House in Portland. The husband of women's suffragist Elizabeth Cady Stanton, he was a well-known writer and orator on abolition and social justice. As he spoke, a "mob of 4 or 5 hundred" surrounded the building and threw stones and mud through the windows. The local press ignored the event.[51]

In October, the Maine Anti-Slavery Society was scheduled to hold its annual meeting in Portland's city hall, but protests caused Mayor Levi Cutter to withdraw permission. The event was held a day late at the Friends Meeting House.[52] Recognizing the likelihood of violence, two prominent White citizens, Ruby's close friend Samuel Fessenden and David Thurston, a founding member of the American Anti-Slavery Society, appealed to Cutter for protection. The mayor replied that "it was his settled belief" that attendees "could not be protected." A mob did form outside the meeting house, jeering and throwing stones, but the meeting went forward anyway.[53]

During that time, Ruby was busy on other fronts, too. A letter he wrote to Reverend Amos Phelps in Boston shows that he was advocating not just for emancipation but for free Black individuals in trouble.

> Dear Sir
> I take the liberty to write to you to Request you
> To go an send to the jayl and see a man by the
> Name of Jermiah Roggers that is put in on
> Pretence of Mutiny on Bord the Brig
> And see what can be done for him if you please
> I should not have trouble you if I had known
> Any one that I could depend on and if it wont
> Be to much trouble you would ablige him
> Verry much I send ten dollars and you will
> Give it to him if you please and I will be good
> To the a mount of fifty dollars if wanted
> Please to write as soon as possable if you pleas
>
> > Yours & c.
> > Reuben Ruby
>
> Please to continue my paper
> Court last Monday in Oct.[54]

The full story behind this letter is unknown, though it's clear that Ruby was extremely concerned for a Black mariner named Jeremiah Rogers. Rogers lived in Portland but had been jailed in Boston on mutiny charges. Ruby sought to use all of his influence to ensure that Rogers was treated fairly and had legal representation. Records show that a case of mutiny did come before the Boston court in early October involving two White sailors and a Black cook on the whaler *Isabella* out of New Bedford, Massachusetts. But the records do not mention Rogers specifically.[55]

The letter, hurriedly written in Ruby's own hand and voice, reveals that Ruby willingly used his network of acquaintances to help individuals in distress. Like the letter he and his neighbors wrote to launch the Abyssinian Religious Society, it shows his deferential style. He apologizes for any "trouble" his request may cause the Reverend Phelps, repeats "if you please" numerous times, and offers money to assist Rogers. He further requests that Phelps "continue my paper," meaning his subscription to the *Emancipator*, of which Phelps was the editor, showing his support for matters dear to Phelps. But underneath Ruby's deferential style is a bold appeal: a Black man asking a prominent White man for a favor.

It's not clear whether Phelps visited Rogers in the Boston jail or helped his case. But Rogers was likely acquitted. Four years later, he was named moderator of Portland's Abyssinian Religious Society, and the next year he attended the Maine State Convention of Colored Persons.[56]

Two important observations emerge from Ruby's letter. African Americans throughout the Northeast communicated regularly and were joined to one another—and to White abolitionists—via an extended network. As a part of that network, Reuben Ruby had a well-developed sense of social responsibility. He worked hard, publicly and behind the scenes, to secure justice for others in difficult circumstances.

IN OCTOBER 1836, ENGLISH abolitionist George Thompson was ending his American tour. He was scheduled to speak at a meeting of Boston's Female Anti-Slavery Society next door to *The Liberator*'s offices. An angry mob formed, determined to stop him. Thompson learned of their plan, escaped to the waterfront, and rowed himself out to the New Brunswick packet to avoid being carried away by the rabble. Publisher William Lloyd Garrison happened to be at his offices and became Thompson's surrogate; he was seized by the mob and dragged through the streets. Mayor Theodore Lyman, an anti-abolitionist, nevertheless stepped in, jailing Garrison for his own safety and advising him to leave town for a while. Garrison and his family fled to Connecticut, where his wife gave birth to a son, whom they named George Thompson Garrison.

Two years earlier, Reuben and Rachel Ruby had had a son whom they named after well-known British abolitionist William Wilberforce. In 1836, Arthur Tappan Ruby was born, named for the New York abolitionist who had helped to form the American Anti-Slavery Society with Garrison. Five years later, the Rubys would name another son for the British abolitionist whom they met in person: George Thompson. The names of the Rubys' sons, like Reuben's and Rachel's participation in multiple activist causes during the 1820s and 1830s, speak to their forthright passion for abolition and civil rights at a time when such views carried a dangerously high cost, even in the far North. At the end of that period, they would move their family to New York City, where the struggle between pro- and antislavery factions was more pronounced and potentially more volatile.

CHAPTER 4

Metropolis of Liberty

The free born inhabitants of the United States may be offered for sale and sold, even in the metropolis of liberty, as oxen.

—Dr. Jesse Torrey, Philadelphia physician, 1834

At the end of the 1830s, Nathaniel Gordon II and Reuben Ruby moved with their families to New York City. Both were seeking opportunity during a devastating economic depression, and what better place to find it than the world's busiest port, where hundreds of ships came and went daily, carrying tons of valuable cargo and hundreds of entrepreneurs, sailors, fugitives, and fortune seekers? Gordon's and Ruby's experiences offer two distinct but connected images of the business capital of the North: a city that was as diverse, chaotic, and divided as the nation itself.

NATHANIEL GORDON II AND his family left Portland for New York in 1838.[1] At home, a massive financial crisis—the Panic of 1837—had caused commerce to screech to a halt; shipping stalled, factories closed, and thousands lost their jobs. In New York, nearly 50,000 of the city's 300,000 residents were unemployed.[2] But the city was now the largest port for the United States, doing more business than all of New England combined and offering seemingly limitless opportunities for a shipmaster and trader.[3]

Throughout the 1830s, Gordon had had a business address in New York, even though his home address was in Maine. But in 1838, he, his wife Mary, and their three children—Dorcas, seventeen; Nathaniel, twelve; and Mary, four—took up residence on Stone Street in Manhattan, just south of Wall Street and a few blocks from the slips clustered along the East River. Nathaniel set up shop as a produce merchant, selling cheese, butter, pork, and ashes on commission, with a business address at 27 Front Street in Brooklyn, close to where the large sailing ships docked.[4] He also continued to work as a shipmaster, transporting goods between the Northeast and the Caribbean.

Less than a year into this new venture, he ran into strong headwinds. On June 25, 1838, Gordon sailed the brig *Dunlap* into New York Harbor. He had captained the ship from Point-à-Pitre, Guadeloupe, carrying four hundred hogsheads of molasses for Portland and thirteen passengers—twelve French and one American mariner—according to the ship's manifest. One passenger was missing from that list: a Black man named George Washington. One of Gordon's White passengers, Lambert Bercier, brought Washington along, and Captain Gordon left Washington off the list of passengers, hoping to slip him through unnoticed.[5] When Bercier and his family went ashore in New York, Washington was ordered to stay aboard the *Dunlap*, dress in sailor's clothing, and look busy about the rigging.[6]

Eight days later, Gordon and Bercier were called into federal court in the Southern District of New York on charges of piracy under the Act of 1820. According to that act, "if any citizen of the United States . . . shall forcibly confine or detain . . . on board such ship or vessel, any negro or mulatto not held to service by the laws of . . . the states or territories of the United States with intent to make sale of . . . such negro or mulatto, as a slave, such citizen . . . shall be adjudged a pirate; and . . . shall suffer death."[5] Failing to record Washington's presence—and disguising him as a sailor—proves that Gordon knew he was breaking the law.

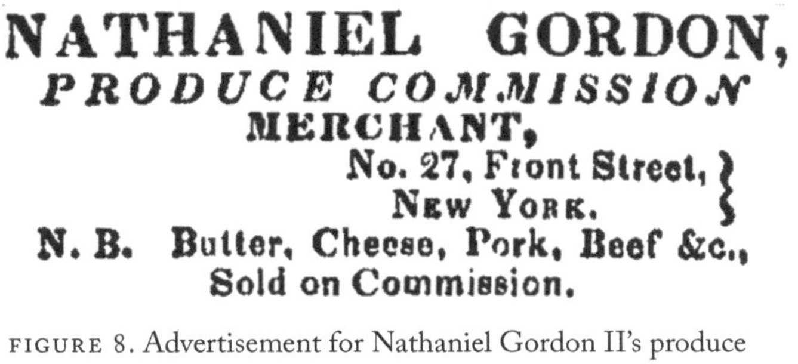

NATHANIEL GORDON,
PRODUCE COMMISSION
MERCHANT,
No. 27, Front Street, }
NEW YORK.   }
N. B. Butter, Cheese, Pork, Beef &c.,
Sold on Commission.

FIGURE 8. Advertisement for Nathaniel Gordon II's produce business in the *Burlington Free Press* (VT), September 28, 1838, http://genealogybank.com.

The U.S. marshal and district attorney seized the *Dunlap* and its cargo. While there's no indication that Gordon himself intended to sell or detain Washington, Bercier readily admitted his intention to do so. As master of the ship, Gordon was also held responsible, and if he were found guilty, he would forfeit the ship and its contents and possibly be sentenced to prison—or death—for slave trading.[8]

It wasn't customs agents who discovered the plot. David Ruggles, an ambitious, educated young African American and the most active and visible member of New York's Committee of Vigilance, reported Gordon to authorities. The committee had been formed in 1835 precisely for this purpose: to thwart the illegal slave trade in New York's busy harbor, prevent the kidnapping of free Blacks into slavery, and force local courts to uphold the laws on behalf of Black citizens and others.[9]

The committee was born of dire circumstances. Its first annual report cited "the alarming fact that any colored person within this state is liable to be arrested as a *fugitive from slavery* and put upon his defence to prove his freedom, and that any *such* person thus arrested is denied the *right of a trial by jury* . . . often without the aid of a friend or a counsellor."[10] Numerous court cases from the period reveal that Blacks were routinely denied the right of trial by jury and the right to testify on their own behalf. This left virtually any person of color liable to kidnapping without recourse, unless a White individual spoke up for them.

Ruggles, who served as the committee's secretary and enforcer, was confrontational and courageous. He and his associates boarded ships, freeing Blacks who were being held against their wills. They demanded that southern slaveholders who were staying in the city emancipate enslaved persons they'd brought with them, and they reported those who had overstayed the nine-month limit to authorities.[11] They assisted, secreted, and advocated in court for runaways. And they daringly challenged kidnappers and bounty hunters who roamed the streets of New York looking for free Blacks to capture and sell south. Ruggles even published the names of kidnappers in his newspaper, *The Mirror of Liberty*. The work was dangerous, nerve-wracking, and often violent. Ruggles received many beatings and many threats to his life. But by 1838, he and the Committee of Vigilance had helped to rescue more than 522 individuals from slavery.[12]

Ruggles regularly walked the docks of New York's busy port, inquiring of Black sailors and others who might be hiding human cargo. And plenty were. Though New York wasn't technically a slave state, it was apathetic to slavery at best, and complicit at worst. Its status as the busiest international port in the United States resulted from the cotton, sugar, tobacco, and rice trades, whose captains, crews, goods—and often, enslaved workers—passed through the harbor. And New York courts reflected those economic interests. According to the Committee of Vigilance, "the laws enacted for the protection of the colored people are continually violated, not only by men in private life, but even by our judges."[13]

Ruggles filed charges against Gordon, Bercier, and the *Dunlap*, recording the details of the case in *The Mirror of Liberty*. Gordon left no written account behind, so his position is seen only through the filter of Ruggles's reporting. But numerous letters reprinted in *The Mirror of Liberty* show that Gordon's and Bercier's friends and associates exerted tremendous pressure on Ruggles to withdraw charges. Horace Dresser, a lawyer who represented fugitives from slavery on behalf of the Committee of Vigilance, wrote to Ruggles stating that Gordon and Bercier would offer "a handsome sum to be relieved of their fix." He recommended that Ruggles accept the money and put it into the committee's treasury.

The *Dunlap*'s consignee, New York merchant M. C. Morgan, wrote to Ruggles, encouraging him to meet with Gordon and William Price, the U.S. district attorney. But Ruggles refused. "Principle," he replied, "is not an article of merchandise, if men are; therefore, it can neither be bought or sold." And Nathaniel Gordon himself wrote to Ruggles, hoping to inspire his empathy. He was a family man, he said, with a wife, children, and a reputation to consider. Still, Gordon had shown little concern for the wife and family that George Washington had left behind in Guadeloupe. Ruggles responded, "My feelings are for you, while my judgment is firmly against you."[14]

As a final recourse, Gordon's supporters attacked Ruggles in the press. An article in the *New York Express* titled "Kidnapping a Brig and Captain" portrayed Gordon as the real victim in the affair: "The colored people have undertaken to kidnap the white!" According to the piece, Gordon had reluctantly brought George Washington on board the *Dunlap* at Bercier's request, believing him to be a free Black. Gordon had told Bercier to obtain the necessary passage papers from the American consul in Guadeloupe, but the consul had recently died. Thus, "resting in good faith upon the assertion of the Frenchman, that the negro was not a slave, [Gordon] took him on board . . . and brought him to New York." The writer then asserted that Ruggles and the Committee of Vigilance were guilty of corruption: "Abolitionism is nothing but a pick the pocket business, by which traps are to extort costs, or bribes from captains and owners of such vessels."[15]

The case was finally sent to a grand jury. Though Ruggles had managed to engage five sailors from the *Dunlap* as witnesses for the prosecution, District Attorney Price never appeared. Not surprisingly, the grand jury dismissed the case against Gordon and Bercier.[16]

David Ruggles, bitter after his exhaustive efforts, wrote, "the public may judge as to whether gold or justice turned the scales in the matter."[17] Since he'd been offered a bribe to withdraw charges, he believed that a similar bribe had helped keep the district attorney at home, allowing the grand jury to render the only decision it could. Whatever occurred behind the scenes, Gordon and Bercier went free, and the *Dunlap* was released. What happened to George Washington, the hapless captive aboard the brig, is unknown.

GORDON'S CASE WAS SANDWICHED between two others that show how captains, slave traders, and New York courts conspired to work around the 1820 piracy law. In December 1836, the brig *Brilliante*, under Brazilian captain Joao De Souza, arrived in the city for repairs and provisions. Suspecting that De Souza was a slave trader, Ruggles visited the ship, found five enslaved men aboard, and reported his findings to authorities. De Souza was arrested, and his captives were detained as witnesses.

In court, De Souza argued that he was merely passing through New York, had no intention of selling the men locally, and claimed that they were "bona fide seamen." The judge agreed, saying that the men "had not been brought here to be sold or held to labor, but only during the temporary stay of their master." They were escorted back to the *Brilliante*.[18]

Four days later, as Ruggles lay asleep in his house, the mate of the *Brilliante*, Joseph Michaels, and a policeman named Daniel Nash broke in and tried to carry him away. A watchman heard the ruckus and arrived to intervene and arrest Nash and Michaels. A search of the pair turned up a writ indicating that they intended to carry Ruggles to the *Brilliante* so he himself could be shipped to Brazil and sold.[19]

Later, when Ruggles went to the police station to file a complaint against Michaels and Nash, he was arrested by Nash's partner in crime,

Tobias Boudinot, and jailed. Ruggles was ultimately freed, as was Captain De Souza. After only a slight delay, De Souza and the *Brilliante* sailed for Brazil on February 20.[20] Apparently, bringing kidnapped Africans into the Port of New York was legal as long as captains didn't sell their captives on the streets of the city.

THREE WEEKS AFTER NATHANIEL Gordon II was accused of piracy in New York, David Ruggles filed another complaint with the New York federal court against another Maine sea captain, Ebenezer Farwell of Vassalboro. Farwell, master of the ship *Transit*, was charged with "bringing four Africans here from the coast of Africa, contrary to law," and was taken into custody by the U.S. marshal. He had brought one of the Africans to his father's home in Maine, saying that the man was ill and "would be carefully attended to until he recovered."[21] Farwell defended his actions, claiming that, "being in want of seamen while he was on the coast of Africa, he shipped the four Africans as part of a crew, at the regular wages given to seamen." But this was an old trick, used long before the Act of 1820 became law, when states such as Massachusetts and Rhode Island had had their own laws that banned importing Africans for the purpose of enslaving them. In 1787, Rhode Island abolitionist Stephen Hopkins noted that "Capt. Moses Smith of Providence . . . shipped two free Negroes as seamen on board his vessel." But when his ship arrived in Newport, "instead of paying them their wages," Smith "sold them for slaves."[22]

There was no clear proof that Farwell had recruited the Africans with the intent to sell them. In fact, he had freed—or at least abandoned—three of them upon arrival in New York; they were found hungry and destitute, wandering the streets of Manhattan. The court determined that the African sent to Maine—known only as Yazee—had joined the crew of the *Transit* reluctantly. But he had gone to Maine "by his own consent," where he was employed as a "free laborer."[23] Several newspapers concluded, "The act under which Captain Farwell was accused, applies only to cases in which persons are brought into the country with intentions to make them slaves, and as there was no appearance of such intent on the part of the Captain, the complaint was of course discharged."[24]

Proving any sea captain's intent was nearly impossible. American slave captains employed many schemes for denying the obvious: employing

Africans aboard their ships as "sailors"; flying foreign flags; posing as passengers while allowing non-Americans to take over their captain's duties; discharging their captives in Cuba or Brazil before returning to U.S. ports; waiting until they were in African ports to actually fit out the ship for captives; running ships to Africa or Cuba and then selling them to a third party; refitting, renaming, and burning ships so they couldn't be found out. Because shipmasters were prominent and well-connected members of their communities, courts were inclined to give them special privileges. And as David Ruggles implied in the *Dunlap* affair, merchants and captains often used money to encourage courts and prosecutors to look away.

The *Transit* case was merely the tip of the iceberg for Farwell, who was a fixture in New York courtrooms. Less than a year earlier, he had been called into circuit court for "inflicting cruel and unusual punishment on John Brown," a Black steward and cook on the brig *Mercandy*, "by which treatment it was alleged he caused or accelerated the death of the said Brown." In that case, White members of Farwell's crew had brought the charges and testified against him.

Farwell had hired Brown as a cook, but despite being "a bright mulatto man," Brown wasn't cut out for the job. The crew complained about his food and his slovenly habits. His hair was often found in the dishes he was serving, he would drag his sleeves in the food, and his trousers were so long that he frequently tripped in the galley and broke dishes.

A few days into the voyage, Captain Farwell removed Brown from his duty as cook. He then began to treat Brown "with great severity . . . and cruelty," according to crewmembers. He cut off Brown's sleeves and pantlegs. In very cold weather, with other sailors wearing foul-weather gear, Brown was ordered to wear just his short sleeves and short pants and "had no shoes, or stockings, or boots, or coat or hat on." His shipmates testified that the captain "had repeatedly flogged him—two or three times a day—20 or 30 times in all." Farwell made Brown "tie himself to the rigging" and sent him to the main topmast in "cold and sleety weather . . . after he was taken sick." When Brown grew too ill to work, the captain ordered him into a longboat with several pigs in it, exposed to the weather. After enduring a steady diet of brutality, Brown died twenty-six days after the *Mercandy* left port. "The captain read prayers over him," witnesses recounted, "and he was thrown overboard."

The Act of 1835 had made it illegal for sea captains to beat, wound, or imprison sailors or inflict cruel and unusual punishment without sufficient cause.[25] Yet several powerful men took Farwell's side. Maine's governor and secretary of state, a U.S. senator, and two state senators sent depositions testifying "to the general good and excellent character of Capt. Farwell."[26] The judge then instructed the jury that, to convict Farwell, the prosecution would have had to show that the punishment had been "inflicted from anger, hatred, or malice on the part of the captain." To ensure that the jury came to the correct conclusion, the judge noted that "there was no evidence to prove that it had been done maliciously." According to the *New York Morning Herald*, "the jury without leaving their seats or deliberating two minutes returned a verdict of *Not Guilty*," and "Captain Farwell . . . left the Court in company with a large number of friends by whom he was warmly congratulated." The *Herald* praised Judge Smith Thompson for presiding over a trial that was "lucid, fair and masterly." He had "instructed the jury without dictating to them."[27]

A year later, the *Herald* was less confident of Farwell's innocence. "The accused only escaped a charge of manslaughter by the skin of his teeth," wrote a reporter, referring to the Brown case. This change of heart had likely been inspired by mounting evidence that Farwell was a bully with a bad temper. A White steward and White first mate who had served with Farwell aboard the ship *Franklin* testified in yet a third trial to his "cruel and unusual punishment" and his threatening to run the mate "through the heart with a cutlass."[28] In that case, a New York court fined Farwell $27.69 damages—not for threatening or cruel and unusual punishment, but "for not supplying his crew with a sufficiency of good and wholesome food" on a voyage to Liverpool. Never questioning Farwell's suitability as a captain, the *Lincoln Telegraph* of Bath, Maine, printed the decision as a "Caution to Shipmasters."[29]

Justice in the United States—even in the North—continued to favor White over Black and the powerful over the disenfranchised. But in Africa, things were more complicated. Farwell continued to make trading trips there, despite his close call in the *Transit* case, and the failure of federal courts in New York to hold him accountable would bring dire consequences. In December 1842, Abel P. Upshur, the secretary of the U.S. Navy, wrote an open letter to President John Tyler that was published widely in the press. In describing American trade on the African coast, he noted, "Several of our vessels have been captured by the natives, and their crews barbarously murdered. The last aggression of this sort was upon the schooner Mary Carver, [commanded by] Captain Farwell, in the district of Berribee, ninety miles south of Cape Palmas." Farwell, it seems, had pressed his luck one time too many.[30]

Sensational reports of the *Mary Carver* incident flooded American newspapers. An account from North Carolina referred to the residents of Béréby, in present-day Ivory Coast, as "cannibals."[31] The *Baltimore Sun* published a first-person account from the captain of a brig lately arrived in Baltimore from Liberia, who reported that Béréby was "inhabited by natives of a very savage character." According to the account, Farwell had been lured to shore to examine some camwood, which the local inhabitants wanted to sell him. Once on shore, locals seized the captain, who was allegedly stripped and beaten by women and children. Farwell begged for his life "on account of his absent wife and child," but the attackers, being "ruthless savages, had no ears for his entreaties." Meanwhile, local men boarded the *Mary Carver*, massacring the crew and plundering the vessel. The *Sun* was careful to point out that the violence was gratuitous: "no dispute had occurred, as previously reported, between Captain Farwell and the natives."[32]

There's no proof that Farwell was engaged in man stealing or slave trading. That he was innocent of bringing the Africans' wrath upon himself and his ship is doubtful, given his character. In recounting the story, the *Vermont Telegraph* editorialized, "What less could be expected? It is no cause for wonder that such awful retaliations should occasionally appear on that devoted coast, which has so long been the theatre of brutal and diabolical outrage, where the white man has prowled for human prey. It is rather to be wondered at, that a white man can step foot on the coast and escape with his life."[33]

In October, another sea captain, recently arrived in Philadelphia from Liberia, added to the growing hue and cry for revenge on behalf of Eben Farwell and the crew of the *Mary Carver*. The inhabitants of Béréby, he wrote, "are a bad race, and deserve to be severely chastised. . . . They can easily be castigated; the landing is fair, having myself landed there often while trading with them a few years back."[34]

In response, the U.S. Navy launched an expedition to further investigate the matter comprising four ships and two hundred marines and sailors commanded by Commodore Matthew Perry. But Perry's letter to Secretary of the Navy Upshur clearly states his actual mission: "Arrangements are in place for chastising the natives of Berriby . . . for the murder of the master of the Schooner Mary Carver."[35] On arrival, the commodore met with the local king, Ben Cracko, but after a short while, talks broke down. As a result, a naval detachment mortally wounded the king, killed a number of his subjects, and burned seven villages to the ground.[36]

Such was the appalling path of destruction left by the brutality of one Mainer, Eben Farwell. But the incident also speaks to the long-held views of Americans; to look good politically at home, American interests—including American ships and crews trading in humans—must be defended abroad. And there was minimal cost in doing so: who was going to make Commodore Perry and his detachment pay for their overreaction? American newspapers and shipmasters who had traded in Africa chose to report the original incident as an unprovoked massacre by the violent and predatory inhabitants of Béréby. Farwell's reputation as a cruel and ruthless captain and probable slave trader was ignored. But it's easy to understand how his well-documented character flaws and the failure of New York courts to hold him accountable had encouraged the disaster.

LIKE DE SOUZA AND Farwell, Nathaniel Gordon escaped the New York court system unscathed. The 1820 piracy law had minimal value in stopping the international slave trade. Judges and juries ignored its clear language and avoided its heaviest penalty, while prosecutors were reluctant to press charges. These tendencies would play into an even more important and explosive court case in New York some twenty years later.

After only a year, Nathaniel Gordon II left New York and returned to Maine with his family.[37] The *Dunlap* incident had undoubtedly influenced that decision, and it seems to have been a turning point for Gordon. He abandoned his ambition of becoming a trader and focused on running cargo between Portland and the West Indies. Less clear is the impact the incident had on his family, including his wife, daughter, brothers, and his twelve-year-old son, Nathaniel III, who would follow in his father's footsteps as a shipmaster.

LIFE IN NEW YORK in the 1830s and 1840s was complicated. The ships and captains transiting New York harbor frequently ignored antislavery trafficking laws, and foreign investors in the slave trade were beginning to take up residence there, given its tolerant attitude.[38] But New York was also a magnet for people who were escaping from slavery, many of whom arrived with the help of sympathetic mariners. Some White ship captains willingly secreted fugitives on their way north, and Black sailors carried letters between southern fugitives and Underground Railroad operatives in New York and beyond. In 1826, a local newspaper complained that New York City had become "the point of refuge to all the runaways in the Union."[39]

New York had numerous boardinghouses for Black sailors, at least some of which harbored fugitives. The most prominent was the Colored Sailors' Home, managed by William P. Powell, Sr., a free African American. A former sailor himself, Powell was a member of the American Anti-Slavery Society and made no secret of his views. He placed a picture of Crispus Attucks, a Black stevedore and the first casualty of the American Revolution, in the dining room of his house. He provided a library and reading room on site, held abolitionist meetings there, and, like so many in the abolitionist movement, forbade drinking. Powell actively recruited seamen to help rescue fugitives, and he is believed to have harbored hundreds of runaways on their journeys north.[40]

Charles B. Ray and Henry Highland Garnet, both Black residents of the city, also housed fugitives. Garnet, a clergyman and abolitionist, had himself escaped from slavery in Maryland as a boy. "One hundred and fifty, in a single year, have lodged under my roof," he later wrote.[41]

In early September 1838, just a month after Nathaniel Gordon II's appearance before a New York grand jury, Fred Bailey, a fugitive from slavery in Maryland, landed in Manhattan. He was dressed as a sailor and had traveled by train and boat. Without friends or shelter, he slept on the docks for a night, "afraid to speak to any one for fear of speaking to the wrong one." But the next day, David Ruggles heard about Bailey and sought him out. He took the fugitive to his home at 36 Lispenard Street. There, he gave Bailey shelter and a new last name: Johnson. Fred Johnson sent word of his escape to his fiancé, Anna, who was a free African American. Anna quickly traveled to New York, and the couple were married at Ruggles's home. But Ruggles thought New York too dangerous for them, so he packed the Johnsons off to New Bedford, Massachusetts, with a $5 bill and a letter of introduction—to begin a new life. In New Bedford, the fugitive changed his name one last time: to Frederick Douglass.[42]

REUBEN RUBY MAINTAINED HIS hack business in Portland through 1837, but with the severe economic depression, most Portlanders were walking, not hiring cabs.[43] A series of lawsuits also show Ruby's growing estrangement from the Abyssinian Religious Society. In 1837, he and other members had published a newspaper notice warning that the church's pastor, Samuel Chase, was fundraising without the approval of the congregation. Chase sued them for libel and won. Ruby was able to pay the $150 fine, but Abraham Niles, a deacon at the Abyssinian, couldn't, and city officials seized his home.[44]

A year earlier, Ruby had sued the Abyssinian Society, saying that they owed him for improvements he'd hired others to make to the unfinished meeting house. The society countered, arguing that it hadn't authorized him to make those improvements. It was a sore spot for Ruby, who had put his heart and soul into the Abyssinian at the start, but felt his generosity was being abused.[45] He still held the land the meeting house sat on in mortgage, and bitterly declared that "The Society should not have it if they paid a thousand dollars." He later said that, if they paid the mortgage, he "would have nothing more to do with them." The case continued for three years, and was a major source of anger and frustration for Ruby. While a local court initially awarded him $900, the Maine Supreme Judicial Court later set that judgment aside.[46]

All these matters may have shaped his decision to leave Portland. So in 1839 or 1840, Ruby moved to New York with his young family: his wife Rachel and sons Frederic, nine, William, six, Arthur, four, and daughter Sarah, eight. Shortly after arriving, Ruby started a "refectory," or restaurant, in lower Manhattan. New York in the 1830s and 1840s was a boomtown for eating establishments.[47] And cooking, catering, and operating restaurants were among only a handful of trades open to free Blacks.

Although the nation was in the midst of a depression, restaurants in New York were springing up like weeds. Workers in Manhattan's business district were no longer going home for lunch, and many individuals ate breakfast, lunch, and dinner outside the home. Refectories and eating houses were designed to feed large crowds at low prices; some served between 1,000 and 3,000 diners at lunchtime.[48] On Nassau Street, where Ruby's refectory and a host of others were located, "a plate of anything may be had for sixpence," declared the *Broadway Journal*.[49]

One prominent African American restauranteur served as a model for Ruby. Thomas Downing, the son of parents released from bondage, had succeeded—perhaps even beyond his own imagination—in the business. From 1825 to the 1860s, Downing's Oyster House was the most famous restaurant in New York apart from Delmonico's. Occupying numbers 3, 5, and 7 Broad Street near Wall Street, Downing's Oyster House was known to procure the freshest oysters and to serve them in style.[50]

Downing knew oysters. He'd grown up on Chincoteague Island, Virginia, fishing, oystering, and clamming. He eventually made his way to Philadelphia and then to New York, where, in the 1822 directory, he is listed as an "oysterman."[51] Soon Downing opened his own refectory. While the majority of oyster houses or "cellars" were dark and dirty—at the time, the bivalves were anything but a delicacy—Downing's evolved into a large, carpeted, well-lit space that catered to well-to-do businessmen, bankers, brokers, and lawyers in the Wall Street neighborhood who devoured oysters by the ton: stewed, raw, fried, or baked in pie. Downing himself rowed over to the Jersey Shore at all times of day to personally inspect and purchase oysters. His restaurant was extremely popular, as was its owner. English novelist Charles Dickens dined on Downing's oysters on a trip to the United States, and Queen Victoria partook of some of his choicest oysters, which Downing himself shipped to her. New Yorkers appreciated him, too; the New York City Chamber of Commerce closed on the day of Downing's funeral so that members could attend.[52]

While businessmen were frequenting the well-appointed restaurant, fugitives were hiding out in its basement and back rooms. Downing was careful about harboring runaways, but he was forthright about where he stood on slavery and equality for Blacks. In 1836, he helped to found the United Anti-Slavery Society of the City of New York. He and his son George also worked hard for equal suffrage for African American men, petitioning the state government numerous times.[53] He was a prominent figure in the Colored Convention movement and had attended the 1835

Convention of the Free People of Color in Philadelphia, where Reuben Ruby had presided.

Ruby knew and respected Downing, and because he was ambitious, he may have seen Downing's Oyster House as a model for what he might accomplish. In fact, some of Ruby's advertisements referred to his restaurant as "Oyster and Eating Rooms."[54] But he would have learned about Downing's from papers and talk on the street, or perhaps from visiting the kitchen through a back entrance; Downing's, like most of Manhattan's eating houses, served only White clientele.

Segregated restaurants were the norm in New York, though some activists balked at the practices that restricted Black diners. In 1837, Ruby's friend Samuel Cornish visited a New York restaurant run by a Scottish abolitionist where he was "refused a cup of tea, on the account of my color." Outraged, Cornish publicized the incident in *The Colored American*: "It remained for a foreigner, in a cellar cook-room, to insult a native citizen . . . and to deny a minister of Christ, of gray hairs, and twenty-five years' standing in the Presbyterian church, a cup of Tea."[55]

It's unlikely that Ruby's restaurant served both Black and White diners, given the disposition of most Whites on the matter. And at the time, New York's White population held most of the disposable income. But Ruby's advertisements in local newspapers portray an eating house consistent with his beliefs. The refectory served dinners, breakfasts, and tea. Advertisements also promised to "provide dinners for families and send them to their house, at short notice," perhaps allowing Black families, barred from Manhattan's best eateries, to enjoy prepared meals. Ruby also billed his as a "Temperance Eating House," where patrons could look forward to tea, "pure milk" and "[p]ure spring water at the bar," but "no intoxicating liquor." [56] Like many of his activist peers, Ruby believed that drinking alcohol aggravated discrimination and would slow Blacks' progress towards equal rights. David Ruggles, too, refused to sell liquor in his Manhattan grocery store.[57] *The Colored American* newspaper wouldn't accept restaurant advertisements because most New York eating houses offered "liquid death, both for body and mind," rather than "wholesome food for the body." Its editor Samuel Cornish wrote, "As we cannot participate at all in this kind of traffic, we shall not advertise any place, under what ever name, in which is to be sold ardent spirits."[58]

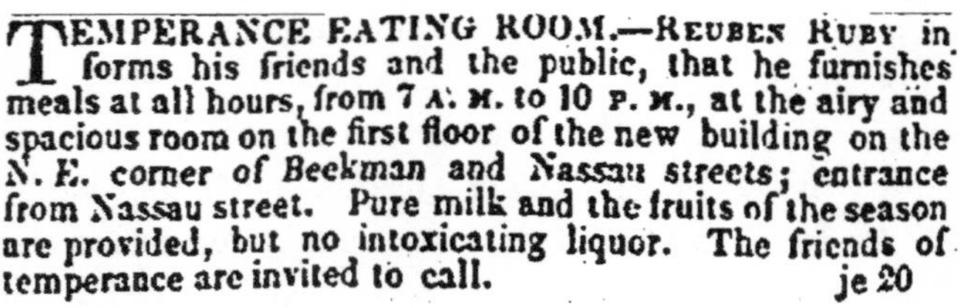

TEMPERANCE EATING ROOM.—REUBEN RUBY informs his friends and the public, that he furnishes meals at all hours, from 7 A. M. to 10 P. M., at the airy and spacious room on the first floor of the new building on the N. E. corner of Beekman and Nassau streets; entrance from Nassau street. Pure milk and the fruits of the season are provided, but no intoxicating liquor. The friends of temperance are invited to call.   je 20

FIGURE 9. Advertisement for Reuben Ruby's Temperance Eating Room in the *New York Observer*, September 12, 1840, http://genealogybank.com.

Ruby opened his restaurant at 137 Nassau Street, on the corner of Beekman, a location that speaks volumes about his life in New York. The street was home to numerous eating houses, newspapers, and antislavery societies, including the *Broadway Journal*; the abolitionist *New-York Tribune*, founded by Horace Greeley; the *New York Leader*; the American Moral Reform Society, with which Ruby had been briefly affiliated; the American Anti-Slavery Society and its newspaper, the *National Anti-Slavery Standard*, whose offices were said to be a haven for those fleeing slavery; and the Temperance Union.[59] The abolitionist American Missionary Association and the American and Foreign Anti-Slavery Society, where fugitives were also known to gather, could be found on John Street, just around the corner from Ruby's refectory.[60] William Powell's Colored Sailors' Home sat at the corner of John and Gold Streets. David Ruggles's Committee of Vigilance was also located on John Street, and *The Colored American* was published on nearby Frankfort Street. Ruby undoubtedly mingled, discussed, and worked with both White and African American abolitionists in New York, and his social and political beliefs, perhaps even more than his culinary interests, likely drew him to the city.

In 1840, Ruby began attending meetings of the Manhattan Anti-Slavery Society and was elected president. In November, he presided at a meeting of New York's Black citizens to discuss how best to persuade the state legislature "to extend the elective franchise to all her citizens irrespective of color or condition." Stringent property ownership requirements for Black New Yorkers—but not for Whites—made it nearly impossible for them to vote. In 1835, only sixty-eight registered Black voters were recorded in the city, despite a Black population of some 16,000.[61] Both Thomas Downing and Henry Highland Garnet were deeply involved in the voting effort. Attendees at the meeting took assignments to secure signatures from their respective wards. Ruby covered Ward 4, along the East River.[62] By February 1841, the state legislature had received petitions for suffrage signed by some 1,300 Black and 400 White New Yorkers.[63]

In the meantime, Ruby had also become friendly with David Ruggles. He began participating in Ruggles's projects, attending the National Reform Convention of the Colored Inhabitants of the United States in Hartford in 1840 and joining the American Reformed Board of Disfranchised Commissioners, a short-lived organization that sought to unify all Blacks in the antislavery cause.[64] Reuben's wife was active in antislavery affairs, too; Rachel Ruby's name is listed as an organizer of a benefit for the Manhattan Anti-Slavery Society, alongside that of the influential abolitionist Lydia Maria Child.[65] In addition to writing *The American Frugal Housewife* (1832) aimed at American women, Child had published *An Appeal in Favor of That Class of Americans Called Africans* in 1833. She became the editor of the *National Anti-Slavery Standard* in 1840 and would later edit Harriet Jacobs's autobiography, *Incidents in the Life of a Slave Girl*, published in 1861.

ALTHOUGH NEW YORK HOTELS, dwellings, and restaurants were segregated, New York neighborhoods, especially in lower Manhattan, were mixed.[66] And they housed plenty of Black-owned businesses like Ruby's: refectories, boardinghouses, dry-good stores, groceries, pharmacies. David Ruggles sold "free sugar," not produced by enslaved laborers, at his grocery store. He also opened the first Black-owned bookstore in the United States.[67] Like the Colored Sailors' Home and the offices of *The Colored American*, Ruggles's bookstore featured a reading room where educated African Americans could gather the latest news, even if they couldn't afford to purchase books or newspapers.

While Manhattan offered a vibrant social and intellectual atmosphere for the Rubys, it was also dangerous. Kidnappers and bounty hunters—then referred to as "black-birders"—roamed the streets, seeking to capture fugitives from slavery and unsuspecting free Blacks to ship south, a practice now known as the Reverse Underground Railroad. Only Philadelphia attracted more kidnappers than New York. "Every colored person, and every friend of their persecuted race, kept their eyes wide open," wrote Harriet Jacobs, who had escaped from slavery and began residing in New York City in 1842. "Every evening I examined the newspapers carefully, to see what Southerners had put up at the hotels."[68] Anti-slavery newspapers published warnings about kidnappers, often naming the culprits:

> We are informed that the notorious NASH has returned from the South, and is prowling about the city for more victims. Col-ored people should be on their guard. Let no white man into your house unless you know who he is, and what his business is. If he says he is an officer and has a warrant to arrest a fugitive slave, *don't let him in unless he shows a search warrant.* He has no right to go or stay in without [one].[69]

"The notorious NASH" was Daniel D. Nash, who, along with his associ-ate Tobias Boudinot, were city policemen and members of what Ruggles called the "New York Kidnapping Club": the group that had attempted to kidnap him during the *Brilliante* affair in 1838. Nash, Boudinot, and their associates worked the city's streets and the courts, capturing Black individuals and bringing them to Richard Riker, the court recorder, claiming that they were fugitives. Riker would dispatch the victims to the South before they had the chance to present witnesses or lawyers to speak for them. As African Americans, their word in court was worth little or nothing if it contradicted a White person's testimony.[70]

New York courts were stacked against Black individuals. Ruggles wrote that a White man named Ayres had transported a young Black apprentice from Jamaica to New York, intending to sell him in South Carolina. When Ruggles and a counsel for the boy appealed to Judge Irving for an urgently needed writ of habeas corpus, "His Honor declined issuing it upon the ground that he was sick, and should soon leave his office and go to bed." Ruggles then appealed to Irving's colleague, Judge Ulshoeffer, who "refused to allow the writ, as he wanted his dinner and could not attend to it."[51]

In 1836, Peter John Lee, a free Black from Westchester, New York, was kidnapped and sold.[72] In June 1838, a Captain James Dayton Wilson was arrested and charged with kidnapping three young men—Isaac Wright, Robert Garrison, and Stephen Dickerson—and selling them into slavery.[73] Free Black musician Solomon Northup was famously lured away from his upstate New York home in 1841, kidnapped, and enslaved for twelve years.[74]

Children were frequent victims, too, so Reuben and Rachel must have feared not just for themselves but for their four children, all of whom were under ten years old in 1840. Seven-year-old Charles Kelsey disappeared from his home on Beekman Street in Manhattan in 1837 and was believed to have been kidnapped.[75] *The Colored American* published a notice of a missing boy named John, age thirteen, who, it was feared, had been sold south.[76] David Ruggles published this notice in the same newspaper:

> CHILD LOST—Frances Maria Shields, a girl of about 12 years of age, is missed by her guardians and acquaintances. . . . She is middling size, dark brown complexion, short hair, with a scar over her right eyebrow. Her dress was a purple and white frock, white straw hat, lined with pink, and trimmed with straw colored ribbon, mixed stockings, and boots. Any person who will give such information as will lead to the restoration of said girl to her guardian and friends, shall be rewarded.[77]

The notice, with its poignant details, is all the more tragic for what it doesn't say: how her family must have agonized over her safety and mourned her loss. No doubt, free Black parents like the Rubys felt compelled to lecture their children frequently about kidnapping and how to stay safe on the streets of American cities.

White southerners and New York policemen weren't the only ones to be feared. David Ruggles told a gathering of African Americans that they must be on the lookout for kidnappers—White *and* Black— including a Black man named John Wallace who had attempted to lure young Eliza Cummings onto a boat in New York Harbor.[78] Ruggles also noted in his newspaper that a fugitive in New York had been taken back into slavery when "a certain colored man . . . did betray him by writing to his Master."[59] Black kidnappers relied on shared ethnic identity and trust. What could be suspicious about a Black man or woman leading a young Black child screaming and kicking down the street?

IN THIS CHAOTIC, TEEMING metropolis, there were, of course, the bottom feeders: those who professed principles but cared little for North or South, race or creed, morals or law. Among them was Fontaine H. Pettis, who purported to be a lawyer from Virginia who had moved to New York City. He advertised his fugitive-catching services widely in southern newspapers: "In defiance of the Abolitionists, he can cause to be secured any fugitive slave, who shall be North of Mason and Dixon's line."[80]

Members of the Committee of Vigilance and free Blacks like the Rubys were naturally wary of Pettis, but Pettis was as willing to prey upon unsuspecting slaveowners as he was their so-called property. In addition to placing advertisements in newspapers, Pettis wrote directly to slaveowners who had posted runaway notices, using details from their descriptions to imply that he knew where the escapees were: "I take leave to write to you by way of inquiry, whether or not you have recently lost a black fellow? My most confidential spy has this moment informed me that a fellow has just arrived here . . . [with] *free papers*, made and signed by you." Pettis would then ask the enslaver to send him a formal power of attorney and an advance of $20. He claimed that once he had managed to return the fugitive to the enslaver, he would collect an additional $100. Quite a few $20 bills were lost because few, if any, such transactions were completed. Eventually, a slaveowner in Charleston, South Carolina, discovered Pettis's scam. The slaveowner had placed a runaway advertisement, and the fugitive, who had never left Charleston, was quickly returned to him. Soon afterward, he received a letter from Pettis claiming that the escapee was in New York. The enslaver wrote to the *Charleston Courier* to expose Pettis, and the story was picked up by newspapers across the South.[81]

Pettis was an equal-opportunity scammer. Despite posing as a slave catcher, he didn't mind dining at Black-owned establishments in New York. In June 1841, he was arrested for having eaten multiple times at a restaurant owned by a Black resident, Moses Leach, and running up a whopping $125 bill. When the physically impaired Leach demanded his money, Pettis assaulted him. Pettis was arrested and jailed, unable to pay his $300 bail.[82]

ACCORDING TO THE 1840 federal census, Reuben Ruby lived on Manhattan's Lower East Side and was the head of a household of eleven that included Rachel and their four children as well as two males and three females between the ages of ten and fifty-four who weren't part of the immediate family. One was described as a "learned professional engineer."[83] These other individuals may have been relatives, boarders, or both. Manhattan's hotels would not accept Black clientele, except for enslaved persons traveling with their masters, and the city's boarding-houses were segregated. So African American travelers relied heavily on private households that were known to accept Black boarders, many of whom advertised in abolitionist papers such as *Freedom's Journal* and *The Liberator*.[84] It's likely that Ruby sought to bring in extra cash by subletting rooms to other free Blacks.

On July 1, 1840, Rachel gave birth to a fifth child: George Thompson Ruby and, in 1843, to son Horatio. But New York also brought tragedy for the family. In 1842, Arthur Tappan Ruby died of scarlet fever at age six.[85] In November 1846, the Rubys' only daughter, Sarah, drowned. She had found work as a chambermaid aboard the steamer *Atlantic* when it sank in a violent storm off New London, Connecticut. Some forty or fifty of the seventy passengers and many of the crew were lost, including fourteen-year-old Sarah.[86] By age forty-eight, Reuben had already suffered the loss of his first wife and three of his children.

THE RESTAURANT BUSINESS IN New York was booming but volatile. In addition to refectories, dining rooms, and saloons, the streets teemed with vendors selling oysters—a New York staple—clams, corn on the cob, gingerbread, and pies. With so much competition, it was impossible for everyone to succeed. And, indeed, New York directories suggest that Ruby's restaurant foundered in the years after 1842. The 1842–43 directory lists Ruby as a "restaurator" at 95 John Street, no longer at the Nassau Street address. The following year he is listed as a "laborer" residing at 10½ Thomas Street and, from 1844 through 1847, as a "cook" residing at the same address. It's likely that he lost his restaurant sometime in 1843 or 1844 and subsequently found work as a cook in other establishments.[87] His activism diminished, too. He attended none of the local or national colored conventions after 1841 and grew increasingly quiet as an activist in the later years of the decade. He was likely struggling to support his family.

In the early morning hours of July 19, 1845, fire broke out at a sperm oil merchant's and candle factory on New Street in Manhattan, a half-mile south of the Rubys' residence. It spread to a warehouse that held saltpeter, a component of firecrackers and gunpowder, causing a huge explosion that leveled several buildings and could be heard for miles. A second, larger blast followed when a gas reservoir on New Street exploded. "The concussion was so great," reported the *New York Herald*, "as to smash more than half a million panes of glass in the neighborhood." By the next day, three hundred buildings had been leveled, and troops were ordered into the streets to protect property. Four firefighters were killed, along with twenty-six citizens.[88]

Reuben's son, William Ruby, eleven years old at the time of the fire, was fascinated by the fire companies, which were then private, all-volunteer fraternities. Each company recruited young boys to light the streets or help drag the heavy engines and equipment to the fires, all competing to be first at the scene. William served as a torch boy who ran ahead of the fire engines to light their way. His experience in New York and his witnessing the devastating fire of 1845 would prove critical in another fire some two decades later.

FOR THE RUBYS, THE hard times continued. In December 1848, the steamship *New York* anchored off Staten Island with three hundred passengers who had been exposed to cholera and were ordered to quarantine aboard. But not all did. The winter passed without a serious outbreak, but by June 1849 cholera roared into the city. Public schools were taken over as sick wards, and the city health department forbade the selling of fruit, produce, and fish on the streets. By August, more than 5,000 had died, and the city had begun burying bodies in a large trench on Randall's Island.[89]

The cholera outbreak, coupled with economic concerns, spelled the end of the Rubys' nine-year sojourn in New York. The family packed up and returned to Portland—except for Reuben. Having lost his restaurant, Reuben was in need of a financial boost. So in early 1849, he decided to make a risky voyage to California on his own.

CHAPTER 5

Gold Rush

Every man now worships gold, all other reverence being done away.

—Sextus Propertius

ew American families in the nineteenth century could afford not to worry about money. Some sought ways to make a steady and reliable income. Others took risks that promised greater rewards. The discovery of gold in California fanned those flames, producing a condition known as "gold fever," which swept across the United States and soon spread to other continents. Tens of thousands of individuals abandoned their homes and livelihoods to engage in high-risk ventures that could bring huge gains in a short time. Mining was one undertaking that could yield sudden riches. Transporting Africans into slavery was another; many who followed the merchant trade believed that a single shipload of captives landed in the Americas and sold into slavery could make a shipmaster's fortune.[1]

After leaving New York, Nathaniel Gordon II settled into a routine of running molasses from the Caribbean to Maine. Molasses was among Maine's largest imports in the West India trade, and local capitalists— especially John Bundy Brown—were seeking to refine it into sugar. Brown also had his hand in real estate and developed Portland's Western Promenade, which would become one of the nation's wealthiest neighborhoods. In 1845 he and his partners set up a large sugar refinery in Portland. Eventually, the Portland Sugar House grew into one of the largest in the United States, employing some 200 people and processing about 250 barrels of sugar per day.[2]

Most of this sugar was produced on the backs of enslaved laborers. The cotton boom had caused a particularly brutal form of slavery in the

Deep South, but the Caribbean sugar industry, which began in the six-teenth century, was worse in many ways. Deaths were so common among sugar plantation workers that they needed to be constantly replaced with newly captured ones. As Ralph Waldo Emerson wrote, "the sugar they raised was excellent; nobody tasted blood in it."[3]

Portland's Sugar House was profitable for Brown and his employ-ees, and by supplying the raw material for the enterprise, sea captain Nathaniel Gordon II shared in the prosperity. In December 1847, he pur-chased land in Portland's West End and engaged Charles Quincy Clapp, the city's most sought-after architect, to build him a Greek Revival house.[4] The purchase allowed the Gordons to live in comfort and style among the elite.

Although all of the surviving Gordon brothers—Joshua, Morgan, and Nathaniel—were sea captains, not all made their livings in the molasses trade. Morgan was even more ambitious, anxious to make money, and will-ing to take bigger risks with even more lucrative cargo. In 1843, he was cap-tain and owner of the brig *Caballero*, built in Baltimore. He sailed it to Rio Pongo in Africa, on Guinea's central coast. There, he boarded 346 captives and transported them to Cuba. The 339 who remained alive after the gruel-ing passage were sold into slavery.[5] Thomas Turner, a seaman who accom-panied Gordon, described the trip for authorities. But why did Turner, who had been complicit in this scheme, admit what they had done? It's a com-plicated story, but it demonstrates the complex webs of ships, shipmasters, owners, and sailors who conspired to carry out the slave trade.

Turner held a grudge against a third party in the plot: Paul Faber from Virginia. With his Black wife Mary, Faber ran a "slave factory" on the Rio Pongo in Guinea. Their operation involved a trading station, where goods were exchanged for money or captives, and a barracoon, where persons who had been captured inland were brought and held until sold.[6] The intrigue began when Turner shipped aboard the *Caballero* in Balti-more in November 1843. Captain Morgan Gordon had recruited him as a seaman and carpenter and assured him that they were embarking on an ordinary trading voyage to Africa. But in Baltimore, the *Caballero* was denied clearance to sail to Africa, likely because customs officials were suspicious of Gordon's intentions. So Gordon and crew sailed on to New York, where the *Caballero* was cleared for the transatlantic voyage on November 27. This was a notorious dodge on the part of shipmasters intent on running contraband: if customs officials at one port denied them clearance, they would simply sail on to the next.

At Rio Pongo, Gordon moored at the site of Faber's slave factory, sold his cargo, and began taking on wood, water, and rice. He then sold the ship to Faber for $10,000; the name *Caballero* was scratched off the ship's stern. Finally, according to Turner, "we took on 346 slaves" and made for Cuba. Gordon, Turner, and Faber were reputed to be the only White individuals aboard.[7] On her way to Africa, the *Caballero* had flown under the American flag; on the passage to Cuba, she carried no name on her stern nor any flag on her mast.

A naval officer who examined the ship later described the accommodations for the kidnapped men: "Between her decks, where the slaves are packed, there is not room enough for a man to sit, unless inclining his head forward. Their food, half a pint of rice per day, with one pint of water. No one can imagine the sufferings of slaves, on their passage across, unless the conveyances in which they are taken can be examined."[8] As for the fifty Guinean women aboard, they were confined in a cabin built to accommodate six.[9]

On such voyages, sailors witnessed the cries of the captives, the overpowering stench emanating from the hold, and the extreme discomfort, seasickness, filth, and inhumane conditions that captives were forced to endure. How could Gordon, Faber, and Turner ignore what their senses and consciences were telling them?

English slave captain John Newton contended that mariners in the trade became hardened to the suffering around them and acquired "a spirit of ferociousness and savage insensibility, of which human nature . . . is not ordinarily capable."[10] And then there was the promise of potentially huge profits. Perhaps that was enough to allow the threesome to ignore the human cost of their commerce. According to the naval officer who examined the *Caballero*, "a good hearty negro costs but twenty dollars" in Rio Pongo, but "they bring from three to four hundred dollars in Cuba"—a fifteen- to twenty-fold return on investment.[11] Given such profits, the slave trade was itself a sort of gold rush: a venture that allowed sea captains, merchants, and investors to accumulate wealth rapidly, if they were fortunate or shrewd enough to avoid disaster.

The *Caballero* arrived in Cuba after a passage of thirty-five days, landing the captive Africans "about thirty miles to windward of Matanzas."[12]

After selling their human cargo, Gordon and Faber delivered the brig to some unnamed Spaniards.

Sometime between the *Caballero*'s arrival in Cuba in May 1844 and her return trip to Rio Pongo that fall, Captain Peter Flowery from New York took over the ship. He sailed the brig to New Orleans, where it was repainted and given new masts, sails, and rigging, and a new name: *Spitfire*. On November 26, Flowery sailed the *Spitfire* from New Orleans to Havana and from there to Rio Pongo.[13]

Turner, Gordon, and Faber returned to Africa together on a different ship: the *Manchester*. Another ship, the *Devereux*, may have left at the same time. According to one newspaper account, "Capt. Gordon, the commander and ostensible owner of the Manchester and Devereux," left Boston on September 22, 1844, but not without his ships' being extensively searched by customs officials "on suspicion that they were intended for the slave trade."[14] Gordon and Faber, it seems, were well known to U.S. customs officials up and down the East Coast, which suggests this wasn't their first slaving trip.

On the African coast, things took a turn for the worse. The *Manchester* was wrecked on February 24, 1845, at Cape Mount, and though all aboard survived, the ship and cargo were looted by locals. Captain Gordon fell ill with the "coast fever" and was taken with other members of the crew to Faber's slave factory at Rio Pongo to recover.[15]

At Rio Pongo, Thomas Turner asked Faber for his pay. Faber refused. So Turner took revenge. On February 11, he saw the refurbished *Caballero* (renamed the *Spitfire*) at Rio Pongo, awaiting her human cargo. He recognized the brig right away, despite its new name, new rigging, and newly painted light-blue hull and buff-colored interior. He also noted other telltale signs of a slave ship: she had both an American captain and a Spanish captain, she was carrying shooks for constructing water casks, and her cargo had been consigned to Faber.[16]

Turner contacted the U.S. Navy's antislavery squadron in Africa, informing them that the *Spitfire* was being used to carry kidnapped Africans into slavery. When naval officers examined the ship at Rio Pongo, they found evidence that it had been fitted out for taking on large numbers of captives, as Turner had promised. Newspaper accounts noted that "her present crew also testified as to her intention of receiving slaves." The squadron couldn't arrest Faber: he was merely the ship's consignee, not its current owner. Nevertheless, on March 26, the crew of the U.S. Navy ship *Truxton* seized the *Spitfire* and arrested Captain Flowery, his officers, and crew. All were "committed to prison, to await their trial before the proper tribunal."[17]

Flowery and his crew were carried to Boston aboard the *Truxton* to stand trial. The commanding naval officer described Captain Flowery as a "very quiet, respectable man." In Boston, Flowery and his officers were charged with outfitting a ship for the slave trade, a lesser charge than the capital offense of transporting persons into slavery. The ordinary sailors weren't charged because they hadn't known that the *Spitfire* was on a slave-trading voyage when they'd left New Orleans.[18] This was a common tactic among sea captains: they would misrepresent the voyage's purpose in order to muster a crew, since few sailors would knowingly sign onto slave voyages. The sailors, along with Thomas Turner and three other members of the *Manchester* crew, were also brought to Boston aboard the *Truxton*; there, they were detained as witnesses and confined to jail along with the accused.[19]

Despite Turner's efforts, Faber was never brought to trial. He was well protected from the charges, having quickly disposed of the *Spitfire* upon landing in Cuba. Turner's testimony was used against Captain Flowery, but a notice in a Boston newspaper suggested that any satisfaction he may have gained from providing evidence was fleeting: "Turner was in miserable health, when released from jail here, and it is not probable that he will live long."[20]

Flowery was lucky: he hadn't been caught under sail with captives aboard his ship, so he was merely convicted of fitting out a ship for the slave trade. The jury consulted for a short time and returned a verdict of guilty "but recommended the prisoner to mercy." He was given the proscribed sentence of five years and was taken to the jail in Salem, Massachusetts. He stayed there for less than two years: in May 1847, President James K. Polk pardoned Peter Flowery, and he was set free.[21]

Paul and Mary Faber continued their operation on the Rio Pongo until Paul's death in 1851. To better conceal their slave-trading activities, the couple started a coffee plantation on site. After Paul's death, William Faber, their son, continued to acquire and ship captives into slavery at least until 1860.[22] As for Morgan Gordon, despite his having carried at least one documented shipload of Guinean captives to Cuba, he escaped prosecution and any repercussions from Turner's testimony. He died at Rio Pongo in December 1844, age fifty-one, likely from "coast fever."[23] He left behind his widow Frances and three children.

Morgan Gordon and Paul Faber, who had operated his African slave factory for decades, were close friends. The intimacy of at least two Atlantic crossings together—sharing quarters and meals daily—plus the risky and challenging business venture they engaged in jointly, suggest more than a casual acquaintance. And it's likely they were compatible in at least one important characteristic: their willingness to take risks. The slave trade attracted individuals who flirted with danger, enjoyed the thrill of conducting illegal activities under the noses of authorities, and placed profit above compassion.

At fifty-one, Morgan Gordon, who owned a home in Portland's well-heeled West End, probably could have retired. Or he could have taken on less risky coasting voyages or legitimate molasses runs to the Caribbean. But he didn't. And his persistence indicates that he found the slave trade satisfying.

The *Caballero/Spitfire* episode also suggests the lengths to which slave traders went to cover their tracks. Shipmasters involved in the trade were often part of international syndicates: networks of investors, shipowners, traders, sea captains, and outfitters of many nationalities. Fred Drinkwater, who lived just a few blocks from Morgan Gordon in Portland, was a "well-known sea captain," but he served in another capacity, too. A U.S. State Department memo indicates that, while in Havana in 1857, he purchased five ships responsible for landing African captives in Cuba.[24] Selling ships abroad for use in the slave trade, as both Drinkwater and Gordon did, was good business. It allowed American captains to make a profit off their ships while avoiding detection and the risk of trying to bring known slave ships back through U.S. customs.

Yet even the British were wise to Drinkwater, as illustrated by a report from British commissioners stationed in Africa and Cuba to George Villiers, the British foreign secretary: "We understand that an American citizen by name Drinkwater, calling himself a resident at Portland, is the purchaser of almost all of these American vessels, and figures as their outfitter, but there can be little doubt that this person is only put forth by the slave-traders to cover their transactions."[25] The commissioners were right: Drinkwater was merely a cog in the machine. According to Thomas Savage, the U.S. vice consul in Cuba, he "was in the employ of, or in some way connected in business with, Mr. Antonio Cabarga," a notorious slave trader residing in Havana.[26]

In the mid-nineteenth century, slave-ship crews hailed from many different countries, but the majority of shipowners were Portuguese, Spanish, and Brazilian.[27] To them, Fred Drinkwater was a useful middleman: a Yankee with connections to shipbuilders, sea captains, and slave traders who could facilitate business deals among them and refit and move equipment.

Despite the predominance of Spanish, Brazilian and Portuguese bosses, the United States did dominate two important aspects of the slave trade: ships and sea captains. Of the estimated 1,789 slave voyages between 1831 and 1850, U.S.-built vessels were used in about 1,000 of them, or 58 percent.[28] And Maine played a key role in this traffic. Between the War of 1812 and the Civil War, it was the leading provider of wooden sailing vessels in the United States, building more such ships than any other state.[29]

As for mariners, in 1834, Lloyd's of London underwriters admitted that America captains were "more competent as seamen and navigators and more uniformly persons of education" and "more efficient" than British captains. Maine supplied more than its share of these skilled seamen. According to the 1860 U.S. census, 11,375 mariners resided in Maine along with 759 shipmasters, a number of whom were slave captains at one time or another.[30] For instance, almost as soon as Peter Flowery's sentence was handed down, Captain Cyrus Libby of Scarborough, Maine, appeared before the U.S. circuit court in Portland. As captain of the brig *Porpoise*, he was charged with bringing two young men from Africa to Rio de Janeiro, contrary to U.S. piracy laws. Libby was ultimately acquitted.[31]

The United States—and especially Maine—also had readily available raw materials at cheap prices, and its shipbuilders chose to build ships designed for speed above size or durability. Compared to seamen from other nations, American sea captains were willing to take more risks in transporting cargo rapidly from one place to the next. As William Armstrong Fairburn noted in his exhaustive work, *Merchant Sail*, the United States surged ahead of the competition to "design and build better, faster, and cheaper wooden ships than any other country":

It had men trained to sail them faster and get more out of a ship than the officers and crews sailing under any foreign flag. The Europeans called the Americans "crazy Yankees," and they were astounded at the audacious and seemingly reckless way in which the Yankees carried sail, made fast passages, delivered cargoes in good condition, demanded and obtained higher freight rates and reduced time of delivery, and made four or even five round voyages bringing in relatively "huge profits" while foreign ships made only three voyages.[32]

The famed speed of American-built ships helped them escape antislavery squadrons and allowed them to make multiple voyages per year, while intrepid American sea captains like Morgan Gordon were willing to take risks to get the job done efficiently and without detection.

IN 1847, NATHANIEL GORDON III—Nathaniel II's son and Morgan's nephew—was anxious to make a name for himself. He was just twenty-two years old when he captained the schooner *Juliet* of Portland on a trip to Guayama, Puerto Rico, late in the year. A story in Portland's *Daily Argus*, which was picked up by the *Boston Post*, the *New York Journal of Commerce*, and the *New York Herald*, among dozens of other newspapers, described a harrowing experience:

> On the passage out, [the *Juliet*] fell in with a piratical schooner of about eighty tons, having 2 guns and 20 men. She [the pirate schooner] ordered me to send my boat on board; thinking there was no chance of escape, we laid our topsail to the mast, getting the boat ready, waiting for him to come down; he hauled up his topsail, when having a good opportunity, we filled away, shot across his bows, and got clear of him. She chased me 12 hours, firing grape shot at us, which did no damage.[33]

Written in first person, this dramatic account is an "extract of a letter," unquestionably Gordon's. Seeking attention, the young seaman cast himself in the role of intrepid captain who had outsmarted well-armed Caribbean pirates. It's the earliest indication we have of his personality: risk taker and fearless shipmaster—a lot like his uncle Morgan—and self-promoter like his father, Nathaniel II, who had written about his own encounter with pirates for the American press.

Nathaniel III was well known around Portland as "a precocious youth, wild, reckless, and daring." He had begun his career under his father.[34] Working his way up from cabin boy, he had ascended to shipmaster in his early twenties by working for a Portland shipping firm.[35] But predictable, reasonably profitable work in the West India trade didn't satisfy his ambition or need for adventure. In 1848, young Gordon and the schooner *Juliet* became objects of suspicion in their own rights. Nathaniel III set out on a voyage from Portland to Rio de Janeiro to the coast of Africa. Shortly after leaving Rio, the *Juliet* was stopped and boarded by the U.S.S. *Allegheny* of the U.S. Navy's antislavery squadron, which was patrolling the area. The U.S. consul in Rio, Gorham Parks, had told the squadron that the *Juliet* was likely a slaver, and the *Allegheny*'s crew spent eleven hours searching the *Juliet* for evidence. They found none and were forced to allow the schooner to continue on her way. But some weeks later, word on the docks at Rio was that the *Juliet* had arrived back in port captained by a Brazilian and carrying five hundred captive Africans. According to sailors on board, after everyone disembarked, the *Juliet* was set afire, and Gordon escaped back to the States.[36]

American merchant vessels arriving at the port of Rio were automatically suspect. As Consul Parks wrote, "there is no trade between either the west or east coast of Africa and Brazil, excepting what is connected directly or indirectly with the slave trade." And business was brisk: "The number of American vessels which, since the 1st of July 1844 until the 1st of October last [1849] . . . sailed for the coast of Africa from this city, is ninety-three. . . . Of these vessels, all except five . . . have been engaged in bringing over slaves, and many of them have been captured with the slaves on board."

The *Juliet* was among those listed by Parks, even though she was seized after her captives had disembarked. And Parks explained why so many American ships were involved: "As our government does not permit vessels carrying our flag to be searched, our vessels are preferred to most if not all others, by the slave traders, as offering the perfect protection for the traffic from the dreaded enemy."[37] Shipmasters like young Gordon were well suited to the trade. They were schooled in strategies for smuggling and avoiding detection and had no qualms about carrying contraband or providing vessels and logistical support for illicit activity. Nathaniel Gordon III was prepared to pick up where his Uncle Morgan had left off.

UPON ARRIVING IN NEW York, Reuben Ruby had been active in promoting abolition and civil rights. As time went on, however, he spent most of his waking hours trying to support his family of seven. He had worked in the eating establishments of New York City throughout the 1840s, but hadn't gotten rich doing so. His need for money impelled him to set off on a risky trip to California's gold fields in early February 1849. He was not alone. Many thousands of men from the States, Mexico, South America, Europe, Australia, and Asia were drawn to California by the promise of gold. Like most prospectors, Ruby traveled without his wife and children. He may, however, have traveled with a "mining company," an informal group of men who traveled and prospected together.

All of the forty-niners encountered hardship, deprivation, and danger. But for Black prospectors, those challenges were amplified. In lawless California and along the way, they faced bullying and violence, risked kidnapping and sale into slavery, and were likely to be denied food and accommodations because of their race. Nonetheless, Ruby, like so many others, could not resist the thought of making a quick fortune.

"The accounts of the abundance of gold in that territory are of such an extraordinary character," stated President James K. Polk in his annual report to Congress in December 1848, "as would scarcely command belief were they not corroborated by . . . officers in the public service who have visited the mineral district."[38] Though Easterners had remained skeptical and at home throughout 1848, the rush had already reached a fever pitch in California, as the president described:

> Labor commands a most exorbitant price, and all other pursuits but that of searching for the precious metals are abandoned. Nearly the whole of the male population of the country have gone to the gold districts. Ships arriving on the coast are deserted by their crews and their voyages suspended for want of sailors. . . . soldiers can not be kept in the public service without a large increase of pay. Desertions . . . have become frequent.[39]

This was a trend too compelling to resist, and, intentionally or not, the president's message served to increase the frenzy. People raced to California to stake their claims.

There were two basic routes to California: over land and by water. Although both were treacherous for men of color, the overland route took three to seven months; the water route, one and a half to three months, depending upon conditions and whether ships sailed around Cape Horn or deposited passengers at Panama, where they would walk across the isthmus and catch another ship for California on the Pacific side. Ruby and most of his peers wanted to get to California as quickly as possible, make their fortunes, and return home. So the water route was fastest. For Black persons, it was also the safest. Black sailors were common, and although their movements had been increasingly limited by discriminatory laws in some ports, Black travelers likely still felt more secure aboard ships than chancing a long trip through unknown territories of the expanding United States.[40]

The newly established mail packets to California offered the most reliable transportation, particularly in the early months of the migration. In 1848, Mexico had ceded Alta California to the United States as part of the treaty ending the Mexican-American War. Almost immediately, the government and enterprising businessmen began creating mail routes that linked the region with the East Coast. The U.S. Mail Steamship Company offered service aboard the S.S. *Falcon* and other ships, which sailed between New York and Chagres, a village on the Atlantic coast of Panama. The Pacific Mail Steamship Company connected Panama City, on the Pacific side of the isthmus, with Monterey, San Francisco, and Oregon. Three steamers for that portion of the trip, the *California*, the *Panama*, and the *Oregon*, were launched in 1848.[41]

Ruby set sail aboard the *Falcon* in early February 1849, likely in steerage.[42] The *Falcon*'s usual route included Charleston, Havana, and New Orleans on its way to the isthmus. Yet South Carolina and Cuba had laws stating that free Blacks who entered their ports as passengers, sailors, or cooks would be welcomed with imprisonment. "If any vessel shall come into any port or harbor of this State, having on board any free negroes or persons of color as cooks, stewards, mariners," declared a South Carolina law of 1822, "such free negroes or persons of color shall be . . . confined in jail until said vessel shall clear out and depart from this State." Cuba's law of 1837 prevented free Blacks from coming ashore for any reason.[43]

In states and countries where slavery was alive and well, Whites viewed free Blacks with fear and trepidation; their very presence might encourage those in bondage to try to escape. A White shipmaster from Boston testified to Congress that "I have often seen colored seamen from northern vessels carried to prison," and that "a list nearly as long as the longest abolition petition could be made out of names of free colored men who have been taken out of ships in Charleston, Mobile, and New Orleans for only being black." He continued, "The trouble it makes is enough to exasperate any shipmaster in the world."[44] In visiting such ports, shipmasters who had hired Black crewmembers were forced to delay their voyages, replace the men, or pay fees to release them from jail.

Ships to California carried more than passengers and cargo; disease was another hazard that Ruby and fellow travelers faced. Bayard Taylor, a correspondent for the *New-York Tribune*, traveled on the *Falcon* in June 1849, just a few months after Ruby did. Although the steamship anchored in both Charleston and Havana harbors, passengers, regardless of race, weren't allowed to disembark at either port because of the fear of spreading disease. "On account of the cholera at New York," wrote Taylor, when the *Falcon* reached Havana, "we were ordered up to the Quarantine ground and anchored beside the hulk of an old frigate, filled with yellow-fever patients. The Health Officers received mail and ship's papers at the end of a long pole, and dipped them in a bucket of vinegar. . . . After sunset, the yellow-fever dead were buried and the bell of a cemetery on shore tolled mournfully at intervals."[45]

Epidemics were a significant hazard for forty-niners and, indeed, for most travelers and city dwellers during the century. Taylor spent four days in New Orleans before leaving for Panama, but it's not clear whether Ruby would have been allowed onshore once he reached the Crescent City. Between December 1848 and February 1849, when Ruby departed, New Orleans had endured a serious outbreak of cholera that had brought business and steamboat traffic to a halt. "The cholera is progressing fearfully at New Orleans," a newspaper account stated in January. "The city is deserted by all who have been able to leave. Vessels and steamboats are unable to discharge their cargoes as there is no one to receive them."[46]

Things were little better when Ruby landed in Panama. In January 1849, a correspondent from the *New York Herald* reported several cholera cases of "great violence" among his co-travelers that killed victims in less than twenty-four hours. In addition, malaria and yellow fever were endemic. "One word to our friends in the United States who are feverish to go to California," wrote the *Herald* correspondent: "1st. Stay at home. 2d. If you go there, take any route but this."[47] Reuben Ruby likely missed that last-minute advice.

Cost for travel aboard the *Falcon* ranged from $70 for a passage in steerage to $150 for a stateroom. But enterprising individuals might manage to get a trip for free if they agreed to work aboard as waiters or laborers. Given Ruby's experience as a cook and waiter, he may have snatched such an opportunity. Still, such arrangements had a cost. To pay their passage aboard the steamship *Pacific* on its first voyage from New York to California via Cape Horn, two Black men, known only as Charlie and Primus, signed on to work as waiters. When the captain, Hall J. Tibbetts, reportedly saw them relaxing, he "took a rope's end to them." But as it turned out, the two were enslaved, and their masters on board the steamer didn't appreciate the captain's liberties with their so-called property.[48] In 1849, California was not yet a state, but it was a free territory, meaning that slavery was officially banned. Nevertheless, plenty of slaveholders risked trips to the gold fields along with those they had enslaved. It's likely that Ruby traveled among enslaved individuals on the *Falcon* to Panama.

Within a week of leaving New Orleans, Ruby would have seen the lush tropical landscape of the isthmus of Panama. The *Falcon* anchored at Chagres, at the mouth of the river of the same name, which drains the continental divide. Previously a sleepy village, Chagres was then in the midst of a boom from the overflowing traffic of gold seekers on their way to California. Dr. Augustus Campbell, a physician who traveled to the gold fields in early 1849, described Chagres in a letter to his mother: "The inhabitants are a mixture of Spanish, Negro, and Indian, speaking the Spanish language. They are honest but will drive a hard bargain." The town itself contained "between two and three hundred huts made of bamboo poles and covered with the leaves of palm," he wrote. "Every house is a sort of groggery where you can get some poor rum and a kind of stuff they call brandy and cakes of the cane sugar. Also, cocoa, cocoa nuts, oranges, bananas, plantains & etc., can be purchased."[49] In addition to the huts, guest houses, saloons, and eating houses were beginning to appear along Chagres's muddy paths. Visitors spent their time in drinking and debauchery. "Most persons at Chagres become dissipated in a few weeks," wrote a resident to a friend in New York, "and between drinking too much, running after women, or gambling, exhaust all their energies, and when they get sick, they have no vitality left in their systems to recover."[50]

From Chagres, those going to California had to hire local boatmen to take them upriver to Gorgona or Cruces, a three- or four-day trip. Typically made in dugout canoes, the trip cost between $30 and $40. Because many of the local boatmen were Black, Ruby may have been able to find sleeping quarters—from very basic guest houses, to shacks, to hammocks in the trees—as well as "bad food at high prices" along the way.[51] Still, he would have had to surmount the language barrier.

Ruby arrived in Panama during the dry season. Later in the year, the constant bone-drenching rains would have made the trip through the fast currents of the Chagres miserable and dangerous. But even during this relatively dry period, Ruby would have seen, heard, and smelled plenty of sensations he'd never experienced before, including the continually oppressive heat and humidity and animals and insects of all kinds. One traveler described the Panamanian landscape as a "deluge of vegetation," with "all the gorgeous growths of an eternal Summer . . . mingled in one impenetrable mass."[52] Another witnessed a "great variety of birds with most beautiful plumage."[53] Still a third wrote, "Game is in great plenty upon the river. A number of wild turkeys were shot from the boats on our passage, and quite a sprinkling of small alligators. . . . A great number of iguanas were shot. . . . One of the New Hampshire mining company shot one of about six feet long."[54] There were passionflowers, orchids, and wild cashews; toucans, macaws, and quetzals; spider monkeys, night monkeys, capuchins, sloths, anteaters, river otters, and jaguars.

The Trans-Isthmian Railroad wasn't begun until 1850, so once Ruby arrived at Gorgona or Cruces, he would have had to walk or hire a mule and guide to cover the remaining distance to the port of Panama: roughly twenty-five miles through the steamy, insect-ridden forest. One forty-niner wrote that a co-traveler had counted fifty-two dead mules along the route.[55]

At Panama, conditions likely improved. Panama had been occupied by the Spanish between 1519 and 1821. In 1849, it was a village of 10,000. The center of town, known as Casco Viejo, sat on a small point of land fortified with walls containing a central plaza. Houses within the walls were built of stone and brick covered in plaster and tile with balconies extending over the streets.[56] Here, most travelers busied themselves with waiting. There were more people than places available aboard the arriving steamships, so would-be passengers spent days, sometimes months, waiting for a space. According to Augustus Campbell, "when we first arrived there was but one vessel in the harbor" and "between two and three thousand persons waiting for a passage." Steamships to California were frequently delayed because they couldn't muster crews; a seaman's pay couldn't compete with the possibilities offered in the gold fields. "The steamer California, which has been due for some weeks," wrote Campbell, "has not yet returned. It is presumed that the hands have deserted."[57]

Once ships did arrive, space was at a premium. After the journalist Bayard Taylor caught the steamer *Panama* to San Francisco, he reported, "Our vessel was crowded fore and aft: exercise was rendered quite impossible and sleep was each night a new experiment."[58] And the trip from Panama to California lasted twice as long as the trip from New York to Chagres.

Once in San Francisco, Ruby likely found tent cities and houses filled with migrants—whom one forty-niner described as being "packed away in rooms like shad." That traveler paid a dollar to sleep on a bowling alley after the bowlers had finished, "near two o'clock in the morning."[59] When awake, the miners busied themselves with gambling and drinking. "We frequently saw miners lying in the dust helpless with intoxication," wrote one observer. Such men were systematically relieved of any gold or cash they'd been carrying.

> The bar-rooms and hotels were crowded with revellers—money, wines, and liquor flowed like water. Gold dust, doubloons, and dollars were the only currency men would look at, old miners often scattering smaller coins in the streets by handfulls, rather than to count or carry them. . . . Gambling prevailed to an extent heretofore unheard of and unknown. The monté and roulette tables, encircled continually day and night by a dense mass, were covered with bags of gold dust and heaps of doubloons and Mexican dollars, which were incessantly changing hands in enormous amounts. Pistols and revolvers . . . made the air musical with loud reports or whistling messengers, while . . . intoxicated men, mounted on fleet horses, were rushing to and fro through the streets, or tramping over the portico of the City Hotel.[60]

Ruby soon left the city, moving due east toward the Stanislaus River, perhaps because he thought it might be less crowded than the American River, where gold had first been discovered. But by early 1849, thousands were already mining along the Stanislaus. In the early days of the Gold Rush, a Black man known only as Dick had found a large vein of gold in the Stanislaus region. He is said to have mined ore worth $100,000 and sold out several claims before retiring to Sacramento to enjoy his wealth. But whether through dissipation, robbery, or both, Dick lost his riches quickly. The abuse that he received in Sacramento—particularly after becoming penniless—was so extreme that he was said to have committed suicide.[61]

Ruby was not a typical forty-niner. He had been a steadfast promoter of temperance as a restauranteur and an activist, and the culture of gambling, drinking, and debauchery very likely offended him. And he was already fifty-one years old, not inclined to engage in the wild antics of younger prospectors. He was in California for one purpose only: to make money.

Homesickness and separation from family may have taken its toll, as it did for many. Mail to California was irregular and infrequent, and in many of the mining areas, it was virtually nonexistent. "My great anxiety is for my wife & child," wrote one prospector. "I cannot hear from them. . . . the disarrangement of the Post Office & the distance that I am from one, (50 miles) makes it very difficult to get letters."[62]

Life in the gold fields was difficult. Prospecting required long days of physical labor, rough living conditions, and poor food. Numerous diarists and letter writers mention the frequency of scurvy among the forty-niners, brought on by a diet of salted meat with almost no vegetables or fruit. Diarrhea, agues, and other scourges were common. As one New Yorker wrote to a friend back home:

> If any man has his health & will work, he can make more than ten times as much here as he can in the states in the same length of time. But many, very many, that come here meet with bad success & thousands will leave their bones here. Others will lose their health, contract diseases that they will carry to their graves with them. Some will have to beg their way home, & probably one half that come here will never make enough to carry them back.[63]

EVERYONE RISKED BECOMING A victim of theft or violence. But for nonwhites and foreigners, particularly Chileans, the threat of violence was constant. Early in the gold rush, Chileans had sailed to California in droves, and they became the largest group of migrants from South America. But once they arrived in the fields, their equipment was stolen, they were driven off their claims, and they were brutalized. In July 1849, a bill dispute between a Chilean and an Anglo-American drew the Hounds, a quasi-military group, to Chilecito, the San Francisco neighborhood where many Chileans had settled. The Hounds took it upon themselves to enforce the supremacy of White Anglo-Americans in California. According to the *Daily Alta California*, "they paraded the streets in a body, and under cover of the night commenced their work of destruction, pillaging, tearing down and then burning the then fragile tenements of the poor Chileans, and robbing them of their property. Nor did their violence end here, fire-arms being freely used and several of the unarmed and peaceable foreigners shot."[64]

Eventually, the leader of the Hounds was caught and forced to leave California, and the others were fined and imprisoned aboard a U.S. man-of-war in San Francisco Bay. Still, the nativists in California had the upper hand. In 1850, the first California state legislature passed the Foreign Miners Tax Law, which levied a monthly $20 on any noncitizen prospecting in the new state. Though a revolt caused the law to be repealed in 1851, it was reenacted in 1852.[65]

THREE MONTHS IN CALIFORNIA was enough for Reuben Ruby. But despite his short sojourn, he accomplished what he had set out to do. By August 1849, he was back in New York, where he was interviewed by a writer from the *New-York Daily Tribune*:

> [I saw] California gold, value $600, dug out at Stanislaus River by a *free* colored man, Reuben Ruby, who left here in the steamer *Falcon* on the 1st of February last, and arrived at San Francisco April 1. One queer shaped lump weighs 11 ounces avoirdupois, a real curiosity; another four ounces: the rest are various sizes, from the size of a chestnut down to a grain of wheat. All this he dug, and paid his expenses, in less than four weeks.[66]

BEFORE RETURNING TO MAINE, it's likely that Ruby met up with friends and associates in New York to tell them about his adventures. In November 1849, the *Tribune* ran another piece describing a newly formed mining company of prominent African Americans who may have been inspired by Ruby's publicized success: "Some merchants of this City have formed an association of colored men for the purpose of mining in California.

The company consists of ten men, and is comprised of some of the most intelligent and respectable colored men of our city."[67]

In December, a free Black named Samuel L. Davis wrote to *The Liberator* from California, asserting that "there are colored people in San Francisco" who are making "from one hundred to three hundred dollars per month." Written to boost black migration, the letter also sought to ease Black New Englanders' fear of risk. In an effort to do "something for ourselves toward our future welfare," Davis and some thirty-five other free Blacks had formed the Mutual Benefit and Relief Society to provide relief "for our own benefit and that of newcomers."[68]

When Ruby finally returned home to Maine, he shared his experiences with the *Bangor Whig*: "Mr. Ruby . . . collected about three thousand dollars worth of gold. The hardships of labor, and the oppressive climate, and the prevailing sickness, he felt, were sufficient to cause him to leave, although he was deemed lucky in the mines. He says that no amount of gold would induce him to risk the perils of the mines again. He has seen the Elephant and is satisfied."[69]

As a pioneer in the Black gold rush, Ruby's experience likely encouraged many of the more than 5,000 African Americans who made their way to California. He was also lucky. His trip to California had been successful: he'd found adventure, made money, inspired other African Americans, and managed to escape ethnic violence and deadly diseases.

By 1850, he was working as a trader in Portland and living with his wife Rachel and sons Frederic, nineteen; William, seventeen; George, eleven; and Horatio, seven. His widowed sister, Sophia Ruby Manuel, who worked as a washerwoman, lived next door with her two children: George, fifteen, and Christopher, eleven. While the 1850 federal census lists Sophia and her children as "black," Reuben and his family were listed as "mulatto": class distinctions likely made by the census taker. The Rubys and the Manuels were among 395 Black individuals living in Portland in that year.[70]

PRESIDENT POLK, WHO HAD acquired California as a U.S. territory and whose words had triggered the gold rush in 1848, left office in 1849 after only one term as president. On his farewell tour, he traveled south to the Gulf Coast, stopping in New Orleans on March 21. On March 23, he attended a dinner in his honor, then left for home the next day, "the state of his health being such as to render it necessary for him to decline any invitations to visit the river towns." He steamed up the Mississippi to his newly built mansion, Polk Place, in Nashville. On June 1, 1849, the former president wrote in his diary, "During the prevalence of cholera I deem it prudent to remain as much as possible at my own house." His caution did little good: two weeks later, he died of the terrible disease at age fifty-three. His retirement had lasted just 103 days.[71]

Just a year after President Polk's death in retirement, President Zachary Taylor died in the White House, a mere nineteen months into his term. His doctor ascribed the cause of death to *cholera morbus*.[72] Both presidents were victims of the nation's third cholera epidemic, which lasted from 1845 to 1859. It had entered the ports of New York and New Orleans in December 1848 and from there spread inland via the nation's waterways, railroad lines, and stagecoach routes. By January, it had reached the river cities of Louisville, Cincinnati, St. Louis, and Nashville. The disease followed prospectors and pioneers over land, too, arriving in Sacramento in October 1850.[73]

Despite his travels, Reuben Ruby escaped the disease. But a neighbor wasn't so lucky. On June 19, 1849, two months after returning to Portland from Matanzas, Cuba, with a cargo of molasses, Nathaniel Gordon II succumbed to cholera. He was fifty years old and had just been appointed customs inspector at Portland.[74] Gordon was preceded in death by older brothers William and Morgan. He left behind his eldest brother, Joshua; his wife Mary; his daughters Dorcas and Mary; and his son, Nathaniel Gordon III.

REUBEN RUBY FOUND GOLD in California and had vastly improved his circumstances, at least for a time. But not so the Gordons. Nathaniel II had fallen back on the familiar: transporting sugar and molasses from the Caribbean to Maine. But he succumbed to an unforeseen hazard: cholera. Morgan Gordon ventured much more by trafficking human beings. He died in the process and came perilously close to being arrested, tried, and punished for piracy. Another Gordon—Nathaniel Gordon III—was also driven by the allure of adventure and rapid monetary gain. Just a few days after his father's funeral, he, too, set sail for California.

CHAPTER 6

Fugitives

They are the lovers of law and order, who observe the law when the government breaks it.

—Henry David Thoreau, "Slavery in Massachusetts"

There were plenty of ways to break U.S. laws in the mid-nineteenth century. The laws meant to end the international slave trade created barriers, but weren't foolproof, as the Gordons had demonstrated. And those intended to protect slavery, such as the Fugitive Slave Law of 1850, fostered waves of civil disobedience in the North. States and cities undermined the Act of 1850 with their own laws and created armed vigilance committees to ensure that fugitives wouldn't be apprehended. And the federal government seemed wholly inadequate when it came to enforcement. These trends undermined the republic itself.

IN MARCH 1849, NOT long before he died, Nathaniel Gordon II sold his Danforth Street house to his son for $1,800. Two days later, Nathaniel III sold the house to his mother Mary for $3,000.[1] He needed cash for a new venture: a trip to the California gold fields. At about the same time, he resigned as shipmaster with a Portland firm, sold his interest in a ship, and secured a small brig aptly named *Fortunio*. He sailed it to California, leaving in June, just days after his father's death from cholera. The trip around Cape Horn was known to be dangerous, but Gordon's Portland acquaintances described his voyage as "a miraculous exhibition of skill, good luck and daring. The crew were wonderstruck at his intrepidity."[2]

But the Danforth Street house was still under mortgage, and in the wake of her husband's death, Mary Gordon struggled financially. In 1850, she transferred ownership of her father's New Gloucester farm to one James M. Tufts, "in consideration of good will." By 1854, however, she could no longer pay the mortgage on the Danforth Street property, and the house went into foreclosure. In 1855, the builders sold it.[3]

The younger Gordon didn't strike it rich in California, either. After two years there, he seized an opportunity to make his fortune by means other than prospecting for gold. On June 3, 1851, he advertised in a California newspaper that the *Camargo* was ready to sail from San Francisco for New York, and he offered space to anyone wishing to ship cargo to the East Coast.[4] No one knows how many people took him up on the offer, but those who did lost their goods. The *Camargo* never reached New York.

The *Camargo* was built in Nobleborough (now Damariscotta), Maine in 1846. Dr. Levi Fenner, a physician, and several East Coast partners had purchased the ship to sail to California for the Gold Rush. Once there, Fenner bought out his partners and became the brig's sole owner. He hired Gordon to sail the *Camargo* back to New York with a load of hides and any other cargo the captain could take on.[5] But Gordon had other things in mind. On November 20, the *Camargo* arrived in Río de Janeiro.[6] From there, Gordon commandeered the ship and its crew to sail to Africa on a slaving voyage.

Nathaniel Gordon III was a pirate in the fullest sense. More intrepid than his father or even his uncle Morgan, he engaged wholesale in the illegal transport of Africans to the Americas and was willing to steal a vessel to do so. Although Brazil had strengthened its law banning the international slave trade in 1850, Gordon believed he could easily outmaneuver and outwit Brazilian authorities as well as the American and British antislavery squadrons patrolling Brazil's coast.[7] And he had a tremendous financial incentive. As the American ambassador to Brazil explained, because of stricter enforcement, "a single cargo [of captives] successfully landed and sold now would make the fortune of the adventurer."[8] Transporting captive Africans was something Gordon knew well; to him, it was a better risk than prospecting for gold.

Brazil had banned importing Africans for the purposes of slavery, but the need for free labor among the country's coffee plantations was acute. And the biggest market for Brazilian coffee was the United States. The demand for coffee, like the demand for cotton, sugar, rice, and tobacco, was driven largely by American consumers and supplied by enslaved laborers.

In spring of 1852, Henry Southern, the British minister to Brazil, wrote to his superiors that he suspected two U.S. ships, Gordon's *Camargo* and the *Mary Adeline*—captained by another Portland, Maine, native, Appleton Oaksmith—of being engaged in the slave trade. Southern also stated that George Marsden, an American broker, was "getting up and aiding these speculations,"[9] no doubt with the help of wealthy Brazilians.

The two voyages had mixed results. In June, Oaksmith sailed the *Mary Adeline* up the Congo River, but the brig ran aground on a sandbar near the mouth of the river and was stuck fast. The next morning, "the river was crowded with canoes, ten to forty natives in each, all armed, and at least two-thirds with muskets," according to the *Nautical Magazine and Naval Chronicle*. "Their movements left no doubt as to their predatory and hostile intentions," the article continued, though the writer didn't speculate on Oaksmith's intentions. Ironically, two vessels from the British antislavery squadron, the *Dolphin* and the *Firefly*, came to Oaksmith's aid, fired cannons and shells at the locals, and managed to pull the *Mary Adeline* off the sandbar. Oaksmith and his small crew escaped with their lives and their ship, but they left Africa without their intended cargo.[10]

After refitting the stolen *Camargo*, Nathaniel Gordon III left Brazil in April. He sailed across the Atlantic and around the Cape of Good Hope to Quelimane in East Africa, where he loaded 550 captives. Although the British antislavery squadron's *Grecian* got wind of the *Camargo*'s presence and searched the rivers nearby, Gordon escaped.[11] On December 12, the *Camargo*, its captain and crew, and its captives arrived safely in Brazil at the mouth of the River Bracuí, some 100 miles southwest of Río. As soon as everyone disembarked, Gordon and the crew set fire to the brig and fled with their human cargo into the mountains.

Brazilian authorities heard rumors of the landing and sent four hundred soldiers to search for the captives among the coffee plantations in the rugged region near Angra dos Reis. They recovered only 38 of the original 550, but they did arrest and imprison four members of the *Camargo*'s crew, along with George Marsden, the American businessman behind the scheme, who was then living in Río.[12] Nathaniel Gordon wasn't among them. He escaped to Montevideo, reputedly by donning women's clothing, his small five-foot-six-inch frame making his disguise plausible.[13]

Thus did Nathaniel Gordon accomplish the last known successful landing of enslaved Africans in Brazil. The problem, complained U.S. Ambassador Robert Schenk to Secretary of State Edward Everett, was that transporting captives into slavery was too easy. U.S. laws and enforcement were weak. "Our flag . . . is the one particularly chosen by these pirates and man-traders for disguise," wrote Schenk. That was because no foreign ships were permitted to search American ships, even when they were suspected of carrying captives. "Unless something more effectual be enacted and done by Congress and the Executive, we must expect to see the instances of crime under its protection soon and often repeated."[14]

Schenk was right: even after they were caught and punished, those engaged in the slave trade often returned to the business. Marsden, Gordon's business partner, did spend five months in a Río jail before being deported to the United States.[15] But once in New York, he returned to the slave trade, purchasing and selling the Maine-built *Gray Eagle*, which landed 584 captives in Cuba in 1854.[16] Nor was the *Mary Adeline* affair Appleton Oaksmith's last brush with the slave trade.

Ambassador Schenk interrogated the imprisoned sailors of the *Camargo* for information that could be used against Nathaniel Gordon in an American court. But nothing came of the effort. In the months that followed, Gordon kept a low profile, focused on his domestic life, and engaged in less risky voyages.

ON MARCH 28, 1855, while residing in Boston, Nathaniel Gordon III married Elizabeth Kinnay. Gordon was twenty-nine and Elizabeth, who had emigrated from London to Boston, was seventeen.[17] It's unlikely that she knew her husband was a fugitive from the law. More likely, she believed she was marrying a man from a respectable family with a respectable vocation.

By 1857, the couple was living in Maine. That year Elizabeth gave birth to their son, Nathaniel E. Gordon (Nathaniel IV), in Cape Elizabeth, just across the river from Portland.[18] By the time Elizabeth's and Nathaniel's young son turned two, however, Gordon was back to his old ways, willing to risk everything to engage in human trafficking. Perhaps he needed money; perhaps he missed the thrill of the chase. Whatever the case, in 1859, he sailed the bark *Ottawa* to Mobile and then to the

Congo River in Africa, where he boarded captives to transport to Cuba. Cuba would remain open to the international slave trade until 1867 and didn't abolish slavery until 1886. Still, it was illegal for Americans to transport persons into slavery, regardless of their final destination, as Gordon well knew.

Gordon had never been prosecuted or pursued for the *Camargo* affair. Nevertheless, by the 1850s, he was notorious among American customs officials and journalists as a serial offender. His departure from Mobile in early 1859, officially for the Caribbean island of Saint Thomas, fooled no one. The *New York Herald* billed news of the voyage as "Another Suspected Slaver": "The bark Ottawa sailed yesterday ostensibly for St. Thomas, but it is believed that her destination is the southern coast of Africa." A Mississippi newspaper stated that the *Ottawa*'s "real destination is the southern coast of Africa" and that the purpose of the voyage was "rescuing some 1800 Africans from barbarism, and transporting them to civilized Cuba."[19]

The *Ottawa* appeared on several lists of known slavers operating along the Congo River.[20] On July 26, 1860, the New York *Evening Post* recorded that the ship was among twenty-six American vessels that had landed human cargoes in Cuba within the last eighteen months. Gordon and the other shipmasters listed weren't even trying to be discreet. U.S. antislavery laws had no teeth, and the slave captains knew it.

Although he escaped capture, Gordon's trip from the Congo was disastrous; only a quarter of the individuals he'd purchased remained alive when the *Ottawa* reached Cuba. Later, he claimed that they had been poisoned by a rival of the slave trader with whom he'd done business on the Congo. While poison was a possible cause of the disaster, disease, dehydration, lack of sanitation, and other horrific conditions aboard the slave ship were likely contributing factors. Once again, after the surviving Africans were taken ashore in Cuba, Gordon burned the ship to destroy all traces of his voyage.[21] Ships—and human lives—held marginal value for him.

ALTHOUGH CONGRESS AND THE courts were lax about the international slave trade and fugitives like Gordon, they clamped down hard on domestic fugitives from slavery. In 1850, Congress passed a law intended to force everyone—slaveholders, their northern sympathizers, abolitionists, and even free Blacks—to help track down and return runaways to their enslavers. The new Fugitive Slave Law had been born of a compromise. Just as a compromise over slavery had facilitated Maine's statehood in 1820, California's statehood in 1850 was part of a similar bargain.

As a U.S. territory, California had leaned antislavery, though perhaps not for moral reasons. Gold ruled in California as cotton ruled in the Deep South, and independent prospectors didn't want to compete with enslaved laborers in the gold fields. Even so, a politically powerful southern minority in California lobbied for all manner of laws permitting coerced labor.[22]

When California petitioned to became a free state, lawmakers from the South balked at the pending imbalance of free to slave states. To placate them, Senator Henry Clay of Kentucky introduced the Compromise of 1850. This law gave California statehood, drew a new boundary between Texas (a slave state) and New Mexico, and allowed New Mexico and Utah to decide the question of slavery for themselves. It also banned the selling of enslaved persons in the District of Columbia.

The most controversial piece of the compromise was the divisive Fugitive Slave Law. Since 1783, the U.S. Constitution had enabled slaveholders to pursue and capture escaped bondsmen and women into free states. Without mentioning the word *slave*, it stated, "No Person held to Service or Labour in one State, under the Laws thereof, escaping into another, shall, in Consequence of any Law or Regulation therein, be discharged from such Service or Labour, but shall be delivered up on Claim of the Party to whom such Service or Labour may be due."[23] The clause directed that any bound laborer who escaped could be recaptured and returned to his or her master. Enslaved or free, Blacks' ability to defend themselves was either limited or nonexistent because, for the most part, only White persons could testify in court.

Most White northerners had ignored the "Service or Labour" clause, pretending that fugitives from slavery were none of their concern. The wording was vague, and the clause was difficult to enforce. But the 1850 Fugitive Slave Law implicated everyone, declaring that "all good citizens are hereby commanded to aid and assist in the prompt and efficient execution of this law, whenever their services may be required." It criminalized giving aid and comfort to fugitives, setting maximum penalties at $1,000 in fines and six months in prison. Anyone who helped, or even knew of, persons escaping slavery could be punished if they failed to report them.[24]

According to the law, special federal commissioners would hear and decide on fugitive cases themselves, without a jury, and due process was quashed: "In no trial or hearing under this act shall the testimony of such alleged fugitive be admitted in evidence."[25] These commissioners, all of whom were White, had an incentive to rule against Blacks, whether they were fugitives or free; they would earn $5 each for cases in which Blacks were set free and $10 for remanding them to slavery.[26] The law permitted no appeals. This left African Americans, free or enslaved, at the mercy of the local commissioner.

Although the Fugitive Slave Law was part of a compromise intended to keep the union together, it effectively drove a deeper wedge between North and South and between those who opposed slavery and those who sought to preserve the Union at all costs. Senator Daniel Webster of Massachusetts walked a thin line. He professed to be against slavery, but he feared that a schism between North and South could lead to war and felt obliged to head it off. As a result, he chose to support the compromise. Speaking before Congress, he declared that citizens of the North exhibited "a disinclination to perform, fully, their constitutional duties, in regard to the return of persons bound to service, who have escaped into the free states. In that respect, it is my judgement that the South is right, and the North is wrong."[27]

Until that moment, Webster had been a prominent and respected voice in the Senate. But in the wake of his speech, Boston abolitionist Reverend Theodore Parker wrote, "No living man has done so much to debauch the conscience of the nation." Massachusetts Congressman Horace Mann likened Webster's agreeing to the bargain to "Lucifer descending from Heaven."[28]

Many northerners were appalled by the Fugitive Slave Law. As the writer Ralph Waldo Emerson reflected, "an immoral law makes it a man's duty to break it at every hazard." Reverend Jermain Wesley Loguen, who had escaped from slavery in Tennessee, spoke to citizens in his adopted hometown of Syracuse, New York:

My neighbors! I have lived with you many years, and you know me. My home is here, and my children were born here. I am bound to Syracuse by pecuniary interests, and social and family bonds. And do you think I can be taken away from you and from my wife and children, and be a slave in Tennessee? . . . I don't respect this law—I don't fear it—I won't obey it! It outlaws me, and I outlaw it, and the men who attempt to enforce it on me.

Loguen's neighbors responded by voting to make Syracuse a sanctuary city, and Loguen later proudly announced that he was "agent and keeper of an Underground Railroad Depot."[29]

Although most northern Blacks were legally free, they had always feared being kidnapped into slavery, and the 1850 law made that prospect even more likely. Martin Delaney, a Black activist, journalist, and physician, wrote, "We are slaves in the midst of freedom. . . . The slave is more secure than we; he knows who holds the heel upon his bosom—we know not the wretch who may grasp us by the throat."[30]

In Portland, activists held several meetings in the Abyssinian Church—"crowded to overflowing by colored and white citizens"—to protest passage of the law. According to the *Portland Weekly Advertiser*, "many, if not most of the colored people are actually and constantly armed, and thus in a very *proper state* of preparation for the slave catcher or his northern minions."[31] An October 8 meeting "was the most enthusiastic I ever attended in Portland," wrote a correspondent to *The Liberator*. "The colored people are determined to resist, to a man—and woman, too—any attempt to take a fellow being back into bondage. . . . Not a man is to be taken from Portland. Our motto is—'Liberty or Death!'"[32]

Two days later, activists met again: this time, to create a vigilance committee "to give notice of the approach of danger; to see that every person is provided with the means of defence and that places of security are selected," and to take "whatever measures may be necessary for our protection." Fifty-two-year-old Reuben Ruby was chosen as a member of that committee.[33]

The November 1, 1850, edition of *The Liberator* was bursting at the seams with accounts of unrest and resistance in response to the new law. The paper printed model petitions for citizens to send to Congress insisting the law be overturned. It reported that the Chicago city council had nullified the Fugitive Slave Law, "releasing the police from obedience to it"; ran accounts of impromptu meetings and gatherings against the law; and, like setting a match to tinder, announced the arrival of George Thompson, the British abolitionist, back in the States.

The Liberator also noted that slave hunters from Georgia had arrived in Boston to pursue two fugitives, William and Ellen Craft. While most fugitives from slavery escaped from border states, this couple had fled more than 1,000 miles from Macon, Georgia, to Boston by means of a daring and clever scheme. Ellen, who was very light skinned, had dressed as a wealthy but sickly male slaveowner. Her husband William had pretended to be her servant. Neither could read nor write, so Ellen had claimed that her right arm was incapacitated and her eyesight poor so that she wouldn't have to sign travel documents and hotel registers.

By 1849, the Crafts were living in Boston, where William, a wood-worker, had started a furniture-making business. But they were also celebrities; they packed lecture halls, recounting their experiences of slavery and their harrowing escape. With the passage of the Fugitive Slave Law, however, the Crafts were at high risk. Two slave hunters named Knight and Hughes arrived in Boston to return the Crafts to their former master, but antislavery activists were ready. Knight and Hughes were arrested for slander against William Craft and charged with conspiracy to commit kidnapping. A sympathetic local posted bail for the pair.[34]

In the meantime, the Crafts were secreted in various houses around Boston until they could leave for Portland, one hundred miles north. According to their memoir, *Running a Thousand Miles for Freedom*, they were forced to spend a few days "in fearful suspense" at the home of one Daniel Oliver while the schooner that was to take them to Nova Scotia was repaired.[35] "Daniel Oliver" was a pseudonym the Crafts used to protect their host from being pursued under the Fugitive Slave Law, which was still in force four years after their book was first published. In fact, the Crafts stayed at the home of Oliver and Lydia Neal Dennett on Spring Street in Portland, a known refuge for those escaping slavery.[36]

Oliver and Lydia Dennett were "engaged heart, soul, and purse in the anti-slavery cause, unpopular as it was," wrote a reporter for the *Portland Daily Press*.[37] Oliver Dennett was vice president of William Lloyd Garrison's American Anti-Slavery Society and an agent for Frederick Douglass's paper, *The North Star*.[38] Lydia Dennett was a member of Portland's Women's Anti-Slavery Society and had helped firebrand

Stephen S. Foster escape an angry crowd in Portland when speaking to the society. She and Elizabeth Widgery Thomas had guided Foster to a back window of the First Parish Church and on to the nearby home of abolitionist friends, the Winslows.[39]

In late November 1850, a newspaper in the mostly pro-slavery town of Bath, Maine, reported that President Millard Fillmore had written to the Crafts' former master, Dr. Robert Collins, assuring him "that any officer who shall fail to do his duty" in pursuing and capturing the Crafts "shall be punished and dismissed."[40] Nevertheless, a network of citizens in Boston and Portland made sure that the Crafts made it safely to Halifax. From there, they left for England, where they lived for nineteen years. *Running a Thousand Miles for Freedom* was published in 1860 and was a sensation.

Two other wildly popular books had already added fuel to antislavery fires. *Twelve Years a Slave: Narrative of Solomon Northup, a Citizen of New-York, Kidnapped in Washington City in 1841, and Rescued in 1853, from a Cotton Plantation near the Red River in Louisiana*, was the autobiographical account of Solomon Northup of Saratoga, New York. As the long title indicates, Northup, a free Black, was kidnapped and sold south only to find his way home a dozen years later. Published in 1853, the account sold some 30,000 copies in its first run—more than Henry David Thoreau's *Walden*, Walt Whitman's *Leaves of Grass*, and Ralph Waldo Emerson's *English Traits* combined.[41]

A year earlier, Harriet Beecher Stowe's *Uncle Tom's Cabin* had become the bestselling novel of the century. Although Stowe wrote the book while living in Maine, she'd had plenty of experience with the issues of race and runaways. As a young adult, she had lived across the Ohio river from the slaveholding South in Cincinnati, Ohio, and she had witnessed both racial violence and the influx of fugitives across the river. Her father, Reverend Lyman Beecher, had been the head of Cincinnati's Lane Theological Seminary in 1834, when students organized antislavery debates, nearly causing a riot. In 1836, Harriet married Calvin Ellis Stowe. The couple hired a Black housekeeper named Zillah. When they learned that Zillah was a fugitive, they helped guide her to a safe house on the Underground Railroad somewhere in Ohio.[42]

In 1850, Harriet and her young family moved to Brunswick, Maine, where Calvin Stowe was hired as a professor at Bowdoin College. There, in a rented house on Federal Street, Harriet and her family harbored another fugitive, John Andrew Jackson of South Carolina, despite the stiff penalties prescribed by the Fugitive Slave Act. Jackson had stowed away on a ship bound from Charleston, South Carolina, to Boston and had settled near Salem, some twenty miles away. But passage of the 1850 law forced him to continue running:

> During my flight from Salem to Canada, I met with a very sincere friend and helper, who gave me a refuge during the night, and set me on my way. Her name was Mrs. Beecher Stowe. She took me in and fed me, and gave me some clothes and five dollars. She also inspected my back, which is covered with scars . . . She listened with great interest to my story, and sympathized with me when I told her how long I had been parted from my wife Louisa and my daughter Jenny.[43]

After Jackson's departure, Harriet settled in to write *Uncle Tom's Cabin*. While Stowe's novel was criticized in many circles for being sentimental and uninformed about southern life, it nevertheless became the most popular book of the time, at home and abroad. And although Maine has frequently been dismissed as far removed from slavery and the Underground Railroad, the experiences of Stowe, John Andrew Jackson, and William and Ellen Craft prove otherwise. The latter three were among the most publicized of Maine's fugitives, but dozens—perhaps hundreds—more sought refuge in the state on their way to Canada and Europe.

REUBEN RUBY HAS LONG been considered Portland's foremost African American Underground Railroad conductor, though no one has named any of the specific fugitives that he and his wives Jeannette and Rachel harbored at their homes, or transported through town via Reuben's hack, or fed or helped secure passages while they were hiding in the Abyssinian Meeting House.[44] Only the rare exceptions have names: a handful of well-known fugitives who escaped slavery and lived to tell their stories, and those who were meticulously recorded by Philadelphia's famous Underground Railroad operative William Still. Keeping quiet about fugitives and abettors was essential for legal and social reasons. Reuben's activism while in New York was evidenced in part by the company he kept; so was his and his family's participation in the Underground Railroad in Portland.

In the early 1850s, Reuben and Rachel Ruby and their four surviving sons were living two doors down from the Abyssinian Meeting House, a known hideaway for fugitives. Reverend Amos Noë Freeman, pastor of the Abyssinian from 1840 to 1851, was also an agent. A half block away, at the corner of Newbury and Mountfort Streets, lived Black barber Charles Frederick Eastman, another of the "regular conductors" of the Underground Railroad.[45]

Many White activists lived nearby. Four blocks away from the Rubys, Samuel Fessenden, a prominent White citizen and a friend of William Lloyd Garrison, harbored fugitives at his home on India Street. Both Ruby and Fessenden had been delegates from Portland to the state's Anti-Slavery Convention in 1834, and both attended meetings against the Fugitive Slave Law at the Abyssinian in October 1850. They undoubtedly conspired together.

Elias and Elizabeth Thomas, who lived at the corner of Congress and India Streets, welcomed fugitives to their home and hosted abolitionist luminaries Garrison and Frederick Douglass.[46] Quaker merchant Samuel Hussey, who lived nearby, at the corner of Pearl and Congress Streets until his death in 1837, also harbored fugitives. According to his granddaughter, he was friends with the local jailer, who would notify Hussey when Black stowaways on ships were captured and put in the Portland jail. Through their collaboration, "the slaves surreptitiously escaped in the night and were sent to Canada."[47] Samuel's three daughters, Sarah Hussey Winslow, Comfort Hussey Winslow, and Thankful Hussey Southwick were all well-known activists and members of women's anti-slavery societies in Boston and Portland.

Farther west on the Portland peninsula, African American George Ropes owned a home and hardware store at the corner of Oxford and Elm Streets, where he is known to have harbored runaways. According to his brother David:

> My brother's house was at times a station on the Underground Railroad. One Sunday morning early there arrived in care of a friend a colored man of about forty years of age, trembling like an aspen leaf, who very reluctantly entered the house. He thought he had caught sight of his master in Boston, and was sent to Portland

on the way to Canada, and could not rest even to eat. He started with a fright at the opening of a door. A carriage soon took him on his way.[48]

The driver of that carriage was likely Reuben Ruby, who, at the time, lived just around the corner from Ropes on Preble Street and operated his hack out of his home and the Elm Tavern three blocks away.[49]

Deacon Brown Thurston, a White printer who lived near the corner of Union and Fore Streets, once sheltered some thirty fugitives at his home.[50] Lydia and Oliver Dennett took the Crafts and many others into their home at 133 Spring Street, as did Lydia's cousins, Josiah and Neal Dow, who lived at 714 Congress Street. Like the Husseys, the Dows were Quakers—a religious group that had done more for the antislavery cause than any other. Josiah Dow's home "was always an asylum" for fugitives who "needed food and temporary shelter while waiting to be escorted farther toward the north star of freedom," wrote his son Neal, who would become the mayor of Portland and the father of Prohibition. "During my boyhood, I saw several of these escaped negro bondsmen." One, a young Black woman who had escaped from a plantation near Richmond, Virginia, spent several years at the Dows' house. In his *Reminiscences,* Dow recalled that the woman had promised "the captain who had brought her to Portland never to reveal either his name or that of his ship, a pledge which she kept until her dying day."[51] On another occasion:

> Several runaways who had reached Portland on a vessel from some southern port, had been sent on their northward way rejoicing, my father and I having rendered some assistance. Our colored people held a meeting in the Abyssinian church to celebrate the event, and some whites, among them myself, had been invited to participate. The colored presiding officer, when he introduced me, . . . [told] the audience that the "underground railroad to freedom runs through his kitchen and backyard."[52]

White and Black Portlanders formed a tight network and collaborated fully and continually to help those who were escaping from slavery. When, for example, the brig *Albion Cooper* docked at Portland's Franklin Wharf with a fugitive from Savannah, Georgia, on board, Black residents, including Charles H. L. Pierre, a hack driver, and White residents Daniel Fessenden and B. D. Peck, a local newspaper publisher, worked together to secrete the stowaway in town and send him on to Quebec.[53]

This work was dangerous and controversial. Even before passage of the Fugitive Slave Law, tensions around slavery and the abolition movement had been increasing in Maine. In 1847, members of Portland's Women's Anti-Slavery Society invited Garrison, Douglass, and Charles Lenox Remond to speak at the Friends Meeting House. As Remond took the podium, violence erupted outside. Rioters began throwing stones and eggs and breaking windows, injuring several members of the audience. The mayor was alerted and sent the militia to protect the speakers. Garrison, Douglass, and Remond were escorted from the building, with the women forming a bodyguard around them. Charlotte Thomas, the daughter of one of the society's founders, was struck with an egg. "It made a much stronger abolitionist of me," she later recalled. "It was a fearful tumult outside, but I was too angry to be frightened in the least."[54]

The social costs of helping and harboring fugitives in Portland were as serious as the penalties prescribed by the Fugitive Slave Law. The Friends Meeting House and the Abyssinian Church were among the few places where abolitionists were allowed to speak.[55] "There were not more than half a dozen houses in town that dared to harbor a slave in those days," wrote Charlotte Thomas. "Newell A. Foster, who owned the [*Portland Daily*] Press, and his brother Stephen came near being tarred and feathered for helping us in other slave cases." Still, a steady stream of fugitives continued to pass through Portland: "As the slaves were coming and going all the time we were all kept busy in the work, and so we didn't notice the social ostracism very much."[56]

Supporting abolition and helping fugitives clearly ran in families. As Sarah Southwick, a member of the Hussey clan, recalled, "My parents, relatives, and best friends were all abolitionists. I was born into the cause, and it would have involved much moral heroism to have differed from them to such a degree as to have apologized for slavery. I owe a debt of gratitude to the anti-slavery cause for my education in it."[57] The Ruby children were raised in a similar environment, and their actions as adults would reflect it.

DESPITE DECLARING THAT HE'D never return to California, Ruby did so in 1854. Legal documents signed in Butte County place him in the state's far northeastern corner and show that he gave his friend Charles Pierre the authority to mortgage the Ruby home on Sumner Street in Portland.[58] Reuben must have been struggling financially, or he wouldn't have subjected himself to the difficulties of prospecting and the risky trip to California—especially given the increased risks posed by the Fugitive Slave Law. Other Mainers were trying their luck in Butte County, so it's possible that Ruby was lured to that part of the Golden State by the Lumbert Brothers of Bangor, Maine, who helped found the town of Bangor, California, in 1855.[59]

It's not clear what Ruby accomplished in California, or whether he made money on his second trip. He returned to Portland by early 1857 and took a job as a cook at Stearns' Metropolitan Dining Room on Exchange Street. His home was still under mortgage, but he managed to pay it off a year later.[60]

IN 1857, THE NATION's Black population faced another historic setback. In March, the Supreme Court ruled in the *Dred Scott* case that African Americans, enslaved or free, were not citizens of the United States. Widely held as the worst Supreme Court decision of all time, the *Dred Scott* decision caused outrage in many corners, but it was especially crushing for free Blacks like the Rubys. According to the New York *Evening Post*, the Court had "annihilated at a single blow the citizenship of the entire colored population of the country."[61] Suddenly, African Americans' right to vote, to sue in court, and to expect protection under U.S. law had vanished.

Dred Scott had been enslaved by an Army doctor, John Emerson, and had traveled with Emerson throughout the Midwest. They spent two and a half years in Illinois, a free state, and then moved on to Wisconsin Territory, also free. There, Scott married Harriet Robinson. Dr. Emerson was then transferred south, and Scott and his wife Harriet stayed behind. Ultimately, Dr. Emerson called the couple to return to him and his new wife, Eliza Sandford, in Louisiana, and they complied.

The Emersons then moved to Missouri, along with the Scotts. Upon the doctor's death in 1847, Dred Scott sought to purchase his and his wife's freedom, but Eliza Sandford would have none of it. Scott subsequently filed suit for his freedom in Missouri on grounds that he and Harriet had been residents of free states and that those taken to live in free states automatically became free. After nearly a decade of rulings and appeals, the case reached the U.S. Supreme Court as *Dred Scott v. Sandford*. The South was well represented on the Court: five justices were from slave-holding families, and seven had been appointed by pro-slavery presidents.[62] Chief Justice Roger B. Taney of Maryland wrote the majority opinion for the decision, contending that, because Scott was Black, he was not a citizen and therefore had no right to sue. Blacks, wrote Taney, were "a subordinate and inferior class of beings" who "had no rights which the white man was bound to respect."[63] The decision also declared the Missouri Compromise unconstitutional, ruling that Congress had no right to limit slavery to specific states or areas.

The press erupted. "If epithets and denunciation could sink a judicial body, the Supreme Court of the United States would never be heard *of* again," wrote a Washington, D.C., correspondent for the *New-York Daily Tribune*. "The decision . . . is entitled to just as much moral weight as would be the judgement of a majority of those congregated in any Washington bar-room."[64] In Washington itself, the *National Era* opined, "Who have hitherto reposed their trust in the impartiality of the Court, and its supposed exemption from political bias, will feel their confidence rudely shaken."[65]

But the nation's capital was an island within the pro-slavery South. The *Baltimore Sun* wrote, "The decision, we are glad to say, seems to be welcomed in most quarters."[66] The *Richmond Enquirer* agreed emphatically: "The *nation* has achieved a triumph, *sectionalism* has been rebuked, and abolitionism has been staggered and stunned." The *Enquirer* particularly relished the defeat of the abolitionists: "In the insanity of their anger and agony, the Abolitionists are uttering curses deep and loud, tearing their hair, indulging in all sorts of grimaces and throwing themselves into every imaginable attitude of contortion."[67]

In the wake of the *Dred Scott* decision, Abraham Lincoln, then a private citizen, offered a graphic and satirical portrait of how American society and government had conspired to extinguish African Americans' last glimmer of hope for freedom:

They have him in his prison house; they have searched his person, and left no prying instrument with him. One after another they have closed the heavy iron doors upon him, and now they have him, as it were, bolted in with a lock of a hundred keys, which can never be unlocked without the concurrence of every key; the keys in the hands of a hundred different men, and they scattered to a hundred different and distant places; and they stand musing as to what invention, in all the dominions of mind and matter, can be produced to make the impossibility of his escape more complete than it is.[68]

Stories abounded of how the decision was perverting legal proceedings. In one case, a Black woman from New York sued her absent husband for divorce and alimony, and the court ordered the husband to pay $100, court fees, and $150 alimony. He failed to comply. When the man was called into court for contempt, his lawyer argued that he was not a citizen and therefore could neither sue, be sued, nor be punished by a civil court.[69] In another case, Ruby's friend Thomas Downing, the esteemed Black restauranteur, was called into a New York court for a debt proceeding. He refused to take an oath, saying that the *Dred Scott* decision did not consider him a person or a citizen. The judge made a special exception for Downing, declaring that, "for the present purpose, he might be considered a human being and a citizen."[70]

The court decision was tumultuous for Maine, forcing the state to reexamine its personal liberty laws, Black suffrage, and the state constitution. The state senate's committee on slavery referred to the decision as "a bold perversion of the Constitution, degrading that charter of liberty to the base uses of slavery extension."[71] Immediately, the Republican-controlled legislature set to work strengthening its personal liberty laws. Jails could not be used to hold suspected fugitives from slavery, municipal courts couldn't hear fugitive cases, and county district attorneys had to provide legal assistance to fugitives and their abettors at the state's expense.[72]

In Maine, free Blacks had voted since the start; the state constitution had reserved the right of suffrage for all male citizens and had always counted its Black residents to be such. But now the U.S. Supreme Court had determined that African Americans were not citizens, and had limited the rights of states to determine their own laws. The Maine Supreme

Court was left to decide the matter, and they rejected Taney's assertion that Blacks could not be citizens and had no rights. Justice John Appleton declared for the majority that, according to Maine's constitution, Blacks born in the state were bona fide citizens and therefore U.S. citizens, and Black men, at least, were entitled to vote. "The people of Maine in exercise of their sovereign power, have conferred citizenship upon those of African descent," wrote Appleton, and "having the required qualifications, they are entitled to vote."[73] It was a small bit of good news for the Rubys and Maine's Black citizens, for whom the 1850s had been a disastrous decade.

ON MARCH 30, 1857, Frederick Douglass, the nation's most prominent former fugitive, spoke to a large crowd at Portland's Central Hall.[74] Despite the very dark times, Douglass declared, "My hopes were never brighter than now. . . . I have no fear that the National Conscience will be put to sleep by such an open, glaring, and scandalous tissue of lies as that decision is. . . . This very attempt to blot out forever the hopes of an enslaved people may be one necessary link in the chain of events preparatory to the downfall and complete overthrow of the whole slave system."[75]

As Douglass observed, the American system of slavery was coming apart at the seams. But it was the North, not the South, that was pulling away. And the situation would get much worse before getting better.

CHAPTER 7

Freebooters

There is no republic where there is no justice.

—Saint Augustine

In the months leading up to the Civil War, the American press and public were fixated on three sensational cases of slave trading involving Maine natives Nathaniel Gordon III, Appleton Oaksmith, and Timothy Meaher. The three shared many traits: none more striking than their disregard for the 1820 piracy law. Their exploits demonstrate that piracy was often a family affair, and that weak and inconsistent enforcement of the Act of 1820 was a prominent symptom of a divided nation.

PERHAPS NATHANIEL GORDON III craved money, but he also craved attention and admiration. A California journalist recalled meeting him in Madeira, where "Gordon passed himself off as a wealthy gentleman, . . . [who] was sailing about for pleasure and recreation in a beautiful Baltimore clipper-built yacht." The journalist noted that Gordon was "well known throughout the whole of that [the African] coast, as he is in Brazil, Cuba, and the extreme Southern States."[1]

Back at home in 1860, Gordon, his wife Elizabeth, and their son Nathaniel IV moved in with Gordon's mother Mary in Portland. Acquaintances recalled that, at the time, Gordon boldly announced that he was a slave captain and "defied the cruisers of the world to catch or overhaul him."[2] Perhaps the occupation was the most efficient means of receiving the attention he craved.

By early April of that year, Gordon left Havana as master of the ship *Erie*, bound for Africa. Typical of slavers, the *Erie* also had a shadow captain, a Spaniard, who would give Gordon cover if they were captured by a U.S. Navy vessel. According to the *New York Herald*, Gordon and the Spanish captain made little effort to disguise their mission: "Her cargo was a regular slave-trading one, including the necessary lumber for forming a slave-deck and the five-eighths iron wire to be converted into shackles. There is not the slightest moral doubt that she has gone on a slave trading voyage."[3]

Gordon had told the crew that they were on a legitimate trading voyage, but thirty days out, crewmembers confronted him, convinced that they were on a slaving mission. He denied it and ordered them back to their stations. Once in Africa, however, Gordon sailed the *Erie* up the Congo River, and on August 7, he and the crew boarded 897 Congolese captives. One-quarter were men, one-quarter were women, and half were children. The captives were stripped of their clothing as they boarded and then stowed on decks with only three feet of headroom. They were forced to sit spoon-fashion, with their legs splayed to permit another person to sit inside their legs, and with their backs against the chests of the persons behind them. Gordon then gathered the crew and asked who was willing to continue with him, offering each sailor a dollar for every captive landed in Cuba.[4] The alternative was to take their chances and try to find passage home from the Congo.

The next day, the *Erie* was at sea with her human cargo when she encountered a naval cruiser. Believing it to be a British naval vessel, Gordon hoisted an American flag, knowing that the ships of other nations were forbidden to search U.S. merchant vessels. But he miscalculated: it was the U.S.S. *Mohican*, of the U.S. Navy's Africa Squadron. The *Mohican* chased the *Erie* and shot across her bow, compelling Gordon to surrender.

The first members of the *Mohican* crew to board the *Erie* were Lieutenant John Dunnington and Midshipman Henry Todd. Todd noted that the ship was so overflowing with captives that there was scarcely room to walk without stepping on them. Many of the Congolese had sores and other illnesses. Todd heard cries and shouts coming from the hold, so he and Dunnington brought some of those below up on deck. They hadn't eaten or drunk anything since departing the day before in sweltering heat, so the naval officers provided them with food and water. The captives had been stored so closely that afterward, Todd couldn't get them back into their places between decks without Captain Gordon's and First Mate William Warren's help.[5]

The *Mohican* escorted the *Erie* to Monrovia, Liberia, some 1,900 miles away. The American Colonization Society had helped establish Liberia as a place to repatriate free Blacks from the United States. Black resettlement began there in 1822, and in 1848, Liberia declared itself a free and independent nation. Reuben Ruby's acquaintance and contemporary, John Brown Russwurm, had emigrated there and served as the governor of the Cape Palmas district.

Once in Monrovia, the captives disembarked and were placed in a holding facility belonging to the American Colonization Society. They had been through hell. After being captured somewhere in the interior of the country, they had been marched many miles to a barracoon on the Congo River, where they had waited for an unknown amount of time. And although the *Erie* was intercepted on August 8, the captives remained aboard under inhumane conditions for twenty additional days as the *Erie* sailed to Monrovia. Reverend John Seys, a U.S. agent for Africans recaptured from slaving vessels, witnessed their unloading: "No language can describe what I beheld. . . . More than thirty had died since the capture, on the 8th August, and a large proportion were emaciated—nay, attenuated to the last degree. The scene was sickening to the heart and nerves of the humane."[6]

August 8 had been a propitious date for the U.S. Navy's Africa Squadron: on that day it had also seized the slaver *Storm King*, carrying an additional 618 kidnapped Africans. Her captives had been deposited at Monrovia the day before the *Erie* arrived, and the sudden influx of 1,500 kidnapped individuals—and quite a few corpses—overwhelmed the city's resources.[7] Though the captives weren't taken to Cuba, they were still in unfamiliar circumstances. Most were bonded out to Liberian families and farms. No attempt was made to repatriate them back to their homes along the Congo River.[8]

Naval officers then sailed the *Erie*, with Captain Gordon and mates William Warren and David Hall as prisoners, back to New York City, arriving on October 3. The three were indicted for piracy and for serving aboard a ship involved in slaving. They were confined in the Eldridge Street Jail, where they were "afforded good accommodations." According to the New York *Evening Post*, Gordon was allowed out on parole and was "'dined and wined' to an almost unlimited extent."[9] No one seemed worried that he was facing prosecution for a capital crime—least of all Gordon himself.

James J. Roosevelt, the U.S. district attorney handling the case, offered Gordon a plea deal: if he revealed the backers of his enterprise, he could plead to a lesser offense. Roosevelt knew that few American sea captains operated on their own. Most were backed by Cuban, Brazilian, Portuguese, or Spanish investors, and Gordon was believed to be working for Cuban slave traders when he sailed the *Erie* to Africa.[10] But Gordon and his attorney, Philip Joachimsen, rejected the deal; they were confident that Gordon wouldn't be convicted, and if he were, that he'd be pardoned. District Attorney Roosevelt had said as much publicly: "If they are tried and found not guilty, (which is highly probable) of piracy; or if they are found guilty, such an outside pressure would be brought to bear upon the President [James Buchanan] as would compel him to pardon [Gordon]; in either case he would go scot free."[11] Roosevelt dragged his feet in preparing the case, thinking it was a lost cause.

IN THE MEANTIME, THE country was lurching toward war. Abraham Lincoln was elected president in November 1860; South Carolina seceded in December, and Mississippi, Florida, Alabama, Georgia, and Louisiana followed in January 1861. In April 1861, secessionists attacked and captured Fort Sumter in Charleston Harbor. By June, Texas, Virginia, Arkansas, North Carolina, and Tennessee had joined the Confederacy.

When Lincoln took office in March 1861, changes were immediately apparent, even in federal courts and prisons. Gordon's afternoons on parole ended, as did his steady stream of visitors. Now only his wife Elizabeth was allowed to visit him. In August, Gordon was transferred from the Eldridge Street Jail to a facility ominously called the Tombs. Known for housing New York's worst criminals, it was a heavy stone edifice built in the style of an Egyptian mausoleum on top of Collect Pond in Manhattan. As a result, the Tombs was miserably damp. As soon as it was completed in 1840, cracks had begun appearing in its foundation, and water constantly leaked and pooled on the floors. "Those [cells] at the bottom are unwholesome, surely?" asked novelist Charles Dickens on a visit to the prison in 1842. "Why," answered his tour guide, "we *do* only put coloured people in 'em."[12] Although the prison housed mostly criminals awaiting sentencing, it also held those who had already been sentenced to death; it featured a central courtyard where they were hanged.[13]

Once in the Tombs, Gordon's demeanor changed. He was for the first time being treated like a criminal, and his swagger was gone. He became thinner and "pale and sallow," noted one journalist.[14] Elizabeth, his wife, was visiting once or twice daily. She and their young son, Nathaniel IV, then four years old, were staying with sea captain David Woodside and his wife Elizabeth in Brooklyn.[15] The Woodsides had been former neighbors of the Gordons in Portland.[16]

IN JUNE 1861, GORDON's trial for piracy finally convened with a new district attorney, Republican E. Delafield Smith, who seemed as anxious to prosecute the case as Roosevelt had been reluctant. But Smith immediately ran into complications. Lieutenant Dunnington, the officer who had boarded the *Erie* and arrested Gordon and the crewmembers, had since resigned from the U.S. Navy to join the Confederate cause. Not surprisingly, he was unwilling to testify at the trial of a slave captain in New York.[17] But Smith still had Henry Todd, the midshipman who had boarded the *Erie* with Dunnington and who had been since promoted to lieutenant in the Union Navy.

At trial, Todd testified that the *Mohican* had pursued and seized the *Erie*, and he recounted for the jury what he and Dunnington had found on board. Todd said that First Mate William Warren "was seen tampering with the negroes," so they had put the mate in irons and confined Captain Gordon to his room until they reached Monrovia.[18] Under oath, Warren stated that Gordon had given up his command to the Spanish captain in Africa before the *Erie* sailed with her human cargo.[19] Todd contradicted that testimony, declaring that Gordon "always spoke of [the *Erie*] as if he was master of her."[20] Warren was no doubt testifying according to script, trying to save his own skin as well as his captain's. He knew that if Gordon were found guilty, his own conviction would follow.

In addition to the Spanish captain ploy, Joachimsen, the defense attorney, offered several other reasons why Gordon should be exonerated. He claimed that the *Erie* had sailed under the U.S. flag but was now under foreign ownership; that it had been seized in Portuguese waters, outside the jurisdiction of U.S. law; and that Gordon had been born at sea while his mother was traveling with his father. As a result, Joachimsen argued, Gordon was not a U.S. citizen and was therefore not subject to U.S. piracy laws. But the attorney offered no evidence that the *Erie* was foreign-owned. Moreover, several sailors with experience on the African coast testified that the ship had been in international waters when it was seized. With regard to Gordon's birthplace, Smith called to the stand Captain Richard Crockett of Portland, who testified that he had known the defendant since he was two or three years old and had "never heard that Gordon was born anywhere but in Portland till to-day [when] I heard he was born in the Mediterranean."[21]

In his instructions to the jurors, Judge William Shipman pointed to the flaws in each of the arguments put forward by the defense. He explained that even if Gordon didn't own the *Erie* and was merely navigating her, the captain was still liable. Shipman then stated that the Congo River was three miles wide as far inland as twenty miles and therefore that the *Erie* had been seized in international waters and "within the jurisdiction of the United States." As for Gordon's citizenship: "If his father was an American citizen, he would be [also], even though born aboard."[22] It seemed like an open and shut case, but this was New York, after all.

The jury was out all night and returned in the morning, unable to agree, seven voting to convict and five to acquit, resulting in a hung jury.[23] Gordon must have felt relieved, although the odds had been in his favor all along. According to the New York *Evening Post*, "it was not . . . expected that he would be convicted, as the most important witness, Lieutenant Dunnington, could not be procured to attend."[24] Precedent was equally important. New York juries had been consistently reluctant to convict slave captains, and even when the crime was obvious, judges avoided sentencing slave captains to the 1820 law's prescribed punishment: death. "The slave-traders in this city have matured their arrangements so thoroughly that they almost invariably manage to elude the meshes of the law," wrote the *New York Daily Tribune* just after the trial. "Now they bribe a jury, another time their counsel or agents spirit away a vital witness. . . . The United States [court] offices in Chambers Street . . . have become thoroughly corrupt." But the *Tribune* foresaw positive changes to come under Lincoln and Delafield Smith: "Fortunately, however, a new class of men now have the direction of affairs, and a stop will be put to this iniquitous complicity with crime."[25]

As the *Tribune* predicted, Smith was not deterred. He prosecuted the case a second time. And this time, he found additional witnesses: four mariners who had served aboard the *Erie* on her trip to the African coast. He also won postponement of the second trial to November of 1861, so that his star witness, Henry Todd, could testify. With the Civil War in full swing, Todd had been assigned to a U.S. Naval blockade of Charleston Harbor.[26]

Though Gordon was now virtually penniless, he, too, upped the ante. To assist Joachimsen, he hired the law firm of Beebe, Dean, and Donohue, which had litigated numerous trials of accused slave captains.[27] In the second trial, the defense argued the same points: that a Spanish captain and crew had been in charge of the *Erie* when it took on captives and proceeded on its way; that the vessel had been sold to foreign interests; that she was in Portuguese, not international, waters when seized; and that Gordon was not an American citizen. But with four *Erie* crewmembers contradicting the stories of mates Warren and Hall, the defense had an even more challenging task.

Despite the many distractions that Gordon's lawyers put forward, Judge Shipman's colleague in the case, Justice Samuel Nelson, offered the jury a simple, straightforward guide: "Were these negroes, that were put on board the Erie, in the Congo river, in August, 1860, forcibly detained or confined, with the intention of making them slaves, and did the prisoner, on board of the vessel at the time, participate in that confinement or detention? If he did, then he is guilty of this offence, under the statute. If he did not, then he is innocent."[28]

The jury was out for only half an hour this time, returning with a guilty verdict. It was an astonishing result and a reversal for the nation as a whole: a New York jury had seen fit to render a sea captain guilty for the capital crime of piracy.[29] The defense immediately moved for another trial, but on November 30 Judge Shipman dismissed their motion. Then he pronounced Gordon's sentence. His statement was carried in newspapers across the country:

> The evidence of your guilt was so full and complete as to exclude from the minds of your triers all doubt. . . . Think of the cruelty and wickedness of seizing nearly a thousand fellow beings, who never did you harm, and thrusting them between the decks of a small ship, beneath a burning tropical sun, to die of disease or suffocation, or be transported to distant lands, and consigned, they and their posterity, to a fate more cruel than death. . . . You showed mercy to none—carrying off as you did not only those of your own sex, but

women and helpless children. Do not flatter yourself that because they belonged to a different race from yourself that your guilt is therefore lessened. Rather fear that it is increased. . . . It remains only to pronounce the sentence, . . . which is, that you be taken back to the City Prison . . . and remain there until Friday, the seventh of February next, and then and there . . . on that day you be hanged by the neck until dead; and may the Lord have mercy upon your soul![30]

The *Union and Journal* of Biddeford, Maine, announced Gordon's conviction and sentence but didn't offer that he was a native of Portland.[31] And while scattered notices regarding Gordon appeared throughout Maine, his hometown press was unusually quiet. Only one Portland paper, the *Daily Advertiser*, dared to print, "The case of Capt. Gordon may excite our pity, but for his fate he alone is responsible; he was aware of the penalty when he deliberately defied the law." The rest of the city papers, and there were a half-dozen of them in 1861, had little or nothing to say—as if, by ignoring the shame of having a native son sentenced to hang as a trafficker in human beings, the problem might go away.[32]

GORDON'S CASE INSPIRED MULTIPLE efforts for a reprieve. His lawyers, Gilbert Dean and Philip Joachimsen, traveled to Washington seeking to meet with President Lincoln to request a pardon.[33] Dean appealed to the U.S. Supreme Court for a writ of prohibition, but Chief Justice Roger Taney, author of the infamous *Dred Scott* decision, denied it. Reverend J. W. Chickering of Portland's High Street Congregational Church wrote to Lincoln, urging mercy on behalf of Gordon's mother: "He is the only son of his mother & she a widow; respectable, estimable. Her distress can be (partly) imagined."[34]

Gordon's mother, wife, and sisters also wrote to the president, asking that the sentence be commuted to life. While his mother "deplored the misguided career, which has brought him to this wretched state," she "crave[d] that the life of her only son m[ight] be spared."[35] Mary Gordon and her daughter-in-law Elizabeth, accompanied by Rhoda E. White, a New York judge's wife and a staunch Lincoln supporter, also traveled to Washington, hoping to gain an audience with the president. Although the three women did visit with Mary Todd Lincoln—then distracted by her son Willie's grave illness—the president refused to see them or to hear his wife's arguments on their behalf.[36] So White wrote to the president personally: "Have the hearts of our people and rulers become so hardened that <u>imprisonment for life</u> will not answer the ends of justice?"[37]

Some 18,000 citizens of Maine signed a petition to the president asking for Gordon to be spared, as did 11,000 New Yorkers.[38] In New York City, placards urged citizens to protest "Judicial Murder."[39] A notice in the *New York Herald* "call[ed] upon the humane, who are in favor of commutation of the death penalty, to assemble at the Merchants' Exchange at three o'clock this afternoon and make themselves heard on [Gordon's] behalf at the White House."[40]

But others lobbied for the hanging to proceed. Senator Charles Sumner of Massachusetts, preeminent abolitionist and advocate against capital punishment, nonetheless approved of Gordon's sentence: "While it helps make the Slave-trade detestable, crime is seen in the punishment; and the gallows sheds upon it that infamy which nothing short of martyrdom in a good cause can overcome." He was said to have discussed the case at length with President Lincoln.[41] In Maine, the *Union and Journal* editorialized, "If capital punishment is justifiable in any case, it is in the case of the slave trader, and if Gordon expiates his high-handed offence against heaven and humanity upon the gallows, no one save his guilty companions and sympathizers will complain."[42] *The New York Times* also urged execution:

> It is to the young, the daring, the unreflecting, the temptation of the slave-trading capitalist is offered. Without the help of that class, their commerce would cease. . . . GORDON has deliberately placed himself where he may legally be presented as such an example. Every consideration of justice . . . demand[s] the execution of the sentence of the law upon this most unhappy criminal.[43]

After saying little, Lincoln finally responded, not with a commutation, but with a stay of two weeks. The president's statement was direct, and while he acknowledged those who opposed the hanging, he said little about his own thoughts:

> A large number of respectable citizens have earnestly besought me to commute the said sentence of the said Nathaniel Gordon to a term of imprisonment for life, which application I have felt it to be my duty to refuse.

In granting this respite, it becomes my painful duty to admon-
ish the prisoner that, relinquishing all expectation of pardon by
Human Authority, he refer himself alone to the mercy of the
Common God and Father of all men.[44]

U.S. Marshal Robert Murray, who was in charge of the prisoner, read
Lincoln's order to Gordon in his cell. Elizabeth Gordon was present and
reportedly fainted at the news.

Later in his term, Lincoln was asked to intercede on behalf of another
slave trader who had served his full sentence but couldn't pay his fine.
This time, the president was more direct about his feelings:

> I believe I am kindly enough in nature, and can be moved to pity
> and to pardon the perpetrator of almost the worst crime that the
> mind of man can conceive or the arm of man can execute; but any
> man, who, for paltry gain and stimulated only by avarice, can rob
> Africa of her children to sell into interminable bondage, I never
> will pardon, and he may stay and rot in jail before he will ever get
> relief from me.[45]

Those were unusually harsh words for a president known for his empathy.

Mary and Elizabeth Gordon elicited a great deal of public sympathy.
Newspapers described Gordon's mother Mary as "a person of exemplary
habits" and "unusual piety."[46] Elizabeth, noted several newspapers, pos-
sessed "much personal beauty." But despite Gordon's four trips to Africa,
which should have made him rich, he and his family were destitute.
"[Elizabeth's] pecuniary means are derived exclusively from benevolent
persons," wrote New York's *Evening Post*.[47]

Gordon's last meetings with Mary and Elizabeth occurred the afternoon before he was to be hanged. At the end of the visit with Elizabeth,
he was said to have "cried like a child." The press rendered the details
in dramatic fashion like a scene from a Dickens novel: "As the shades
of twilight fell upon the gloomy prison walls, they parted for the last
time on earth—and who could describe the parting scene—the utter
despair—heart-broken anguish of the stricken ones . . . ever sorrow-
ing for the loved one, prematurely and ignominiously snatched from
their embrace."[48] Once his family members departed, Gordon spoke
with Marshal Murray about his fears for their welfare. Murray assured

the prisoner that he would find a way to help them, and indeed, he did request and secure donations for Elizabeth Gordon.[49]

As Gordon awaited execution, four jailkeepers were assigned to watch him overnight. In the early morning hours, they heard him groaning and rushed to his cell, where they found him in convulsions. They called a doctor, who pumped Gordon's stomach and plied him with antidotes, stimulants, and brandy, which helped revive him. Gordon admitted to having taken strychnine, which had likely been secreted in a cigar that someone had brought him.[50]

Gordon's hanging was scheduled to take place at two o'clock in the afternoon, but the doctor was concerned that the prisoner might not survive that long, so it was moved to noon. Gordon, too ill to walk to the scaffold alone, had to be supported by men on either side.[51] "He was deathly pale with terror," wrote one observer.[52] But the hanging itself was swift, and witnesses agreed that he "died easily."[53] He was thirty-six years old.

And so it was that the first and last slave captain to face the full penalty of the 1820 piracy law met his end. The *Erie*'s first and second mates on the trip, William Warren and David Hall, were more fortunate; prosecutor Delafield Smith allowed them to plead to the lesser charge of violating the Act of 1800, which forbade slave trading between nations. Because the two had already spent more than a year in jail, Judge Shipman sentenced Warren to eight months and Hall to nine.[54]

GORDON'S SAGA HAD CAUSED a media circus, occupying newspapers for the past year. Some sought to capitalize on the story beyond his death. A notice in the *New York Herald* advertised "A Voice from the Tombs, the Execution of Nathaniel Gordon. His Dying Declarations. Written the night before his execution, and published in no other paper. See National Police Gazette."[55] In March, family friend Captain David Woodside helped to organize a "sympathetic benefit" for Gordon's "widow and orphan child" at the Old Bowery Theater. The benefit included clowns and circus events.

AFTER THE EXECUTION, MARY Gordon returned to Portland, but Elizabeth Gordon and her young son remained in New York. Sometime before the decade was out, Elizabeth married another sea captain, a

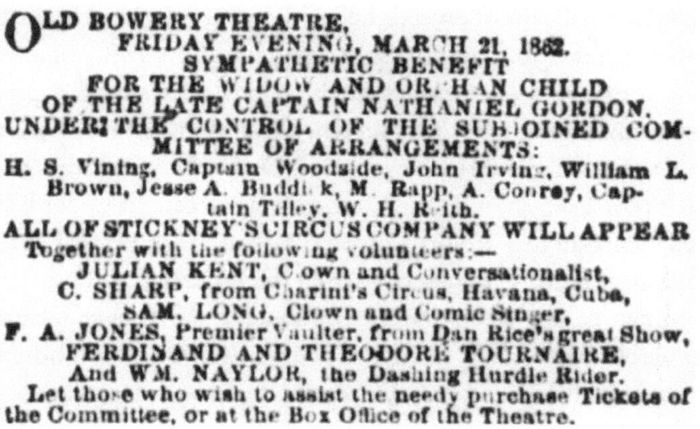

OLD BOWERY THEATRE,
FRIDAY EVENING, MARCH 21, 1862.
SYMPATHETIC BENEFIT
FOR THE WIDOW AND ORPHAN CHILD
OF THE LATE CAPTAIN NATHANIEL GORDON,
UNDER THE CONTROL OF THE SUBJOINED COM-
MITTEE OF ARRANGEMENTS:
H. S. Vining, Captain Woodside, John Irving, William L.
Brown, Jesse A. Buddick, M. Rapp, A. Conrey, Cap-
tain Tilley, W. H. Keith.
ALL OF STICKNEY'S CIRCUS COMPANY WILL APPEAR
Together with the following volunteers:—
JULIAN KENT, Clown and Conversationalist,
C. SHARP, from Charini's Circus, Havana, Cuba,
SAM. LONG, Clown and Comic Singer,
F. A. JONES, Premier Vaulter, from Dan Rice's great Show,
FERDINAND AND THEODORE TOURNAIRE,
And WM. NAYLOR, the Dashing Hurdle Rider.
Let those who wish to assist the needy purchase Tickets of
the Committee, or at the Box Office of the Theatre.

FIGURE 10. Advertisement for an event to benefit Nathaniel Gordon III's "widow and orphan child" in the *New York Herald*, March 21, 1862, http://genealogybank.com.

native New Yorker named Lewis Warren. It's unclear whether there was any family relation to the first mate of the *Erie*, William Warren, also a New Yorker.[56]

MANY BELIEVED THAT GORDON'S execution had ended the slave trade. The *New-York Tribune* called the execution "A Death Blow at the Slave-Trade." The only Portland paper to report at length on the matter, the *Portland Weekly Advertiser*, shared that sentiment: "The traffic in man-kind has received, to-day, a literal death blow." Later, the *Atlantic Monthly* proclaimed that "twenty-five thousand people petitioned Abraham Lincoln to spare [Gordon's] life, and Lincoln refused. All through the little ports and big ports of the United States it was known that the slave trader had been hanged. And when that was known, the American slave trade ended."[57]

Declaring the end of the slave trade was premature. "The conviction of Gordon . . . does not seem to have [had] the effect of restraining other parties from engaging in that nefarious business," wrote the *San Francisco Bulletin* in late December, shortly before Gordon was put to death. Just as Gordon's lawyers were appealing his death sentence, another Portland native was arrested in New York for fitting out another reputed slaver. "The impudence of Appleton Oaksmith, the person just taken into custody by the U.S. Marshal, almost exceeds belief," wrote the *Bulletin*. Oaksmith was caught attempting to fit out the ship *Augusta* in New York, ostensibly for a whaling voyage. He was arrested and brought before Judge Shipman, who had pronounced Gordon's death sentence. But Shipman released Oaksmith and his vessel on bond. Fleeing justice, Oaksmith sailed the *Augusta* to the far tip of Long Island. There, officials again caught up with him and ordered him confined at Fort Lafayette in New York Harbor. "He is now almost sure of getting his deserts," wrote the *Bulletin*.[58]

A contemporary of Nathaniel Gordon III, Appleton Oaksmith was also a native of Portland from a prominent family. His mother, Elizabeth Oakes Smith, was a popular poet and women's rights advocate, and his father, Seba Smith, was a well-known humorist and journalist who had once been editor of the city's *Eastern Argus* newspaper. At about the same time as Gordon was bringing the last shipment of enslaved Africans into Brazil aboard the *Camargo* in 1852, Oaksmith was captaining the *Mary Adeline* to the Congo River, where it ran aground and had to be rescued.[59]

IN LATE DECEMBER OF 1861, Oaksmith was released from Fort Lafayette, only to be immediately rearrested for fitting out yet another vessel, the *Margaret Scott*, as a slaver from New Bedford, Massachusetts.[60] Government officials felt he would be less likely to escape justice in Massachusetts than in New York.[61]

Oaksmith had purchased the old whaler under an assumed name and had paid a man named Samuel P. Skinner to take ownership of the vessel and another, Ambrose S. Landre, to serve as captain. Both were said to be in financial straits and "would not be likely to be scrupulous." Oaksmith relied upon "the temptation of large pay" to keep the officers and crew in line.[62]

But as soon as the *Margaret Scott* left port, she was seized by a federal cutter, whose crew were suspicious of a whaling vessel that was well past her prime. The ship's straw owner, Skinner, was arrested and convicted of fitting the vessel out for a slaver. During his trial, evidence emerged that Oaksmith was involved, along with his brother Sidney and a number of other individuals—Cuban, Portuguese, or Spanish nationals—who operated a firm with Oaksmith in New York and had since fled the country. Captain Landre turned state's witness and identified Oaksmith as the director of the operation.[63] He was convicted on eight of ten counts and was taken to the Suffolk County Jail in Boston.

Although his lawyer requested a new trial, Oaksmith wasn't one to wait around. Instead, on September 11, 1862, he escaped from jail "while the night buckets were being changed."[64] Some reports suggest that he scaled the prison walls. Family members recall that a friend visited him, brought him a bundle of women's clothing, bribed the guards on duty, and the two walked out of the jail arm in arm. His brother Edward was arrested in Boston as his accomplice, but some believed that "the principal instrument" in Oaksmith's escape was Augusta Mason, his cousin, who owned a millinery shop in Portland.[65] The two would later marry.

Wanted notices offering $500 reward for Oaksmith ran in newspapers across the country. The audacious slave trader was said to have a "dark, swarthy" complexion, "long, full beard," "genteel address," and "air of shrewdness."[66] Soon articles appeared stating that he had arrived in Havana, Cuba, where his brother Sidney now resided. Other sources say he spent several months with family in Portland and in Brooklyn and later sailed to England.[67]

THE CASE OF YET another Maine native played counterpoint to Gordon's and Oaksmith's experiences, demonstrating federal courts' wide sectional divide. On July 18, 1860, shortly before Gordon's *Erie* was captured by the *Mohican*, the schooner *Clotilda* sailed into Alabama's Mobile Bay at night. Its crew and captain—a man named William Foster—unloaded 109 captives from what are now Nigeria and Benin onto the steamboat *Czar* and smuggled them into the United States.[68] Towing the schooner to a deserted part of the Mobile River, Foster set it afire. Not until 2019 did archeologists locate the burned and submerged wreck in the riverbed.[69]

Gordon had audaciously used American ships and sailors to transport Africans to Brazil and Cuba. But the *Clotilda* affair was even bolder. Timothy Meaher provided the means and the money for the *Clotilda* operation. It was his idea, born of a discussion with several "Northern gentlemen" who insisted that the 1820 Piracy Act had made smuggling captive Africans into the United States impossible. Meaher begged to differ.

Meaher was master and owner of the steamboat *Roger B. Taney*, which made regular trips between Mobile and Montgomery, Alabama. Named for the chief justice in the *Dred Scott* case, the steamboat may well have been a floating pronouncement of Meaher's thoughts on racial equality. When these "Northern gentlemen," passengers on the *Taney*, asserted that no one would dare import enslaved persons into the States for fear of the death penalty, Meaher "treated this assertion with a levity that astonished his Northern hearers," wrote the special correspondent to the *St. Louis Globe-Democrat*.[70] He took it as a dare and bet the men $1,000 that he could do it.

A resident of Mobile, Meaher was no son of the South; he was a native of Whitefield, Maine. The son of an Irish immigrant, Timothy Meaher had been raised in Maine and moved to Mobile in 1835 with his brother James when they were twenty-three and twenty-five years old. Once in Alabama, he worked as a steamboat deckhand, eventually becoming captain, owner, builder, and planter as well as owner of a prosperous sawmill. Other members of the large Meaher family, including brothers William, Dennis, John, and Patrick Burns, joined him in Alabama, as did sister Abby. John, Burns, and Timothy did well in business and were slaveowners.

William Foster, captain and owner of the *Clotilda*, was a native of Nova Scotia. He, too, had come to Mobile to make his fortune. Meaher found Foster to be a willing accomplice in his plan. In early 1860, Meaher bought the schooner from Foster for $35,000 and then had her outfitted for a slaving trip. The schooner left Mobile Bay on March 4, 1860, with Foster as captain, ostensibly headed to the Caribbean island of Saint Thomas with a load of lumber. But as they began to cross the Atlantic, the sailors aboard the *Clotilda* knew they'd been tricked into a slaving voyage. They threatened mutiny, but Foster offered to pay them double to go along with his scheme. They agreed. The ship arrived without further incident in Ouidah, West Africa, where captain and crew boarded 110 captives.[71]

The return passage took about forty-five days, and the *Clotilda* arrived in Mississippi Sound on July 8. But when Meaher didn't immediately show up to meet the ship and pay the sailors, the *Clotilda* crew threatened mutiny again. They were, after all, in a precarious situation: sitting in U.S. waters with a boat full of West African captives intended for sale.[72] Eventually, the steamboat *Czar*, captained by Meaher's brother Burns, appeared, and Foster and the crew transferred the captives. The *Roger B. Taney* with Timothy Meaher aboard arrived to transport the crew of the *Clotilda*. The sailors were quietly escorted to a private room so that the other passengers would not overhear their conversations, and they celebrated their success over cards and whiskey. The *Clotilda* was towed into a remote bayou, where she was burned and scuttled.[73]

As secretive as Meaher and Foster had tried to be, they were noticed, and the arrival of the kidnapped Africans received wide play in the national press.[74] Not to be denied their fees, U.S. Customs officials chartered a boat, the *Eclipse*, to search for the *Clotilda*'s captives. But Meaher was ready: he sent whiskey to sailors aboard the *Eclipse*, who imbibed freely, and the expedition had to wait until sober sailors could be found to take their places. This gave Meaher time to hide the captives, who were already on the plantations of John Dabney and Burns Meaher, deep in nearby canebrake thickets.[75]

Captain William Foster was charged with failing to report the *Clotilda*'s arrival to U.S. Customs. He was fined $1,000, though the court said nothing about his human cargo. Burns Meaher and John Dabney were each indicted for receiving captives from the *Clotilda*. But U.S. District Judge William G. Jones—a friend of Timothy Meaher's for whom he'd also named a steamboat—stated that the captives could not be found in his district, and therefore, the cases couldn't proceed. Both cases were dismissed in January 1861.

Timothy Meaher was arrested and accused of bringing captives into the country to enslave them, but he had an alibi ready. He hadn't been on the *Clotilda*; he had, instead, carefully documented each trip he had made up and down the Alabama River aboard the *Roger B. Taney*. Given that evidence, Judge Jones dismissed the case. There would be no hangings in Alabama—at least not for slave smugglers.[76]

As for the captives smuggled into Alabama aboard the *Clotilda*, around twenty-five were sold to slave brokers, but the majority remained in Mobile. Thirty-two became the property of Timothy Meaher, twenty went to Burns Meaher, and brother James Meaher enslaved eight. Between five and eight went to William Foster as payment for the trip, and plantation owner Thomas Buford purchased the rest.[77]

After traveling upriver on the *Taney*, the *Clotilda*'s crew were put aboard trains going north to prevent them from spreading rumors in Montgomery. Foster's promise of double pay for sailors who agreed to go along with his slaving trip turned out to be nothing more than a momentary expedient. The sailors received only the original agreed-upon amounts for the trip.[78]

THE CASES OF THE *Erie, Margaret Scott,* and *Clotilda* reveal plenty about the characters and motives of those engaged in the slave trade. Gordon, Oaksmith, and Meaher were, like many criminals, risk takers who thrived on the challenge of breaking the law. As long as they succeeded, no stigma was attached to their actions. "During the time I was engaged in the slave trade, I never had the least scruple as to its lawfulness," wrote English slave trader John Newton, composer of the hymn "Amazing Grace." "It is, indeed, accounted a genteel employment and is usually very profitable."[59] These American slave traders' loyalties were not to any overarching notions of White supremacy or states' rights—not to family, country, or region. Rather, they placed personal gratification foremost: they sought to make great fortunes and they craved adventure, thrilling escapes, and the satisfaction of knowing they'd outsmarted their rivals.

Money was clearly the main objective for most freebooters, yet the adventures of Gordon, Oaksmith, and Meaher demonstrate that the trade did not always result in large profits. John Newton wrote that "there were some gainful voyages, but the losing voyages were thought more numerous." And he described the slave trade as "a sort of lottery in which every adventurer hoped to gain a prize."[80] As with any lottery, only a few managed to beat the odds. The captains of the 1840s, 1850s, and 1860s never made the fortunes that the infamous American captains of the late eighteenth century, such as Rhode Island's DeWolf family, did.[81]

Despite four trips to Africa, Nathaniel Gordon III was penniless when he died, leaving his wife, mother, and young son destitute. It's not clear from any assets or property records he left behind that any of his slaving expeditions made him rich. His bragging about being a slave captain among his acquaintances in Portland shows that the image of daring and defiance was important to him, too. He thrived on the thrill of the chase: "Very many hair-breadth escapes, such as daring sailors delight in, were [Gordon's] fortune," wrote *The New York Times.* "He has confessed to having enjoyed more pleasurable sensations when slipping slily through the cordon of 'slave-catchers' than at any other period of his existence."[82] Gordon was an addict. He felt most alive when outsmarting and eluding authorities. But his need for gratification resulted in his death at age thirty-six.

If Timothy Meaher's scheme was intended to make a profit, it was poorly planned. The truth is, he likely lost money on the trading voyage. The *Clotilda* was small and carried a mere 110 individuals, when most slavers carried upwards of seven or eight hundred. And while twenty-five of the captives were sold for cash, the rest went to co-conspirators. They undoubtedly made money from the enslaved people's labor, but that investment was short-lived: all were set free five years later at the end of the Civil War. One newspaper account declared that, "altogether, the venture cost [Meaher] about $100,000."[83]

Meaher's exploits hit the newspapers even before government officials became aware that he'd broken the 1820 law. And he seemed gratified to have outsmarted authorities. "We fooled them now," he is reported as saying to his wife with a laugh, explaining that while customs authorities were chasing after the Africans near Montgomery, the captives were in a canebrake about a mile from his home near Mobile.[84]

Appleton Oaksmith likely acquired significant assets from his involvement with slave ships, but they disappeared quickly. His failures in the trade were spectacular, and no doubt cost him dearly. Despite being a convicted criminal and fugitive, he engaged in numerous other business ventures, working as a writer and journalist and even serving a term in the North Carolina House of Representatives. Nevertheless, in his later years, he and his family depended wholly upon his wife Augusta's income from a small ship's store she operated in Beaufort, North Carolina.[85]

Oaksmith's capture by authorities—and his escapes—were widely covered in the newspapers of the day, from the East to the West Coast, which no doubt fed his ego. And it's clear that he, like Gordon and Meaher, thrived on deception and cunning. One of his jailers recalled that "he constantly told the wildest stories of the sea, hair-breadth escapes, and adventures."[86] In angling for a pardon from President Grant after the war, Oaksmith supposedly met with the president under an assumed name. Towards the end of their meeting, Grant asked why he was so keen to see Oaksmith pardoned. Without hesitation, Oaksmith replied, "Because I am Appleton Oaksmith."[87]

THESE THREE FAMILIES OF solid Yankee stock modeled, abetted, and shared the transgressions of freebooters. And this speaks to the culture that produced them. Was Maine the free state that it purported to be?

Or was it a sharply divided conglomerate of families, communities, and commercial interests, like the nation as a whole? While Maine's laws—and perhaps a majority of its eligible voters—supported its status as a free state, many of its citizens followed divergent paths, colluding with slaveholders and merchants in the sugar and cotton industries and international slave syndicates. As long as markets for enslaved laborers existed, no state could call itself truly free.

And what about justice? Did Gordon end up on the gallows because he was a Yankee who abetted slavery in a culture that disapproved of it? Hardly. Bad timing, more than anything, spelled his doom, given that so many others from the North, including his father and uncle, had escaped punishment under the law of 1820. In North and South alike, culture and popular opinion made it possible to forgive the crimes of man stealing and piracy. While Gordon's hanging seemed to denote a shift in the wind, he was the only U.S. citizen ever executed as a slave captain. Most, like *Erie* mates Warren and Hall, received reduced sentences; or, like Meaher, had their cases dismissed; or, like Captain Peter Flowery of the *Spitfire*, were granted pardons.

Despite being a fugitive from justice for the duration of the war, Appleton Oaksmith was pardoned by President Grant. In addition to Grant, Presidents Thomas Jefferson, James Madison, James Monroe, John Quincy Adams, Andrew Jackson, James Buchanan, and James K. Polk all pardoned slave captains.[88] That doesn't mean that the death penalty was out of proportion for the crime or for the times; it means that most Americans were willing to forgive those who engaged in it. Without question, many individuals, White and Black, railed against the gross brutality and immorality of the transatlantic slave trade. But the broad voting public, especially in the North, simply preferred to look away.

IT'S IMPORTANT TO REMEMBER the men, women, and children whom these freebooters sought to enslave. Oaksmith's most publicized slaving ventures were preempted by violence and capture, though he was very likely an accessory to numerous successful voyages. The hundreds of Congolese released from Nathaniel Gordon III's last trip likely lived out their days in Liberia as laborers or impoverished refugees. Hundreds more from three previous trips had been enslaved in Brazil and Cuba, and hundreds more had suffered and died aboard his ships. Like fellow

Mainer Ebenezer Farwell, wherever he went, Captain Gordon left suffering and death in his wake.

Timothy Meaher's impact was more complicated. After the end of the Civil War and some four to five years of slavery, the *Clotilda*'s captives became free. They chose to come together in a small community in Mobile, plotting ways to return to Africa. They asked Meaher to pay for their return as compensation for their work; he refused. They contacted the American Colonization Society, which also refused to help. So these formerly enslaved people from West Africa established their own self-governing, self-sustaining community known as Africatown or Plateau, Alabama. Many worked in the shipyards and sawmills of their former owners, including the Meahers, and saved enough money to purchase community land and build a school. They often spoke their native languages and established their own courts and legal structure.[89] Nevertheless, they had been kidnapped and forced to live in a strange and hostile society some 6,000 miles from their communities and families, whom they never saw again.

In 1927, writer and anthropologist Zora Neale Hurston interviewed the last survivor of the *Clotilda*'s captives, Oluale Kossola, whose name upon arriving in Alabama from Benin was changed to Cudjo Lewis. Hurston's many interviews with Lewis were later published in *Barracoon: The Story of the Last "Black Cargo,"* written largely in Lewis's voice. "We cry for home," he told Hurston. "We took away from our people. We seventy days cross de water from de Affica soil. . . . Our grief so heavy look lak we cain stand it. I think maybe I die in my sleep when I dream about my mama."[90] *Barracoon* became one of the last official works of the slave narrative genre. Even so, it recounts a chapter in American history that remains in the forefront of our collective conscience.

TIMOTHY MEAHER DIED ON March 3, 1892, a wealthy man: his money earned from lumber and steamboats, not from slave trading. His death was covered in newspapers across the country. Nearly all noted that he was a "venerable steamboat man." Listed without pause among his accomplishments were building a business empire and bringing the last cargo of enslaved Africans into the United States.[91]

CHAPTER 8

The War within the States

The sectional character of this war was merely accidental and its least significant feature. It was a war of ideas, a battle of principles and ideas which united one section and divided the other.

—Frederick Douglass, 1878

In March 1861, the celebrated actor John Wilkes Booth visited Maine. He was scheduled to perform for two weeks at Portland's Deering Hall, playing, among other parts, Hamlet, Richard III, and Othello—a curious role for an avowed White supremacist. His performances were so popular that he extended his run for an additional three weeks. Helen Western, a resident of Portland who played Desdemona to Booth's Othello, may have also inspired him to extend the engagement.[1] Although Helen had acted since she was a child, it was her remarkable beauty, not her dramatic skills, that attracted notice. The *New York Herald* praised "her fine face and perfect figure."[2] The *Memphis Daily Appeal* wrote, "Few actresses of such limited ability have succeeded in becoming so widely known." She was, according to the newspaper, "very beautiful . . . dark eyed and fair skinned, with glossy black hair."[3]

Booth himself was notoriously handsome. Yet despite the mutual attraction, he left Portland abruptly on April 12. He had heard via telegraph—as nearly everyone had—that Confederate troops had fired upon Fort Sumter in Charleston. The shots marked the beginning of the Civil War. As the actor was leaving town, a collector for the *Portland Advertiser* asked him to pay a printing bill for his performance announcements. Booth referred the collector to his agent, who "referred to his principal; the principal back to his agent; and so like a shuttlecock our collector was batted backward and forward between their falsehoods," the newspaper reported. "In the end, the bill was never paid."[4]

Whatever his reasons for leaving, Booth wasn't fleeing the North because it had suddenly turned hostile for supporters of the southern cause. He continued his tour of northern cities, traveling to Albany, New York, where he watched the newly elected president, Abraham Lincoln, pass in his carriage on the way to the state capitol.[5] Despite Booth's open support for the Confederacy and his disdain for Lincoln, he would continue to book performances in Boston, New York, Chicago, Philadelphia, and other northern cities, packing theaters and receiving warm applause.

THE RUBYS WOULD NOT have been able attend Booth's performances, even if they'd been allowed in the theater's gallery. As a family, they were struggling. In 1854, Reuben had mortgaged the family home to finance a second California venture, finally paying off his debt in 1858.[6] In 1859, Frederic, Reuben's and Rachel's oldest living child, died of tuberculosis at age twenty-eight. By 1860, the family was scattered. Reuben resided at the Elm House Hotel in Portland, where he worked as a cook. Sons William and George, twenty-six and nineteen, were living 130 miles north in Bangor, working as bakers. No records reveal where seventeen-year-old Horatio was. Rachel, Reuben's wife, was residing with her niece, Janette Ruby Freeman, and her husband Aaron Freeman, a dozen miles north of Portland in Yarmouth.[7] In all likelihood, Rachel had contracted tuberculosis and needed someone who could attend to her around the clock while Reuben worked. In October 1861, she died of the disease at age fifty-six.

In December of that year, after eleven southern states had left the Union, secession fever reached Maine. A petition allegedly signed by some 19,000 citizens urged the Maine legislature to consult with the British government regarding "an immediate annexation of the State of Maine to the Canadas."[8] The petition went nowhere: Maine's legislature was overwhelmingly Republican and didn't take up the matter.[9] Nonetheless, it was symptomatic of northerners' widely diverse opinions about the war, secession, slavery, and union.

Two great practical questions dogged northerners: who could fight, and what would they fight for? "My paramount object in this struggle is to save the Union, and is not either to save or to destroy slavery," President Lincoln wrote to Horace Greeley in 1862, in an open letter that was published in several newspapers.[10] Many White Americans felt the same way. But some feared the war would be fought along political rather than regional lines. Benjamin Butler, a pro-slavery Massachusetts Democrat who became a major general in the Union Army, warned Lincoln that the war was becoming "a partisan one." The governors of the New England states were largely Republican, and Butler observed that they were recruiting their political associates to positions of authority in the army. "The Democrats . . . looking substantially upon the war as a Republican war, are taking no part in it," he told Lincoln. He warned that "it would very soon become a party war" with the potential to "bring about a division of the North." To remedy the situation, Lincoln gave Butler the authority to recruit regiments throughout New England. Butler promised that he wouldn't reject any Republican volunteers, but that he would have "four-fifths of every regiment good, true Democrats, who believe in sustaining this country and in loyalty to the flag of the union."[11]

Free Blacks were making their voices heard, too. They were anxious to take part in the struggle to end slavery once and for all, but they couldn't enlist in the Union Army, at least as regular soldiers. In part, Lincoln simply couldn't imagine Blacks as soldiers; in part, he was concerned that border states of Kentucky, Missouri, Maryland, and Delaware would secede if he permitted Black troops to fight. Some sought to force Lincoln's hand. In Boston, Black residents drafted a resolution: "We ask you to modify your laws, that we may enlist—that full scope may be given to the patriotic feelings burning in the colored man's breast."[12] Black activists William Wells Brown and Jermain Loguen argued that Blacks be allowed to fight, as did Frederick Douglass: "This is no time to fight only with your white hand, and allow your black hand to remain tied," wrote Douglass.[13]

Abolitionists were with Douglass. Vice President Hannibal Hamlin, a staunch Maine abolitionist, urged Lincoln to allow African Americans to fight. U.S. Senator William Pitt Fessenden, son of the noted Portland attorney and a friend of Reuben Ruby, advocated for employing Blacks as soldiers and workers, particularly runaways and refugees who entered Union Army camps: "I tell the generals of our army, . . . avail yourselves like men, of every power which God has placed in your hands."[14]

Fessenden's son, Captain James Deering Fessenden, agreed to organize and drill the Union's first Black regiment under General David Hunter in 1862. He wrote to his father, "The fine appearance and good behavior of the men are a source of wonder to everybody." But lacking political support and prohibited from engaging in battle, the unit was disbanded.[15]

The president's views on Black recruitment evolved as the war progressed. In a move that alarmed African Americans and abolitionists, he promised not to interfere with slavery in states that ceased hostilities. It didn't work; not a single state that had seceded responded. Despite what he'd said early on, Lincoln knew that the war was much more than a battle to preserve the union. Even as he sought to "save it in the shortest way under the Constitution," he couldn't keep other matters—like slavery—out of the fight. As the conflict dragged on and volunteers became harder to recruit, he determined that enlisting Black soldiers might be a good idea after all.[16]

The Emancipation Proclamation, which took effect on January 1, 1863, nearly two years into the war, called for enslaved persons in rebelling states to be freed. But it also called for them to be recruited into the Union Army and Navy: "Such persons of suitable condition will be received into the armed service of the United States to garrison forts, positions, stations, and other places, and to man vessels of all sorts in said service."[17] To recruit both White and free Black soldiers, Lincoln signed another bill, the Enrollment Act of 1863. It required all male citizens between twenty and forty-five years old to register with the draft.

In July 1863, Reuben Ruby's youngest sons, George and Horatio, did just that.[18] And in Portland, at least, registration went smoothly. But cities elsewhere, including Boston, Buffalo, and Troy, New York, saw protests. New York City saw the worst week of riots ever witnessed in the United States. The divisions among the city's ethnic and economic groups were sharp and brought on a full-scale battle in the streets.

In New York, unlike Maine, the draft lottery exempted Black men, who were still seen as noncitizens under the *Dred Scott* decision. The Enrollment Act also exempted those who could afford to pay $300 to the government or hire someone to take their place, effectively excusing wealthy citizens. Recent immigrants—most from Ireland and Germany—were required to register if they had applied for citizenship, even if they weren't yet citizens.[19]

New York's working class resented the draft, the ability of wealthy New Yorkers to pay their way out of service, and the notion that the Union was now fighting to free enslaved Blacks. New arrivals from Europe—New York City was one-quarter Irish at the time—were at the bottom of the ladder when it came to jobs.[20] Their main competitors were African Americans. White laborers feared that, if the war succeeded, freed Blacks would swarm into the city and take all the low-wage jobs. Irish immigrants especially, who had often been discriminated against because of their ethnicity, saw themselves being squeezed from both sides.

New York's draft lottery began on Saturday, July 11, just eight days after the Battle of Gettysburg. In the wake of that conflict, most understood that the war would drag on and many, many more would sacrifice their lives. After a Sunday break, the draft continued on Monday, July 13. On that hot and muggy morning, a company of firefighters, along with railroad and foundry workers, congregated near the provost marshal's office, where the lottery was being held. As names were pulled—many of them Irish—the crowd began jeering. As it swelled, the crowd grew angrier. Soon the mob tried to enter the building, and the small police force guarding the office was overwhelmed. Once inside, rioters set fire to the building. They then moved on, seeking new outlets for their frustrations.

At first, the angry throng targeted government and military facilities, attacking an armory and seizing weapons. The New York militia, which might have stopped the crowd, had been deployed to Gettysburg.[21] Symbolically, rioters also attacked the famous clothing manufacturer, Brooks Brothers; in addition to providing clothing for New York's wealthy, it manufactured uniforms for the Union Army. The offices of Horace Greeley's *New-York Tribune*, a Republican antislavery newspaper, also drew demonstrators.

As the violence escalated, Black residents, who weren't being drafted, became targets of the mob's ire. According to the *Brooklyn Daily Eagle*:

> The unfortunate negroes became marked objects for attack. . . . One colored man was hung to a lamp post in Clarkson street and his clothes set on fire.
>
> The crowd made a rush for the negro sailor boarding houses, near the corner of Roosevelt and Chambers street. . . . The whole block

From a print.   Collection of J. Clarence Davies

DESTRUCTION OF THE COLORED ORPHAN ASYLUM, 44TH STREET AND
FIFTH AVENUE.

FIGURE 11. Draft rioters destroy the New York Colored Orphans Asylum, July
1863. New York Public Library Collections.

in Batavia street, from Chambers to Roosevelt, [was] completely
gutted.

A number of colored women applied at the Station House of the
42nd Precinct last night, for protection. They told some alarming stories about crowds coming to sack their houses and kill the
occupants.[22]

By this time, thousands of angry White men were roaming the streets
of New York. Uptown, at Forty-third Street and Fifth Avenue, a large
group burned the four-story Colored Orphans Asylum to the ground.
The staff of the asylum, including Christiana Freeman, the wife of Reverend Amos Noë Freeman, who had preached at Portland's Abyssinian
Meeting House for a decade, helped the 233 children who lived there to
escape to safety at a police precinct nearby.[23]

The insurrection lasted five days, with armed rioters barricading
themselves inside neighborhoods and causing an enormous amount

of damage. They tore up railroad tracks, felled telegraph poles, and destroyed pavement to use as weapons. Fifty buildings were burned.[24] In the midst of war, President Lincoln was forced to divert 4,000 troops from the front lines to New York to stop the violence.[25]

Afterward, one of the rioters wrote to *The New York Times*, expressing his resentment that the Enrollment Act targeted the poor while excusing the rich: "That 300-dollar law has made us nobodies, vagabonds and cast-outs of society, for whom nobody cares when we must go to war and be shot down. We are the poor rabble, and the rich rabble is our enemy by this law." But the rich weren't the only ones whom the rioters resented: "Why don't they let the nigger kill the slave-driving race and take possession of the South, as it belongs to them." The letter was signed "A Poor Man, But A Man For All That," a reference to Robert Burns's egalitarian poem.[26]

One of the victims, a Black sixty-three-year-old whitewasher, had a different perspective. During the violence, he'd been knocked down, kicked and beaten, and left with a broken arm and bloodied face. "I entertain no malice and have no desire for revenge against these people. Why should they hurt me or my colored brethren? We are poor men like them; we work hard and get but little for it."[27]

In fact, the worst destruction was visited upon Black New Yorkers. During the five-day riot, eleven Black men were lynched.[28] Those who escaped found refuge on Blackwell's Island, at police stations, "in the swamps and woods back of Bergen, New Jersey, at Weeksville, and in the barns and out-houses of the farmers of Long Island and Morrissania. At these places were scattered some 5,000 homeless and helpless men, women, and children."[29] Although the riots didn't stop the draft, they did tip the scale in favor of Irish laborers. Thousands of Black residents who had escaped the city never returned. New York's African American population, which had numbered just over 16,000 in 1840, declined to fewer than 10,000 by 1865.[30]

Oddly, New York City's rancor turned to admiration when Black soldiers were finally permitted to enlist in 1864. As the newly formed Black regiments marched through Manhattan on their way to battle, "a thousand men, with black skins, and clad and equipped with the uniforms and arms of the United States Government . . . received a grand ovation at the hands of the wealthiest and most respectable ladies and gentlemen of New-York." The onlookers cheered, waved handkerchiefs, and threw flowers at the newly minted soldiers.[31] *The New York Times* could not refrain from remarking on the irony of the moment:

> Seven brief months have passed [since the Draft Riot], and a thousand of these despised and persecuted men march through the City in the honorable garb of United States soldiers, in vindication of their own manhood, and with the approval of a countless multitude—in effect saving from inevitable and distasteful conscription the same number of those who hunted their persons and destroyed their homes during those days of humiliation and disgrace.[32]

BY THE TIME BLACK soldiers were permitted to enlist in the Union Army as soldiers, Reuben Ruby's eldest surviving son, William, was already serving with the Twelfth Maine Regiment in Louisiana as a mess cook, one of the few roles open to Blacks before the Enrollment Act.[33] The Twelfth Maine had mustered in at Portland in November 1861 under the command of Colonel George Shepley, a Democrat recruited under Benjamin Butler's plan. The regiment traveled by steamer to Mississippi and on to Louisiana. There, Shepley was promoted to brigadier general and made military governor of Louisiana, which surrendered to Union forces in April 1862.[34] The Twelfth Maine went on to capture two Confederate batteries and supplies at Pass Manchac, and it fought at Port Hudson, where it lost sixty-eight soldiers.[35]

If Civil War photos and images are any guide, Black cooks like William Ruby were common in both the Union and Confederate armies. By 1863, their roles were codified in Union Army regulations. Every group of thirty soldiers was accorded one cook and two "colored" assistant cooks. Black assistant cooks received $10 per month. They were recruited in the same fashion as other enlisted men, and their names were to be "entered on the company muster-rolls, at the foot of the list of privates."[36] Yet they were often left off regimental rolls, as William Ruby was.

Somehow, even as a mess cook, William found time for activism while in New Orleans. In January 1864, a French-language newspaper, *L'Union*, recorded that "W. W. Ruby" was involved in a large assembly of the colored citizens of New Orleans in honor of Frederick Douglass.[37] It may be that William had been about to muster out. In October of that year he attended the National Convention of Colored Men in Syracuse, New York, and was elected one of fifteen vice presidents, with Douglass as president.[38]

Concern for Black troops was particularly acute at the convention. Ruby, who had served, and Douglass, whose two sons had joined the famed Fifty-fourth Massachusetts Volunteer Infantry Regiment, undoubtedly influenced that dialogue. Attendees resolved "to have the rights of the colored patriots now in the field respected, without regard to their complexion"—a push for equal pay and fair treatment. Although the Emancipation Proclamation had declared that all African Americans in rebelling states were free, the Black community's worst fear was that this hard-fought victory would be lost or negotiated away: "Should an attempt be made to reconstruct the Union with slavery, we should regard such a course as a flagrant violation of good faith on the part of the Government, false to the brave colored men who have fallen in its defence, unjust to the living who are perilling their lives for its protection, and to be resisted by the whole moral power of the civilized world."[39]

African Americans knew that Lincoln was more anxious to preserve the Union than to secure an end to slavery. Yet they were fighting for emancipation and equal rights at home, whether they were activists, sailors, soldiers, laborers, or cooks. "The free colored man's elevation is at issue, as well as the slave's," wrote Sergeant Charles Singer of the 107th U.S. Colored Infantry.[40] While proclamations like those from the Colored Convention didn't yet have the power of the vote behind them, they did notify the president, Congress, and the courts that the world was watching.

Expressing her apprehension that Lincoln might be tempted to rescind emancipation, Hannah Johnson, the mother of a Black soldier, wrote to President Lincoln reminding him that his actions would be judged by more than just his contemporaries: "They tell me some do you will take back the Proclamation, don't do it. When you are dead and in Heaven, in a thousand years that action of yours will make the Angels sing your praises I know it."[41]

WILLIAM RUBY WASN'T THE only member of his family to serve in the South. Horatio, the youngest of the three surviving brothers, also enlisted. He served in Louisiana with the Western Army, though it's not clear in what capacity. Horatio participated in five or six engagements, including the siege of Port Hudson, just upriver from Baton Rouge, in May through July of 1863.[42] Port Hudson became the proving ground for the first Black Union troops permitted to fight. The First Louisiana

Native Guards, a Union regiment comprised of Black and Creole soldiers, fought bravely against Confederate artillery and sustained heavy losses while contributing to the Union victory. That battle, along with the Confederate surrender at Vicksburg, spelled the end of the Confederacy's control of the lower Mississippi. General Butler, then commander of Union troops in the gulf region, wrote to the War Department about the Native Guard's performance: "The history of this day proves conclusively that the Government will find this class of troops effective supporters and defenders."[43] The change in Butler after seeing African American soldiers in action was palpable; he'd come a long way since his days as a pro-slavery Massachusetts politician.

George Ruby, now Reuben's middle son, accepted a position as a body servant to an officer in the Army of the Potomac but was unable to join up. His father had secured a position as a porter and messenger at Portland's Custom House, and when Reuben became ill, George was forced to remain at home and fill in for him for several months, allowing Reuben to keep his job.[44]

AMONG THE GORDON FAMILY, only two men of recruitment age remained in 1863: Morgan's sons, Charles and George, were twenty-six and twenty-three, single, and therefore eligible. Like their father, both were merchant sea captains. Like the Rubys, the two registered for the draft in Portland in July, though no records indicate that either was drafted or enlisted.[45] As a civilian, however, Charles Gordon was involved in the only Civil War engagement to take place in Maine.

On June 27, the revenue cutter *Caleb Cushing*, which enforced import duties and legal trade in Portland Harbor, went missing from its berth. Between five and six o'clock that morning, the crew of the *Forest City*, a passenger steamer returning from Boston, noticed rowboats towing the *Cushing* out of the harbor. The winds were calm, so the steamer's crew thought nothing of it. But when the *Forest City* docked, crew members saw the *Cushing*'s master-at-arms—who was supposed to be aboard whenever the cutter sailed—on the dock. They raised the alarm immediately.

Word spread quickly. The *Forest City* and another passenger steamer, the *Chesapeake*, prepared to chase the *Cushing*, and hundreds of angry civilians, hearing of the cutter's disappearance—presumably at the hands of Confederate raiders—swarmed the waterfront, seeking to board the boats and join the pursuit. The *Forest City*'s captain pleaded with the swelling crowd, telling them that too many would sink the steamer. He and his crew were forced to turn water hoses on the men.[46] Still, many civilians did board and were given arms by Mayor Jacob McLellan. Thirty men of the Seventeenth Maine Artillery also boarded the *Forest City*, and cannons were put aboard both steamers. Other soldiers manned the guns at Fort Preble, overlooking Portland Harbor.

Mayor McLellan commandeered the *Chesapeake*, taking with him about thirty soldiers of the Seventh Maine and thirty civilians with their own weapons. The civilians came from all walks of life: fishermen, journalists, stevedores, a baker, a minister, a college professor, an artist.[47] Charles Gordon was one of several mariners who joined the chase.[48]

The two steamers were directed to the *Cushing* by flags flown aloft from the eighty-six-foot Portland Observatory on Munjoy Hill. Enoch Moody's powerful telescope allowed him to view the *Cushing* and point the way to the pursuing ships.[49]

So who stole the *Cushing*? Before reaching Maine, Confederate lieutenant Charles Read and a small crew had been marauding up and down the East Coast in the ship *Tacony*. Between June 12 and 24, Read and his crew had disabled or burned nineteen ships.[50] Pursued by the Union Navy into the Gulf of Maine, the Rebel sailors commandeered a fishing vessel, the *Archer* of Southport, Maine. They loaded their gear onto the *Archer*, burned the *Tacony*, and continued their raids, disguising themselves as fishermen.

In Portland, they sought to cripple the port by destroying two Union gunboats under construction and as many merchant ships as they could. En route, they picked up two local fishermen to pilot them through perilous ledges into the harbor. But though Read claimed that the fishermen cooperated after being plied with cigars and liquor, both denied it.[51] Between one and two o'clock in the morning, the Confederates entered Portland Harbor and, with pistols and knives, secured the *Cushing*, placed its twenty crewmen in irons, and headed for the open ocean.

With its engines already firing, the passenger vessel *Forest City* was the first of the steamboats to catch up to the *Archer* and the *Cushing*. At about noon, the Confederates aboard the *Cushing* began firing at the *Forest City*, forcing her to lay to. Because they couldn't find the cutter's stores of ammunition, however, the rebels "were obliged to fire stones and pieces of iron." Then the *Chesapeake* arrived.

The wind was now against the cutter, which was running out of ord-nance, so Read knew the *Cushing* would soon be boarded. He put his captives into one lifeboat while he and the crew boarded another. They then set the *Cushing* on fire. Within minutes, an enormous explosion, which shook buildings in Portland more than ten miles away, proved that the *Cushing* actually had a significant store of artillery.[52] Moody, who saw all this from atop the observatory, sent updates to the crowds on the Eastern Promenade and shoreline below, who shouted and cheered.

The lifeboats and the *Archer* were easily captured, and twenty-three Confederate sailors were taken to Fort Preble in present-day South Portland.[53] "Such was the indignation of our citizens that [the Confederates] would have been murdered had they been brought up to the city," wrote the *Portland Daily Press*.[54] The event, it seems, helped to galvanize support for the Union among Portland's citizens.

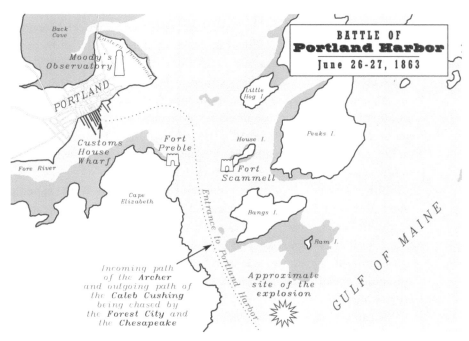

FIGURE 12. Map shows Portland Harbor's narrow entrance—the channel is sur-rounded by ledges—and the approximate site of the battle between the hijacked customs cutter *Cushing* and the steamboats *Forest City* and *Chesapeake*. Map by Andreu Comas. Used with permission.

PORTLANDERS HAD SUCCEEDED IN capturing the Confederate raiders; still, they felt a prevailing sense of unease and panic. Were more Confederate ships waiting to attack? Had members of the Revenue Service been complicit in the event? Truth was, it was the first and last such battle to be fought in Maine during the War, and it spelled the beginning and end of Charles Gordon's participation in the hostilities.

ALTHOUGH HE NEVER ENLISTED, George Gordon, Charles's younger brother, played a more active role in the war—on the opposing side. According to an 1864 article in Portland's *Daily Eastern Argus,* "Capt. George Gordon, of this city, is master of the blockade running steamer *Despatch,*" and New York's *Journal of Commerce* confirmed as much.[55] The *Despatch* was a blockade-runner for the Confederacy, known to have made several successful trips between Charleston and Nassau in 1862 and 1863, and it likely made many other undocumented trips in 1864 with Gordon at the helm, since its purpose was to travel in secret.

Early in the war, the U.S. Navy had attempted to blockade southern ports from Virginia to Texas to starve the Confederacy of income, weapons, and food. This was General Winfield Scott's "Anaconda Plan." But southern planters and businessmen, with the help of British ships, capital, and sailors, ran around and through the blockades, carrying cotton, turpentine, and tobacco on outbound trips and weapons and provisions on inbound ones. As hostilities continued, British shipyards began building sleek and fast steamships designed to run the blockade to secure southern cotton for England's booming textile factories.

Built in Ireland, the *Despatch* was neither sleek nor fast. The captain who sailed it to America in 1862 called it "a second-hand Irish cattle-boat with boilers nearly worn out and engines sadly neglected."[56] The U.S. consul at Liverpool advised officials in the States that the *Despatch* had been sent "by the persons here so actively engaged in sending aid and munitions of war to the people at the South in rebellion against our Government."[57]

The captains and crews of blockade-running ships could make handsome profits if they could outrun or outfox Union ships. A single round trip to the Bahamas, Bermuda, or Cuba of less than a week could net profits as high as $300,000, and captains like George Gordon could earn as much as $5,000—an enormous sum for the times.[58] Blockade running also provided the thrill that some sailors craved. "We enjoyed the excitement in the same way as a man enjoys fox-hunting, only . . . we were the fox instead of the huntsmen," wrote one English captain.[59] George Gordon, it seems, had inherited some of the contrarian, thrill-seeking tendencies of his infamous cousin Nathaniel and his father Morgan, a slave trader and a gun-runner during the Peruvian War of Independence.

GEORGE GORDON WASN'T THE only northerner engaged in running contraband. Appleton Oaksmith was another. The Maine native convicted of fitting out a slaver in 1862 managed to escape from jail and go into hiding. And while most convicted criminals would've laid low, fearing rearrest and prison, Oaksmith compulsively sought out adventure—or trouble. Sailing from Havana on June 1, 1864, he captained the steamer *Caroline* through the Union blockade to Galveston, Texas, with supplies for the Confederacy. Several weeks later, Oaksmith and crew loaded cotton destined for England's textile mills onto the *Caroline* and set off. But three Union gunboats pursued him, forcing Oaksmith and crew to abandon both ship and cargo and return to Galveston on foot. In September, he attempted to sail another steamer, the *Matagorda*, from Galveston to Havana with yet another cargo of cotton. Once again, his vessel was pursued in the Gulf of Mexico. As a U.S. naval ship caught up to the steamer and sailors began to board her, Oaksmith escaped over the gunwale on the opposite side into a small boat, again leaving ship and valuable cargo behind.[60]

TIMOTHY MEAHER, THE MASTERMIND of the *Clotilda* scheme that brought the last cargo of captives meant for slavery into the United States, was never convicted. In Alabama, Meaher was celebrated as a hero who stood fast for the values of the Confederacy. Because the law stipulated that any man owning a plantation with more than twenty enslaved persons was exempt from joining the army, Meaher never had to take up arms for the South.[61] But he did his part as a blockade runner. Meaher loaded his steamboats with cotton—much of it grown on his own lands by enslaved laborers—and sailed for Havana at night to avoid the Union Navy ships patrolling Mobile Bay. In Havana, he traded the cotton for weapons, provisions, and European goods to support the Confederacy.[62]

On December 31, 1863, Meaher was at the helm of his steamer *Gray Jacket* when it was intercepted by the U.S. Navy ship *Kennebec*, some forty miles outside Mobile Bay. Loaded with five hundred bales of cotton and destined for Cuba, the steamer was boarded and escorted to New Orleans, where it and its contents were sold. Meaher didn't take this loss lying down; he sought remission of the *Gray Jacket* through the courts, swearing in an affidavit for the U.S. Supreme Court that he "opposed secession, and . . . gave it no aid or assistance in any way whatever." Although the first mate of *Gray Jacket* stated that half of the profits from the cargo were intended for the Confederate government, Meaher claimed that he had been forced into the deal. He argued that he had been trying to get his property away from a war zone when his steamer was captured. He intended to return to Maine, he said, where he had been born and where his mother still lived.[63]

It was a tall tale, full of holes: one that illustrates Meaher's shifting alliances. He had never considered going home to Maine. In fact, he had left his wife and children behind in Mobile, although this, he said in court, was merely to disguise his intentions. But the most glaring evidence was the name of his steamer: *Gray Jacket*. Like the name of another of his steamboats, the *Roger B. Taney*, it was a signpost for his beliefs and alliances.

Or was it? The names of his steamboats were meant to disguise his Yankee upbringing and persuade his southern business associates and the Mobile community of his allegiance to the South. But when Meaher stood to lose his asset, he denied sharing any principles with the Confederate cause. His true allegiance, it seems, was to himself and his bottom line. The U.S. Supreme Court paid little attention to Meaher's story, for that was all it was. Justices confirmed the decision to condemn the *Gray Jacket* as enemy property.[64]

Despite the much-vaunted rift between North and South, the war was not fought along strictly geographical lines. For some, profit outweighed loyalty to country or state, race, region, or party. For Mainers George Gordon, Appleton Oaksmith, and Timothy Meaher, war was not a moral battle nor a contest to win, but an opportunity to seize.

MAINE'S MOST FAMOUS CIVIL War soldiers were the Medal of Honor recipients Otis O. Howard and Joshua Chamberlain. They represented the political dichotomy among Mainers when it came to war, abolition, and equality. And both Howard and Chamberlain would play leading roles in Reconstruction and postwar politics and society.

O. O. Howard of Leeds, Maine, commanded the Third Maine Regiment at the First Battle of Bull Run, and was promoted to brigadier general. He lost an arm in the Peninsula Campaign and was later promoted to major general. But in 1863 he and his men endured a series of defeats, including routs at Chancellorsville and Gettysburg, which earned him the nickname "Uh-oh Howard."[65] He was a graduate of Bowdoin College and West Point, and was a devout Christian and fervent abolitionist.

Joshua Chamberlain, born in Brewer, was also a Bowdoin graduate. He was pro-Union, but neither a strong abolitionist nor likely a believer in racial equality. He supported emancipation, not as a moral imperative, but as a strategic move: it would help bring the South to its knees.[66] Not even Harriet Beecher Stowe, whom he'd met at Bowdoin, could convince him of the moral necessity of freeing enslaved individuals. After the war, he said that he hoped "the best blood in all the land" had not been spilled "so that negroes might have no one to stop them in going to the polls."[67] Still, Chamberlain and his Twentieth Maine became the heroes of Little Round Top at Gettysburg, a military moment that has been mythologized and called the turning point of the war.

Some 83,000 not-so-famous Mainers also fought for the North; a greater proportion of the population than any other state could claim.[68] Chamberlain's perspective was likely more common among Maine's White soldiers than Howard's was. Most were in it for the Union. They supported emancipation for Blacks as a military strategy, but political and social equality were steps too far.[69] Maine soldier Gardner L. Hatch wrote to his mother, "I enlisted to help put down the rebellion."[50] John Monroe Dillingham, a young mariner from Freeport, Maine, joined the Union Navy. But it was the dissolution of the Union, not the cause of emancipation, that inspired him. Referring to the Emancipation Proclamation, Dillingham wrote to his mother in March 1863: "there is one thing I cant get over that is Lincoln's d——-d nigger proclamation that sties me."[51]

Among many soldiers, the notion that the Union was fighting against slavery was incendiary. Laura Towne, a woman from the North who taught freedmen behind Union lines on Saint Helena Island in South Carolina, wrote in her diary, "Anti-slavery is to be kept in the background for fear of exciting the animosity of the army, and we are only here by military sufferance."[52]

Naturally, there were exceptions. One of those was Walter Stone Poor, a teacher and well-educated White native of Andover, Maine, who enlisted in the Tenth New York Volunteers. Fighting for the Union, he wrote to his sister, was "nobler even than the Revolution for they fought for their own freedom, . . . [and] we fight for that of another race." If slavery could be wiped out "by any sacrifice of mine," he added, "it shall be cheerfully made."[53]

Civilian Nathaniel Austin of Damariscotta, a merchant and ship-builder, thought that the war could—and should—have been avoided. In a letter to his half-brother, Moses B. Lakeman, a colonel in the Union Army, he wrote, "About the war we are now whare we have No Other way but to fight it out the trouble was Brot on no doub by Improper Conduct of our folks the Abolition party and other Imprudent polititions + now the matter must be settled by the Sheding of blod."[54]

Charlotte Thomas, active in the Women's Anti-Slavery Society of Portland, recalled that the Civil War "was not started to aid the slave, but simply because our flag was pulled down and insulted. There was no thought of freeing the slave when that began." She declared that "Portland was never anti-slavery until the close of the war, and then circumstances forced it to be."[55]

Maine's Black community likely saw things differently. William and Horatio Ruby were only two of many African Americans from Maine to serve in the war. In December of 1863, three Peters cousins from the town of Warren—Daniel, Dexter, and James—enlisted in the all-Black Fourteenth Rhode Island Heavy Artillery Regiment, believing that a White Maine regiment wouldn't have them. In January 1864, their cousins William and Reuben Peters joined them.[76] Three more family members—Abraham, John, and Mariel Peters—served in the Union Navy, along with seventy-two other African Americans born in Maine.[77] Ninety-three Black Mainers enlisted in the United States Colored Troops, while others took their chances and enlisted in predominantly White units, including the First Maine Heavy Artillery, which lost more men in a single battle than any other Union unit.[78]

While the thoughts of these Black Mainers haven't been preserved, those of other Black soldiers have. "If I fall in the battle anticipated, remember, I fall in defense of my race and my country," wrote a member of the Fifty-fifth Massachusetts Regiment, fighting at Folly Island, South Carolina.[79] A soldier from Indiana wrote home, describing his homesickness, "but [I] soon rally when I think on what principal I am fighting which is for the benefit of my race." And he added, "If it is necessary I will give up my life most willingly to benefit the Colored Race."[80] "I am more than one year in the army, and do not wish to go home till every slave in the South is set free," wrote Sgt. William Watson of Pennsylvania while fighting with the Twenty-fifth U.S. Colored Infantry in Barrancas, Florida, in 1865.[81]

Across the nation, nearly 198,000 Black men fought with the Union Army and Navy.[82] And their contributions were clearly outlined by the commander-in-chief himself. Forced to defend his decision to finally enlist Black soldiers, Lincoln said, "There are now in the service of the United States near two-hundred thousand able-bodied colored men. . . . Abandon all the posts now garrisoned by black men; take two-hundred thousand men from our side and put them in the battlefield or the cornfield against us, and we would be compelled to abandon the war in three weeks."[83]

Those African Americans contributed mightily to the Union victory on April 9, 1865, the day that Robert E. Lee surrendered to Ulysses S. Grant at Appomattox Courthouse in Virginia. General Grant chose Joshua Chamberlain to receive the weapons and colors of the surrendering Army of Virginia. As the Confederates came forward with them, Union soldiers met them with silent salutes.

Five days later, John Wilkes Booth assassinated Abraham Lincoln. Booth was pursued and tracked down by federal agents, and twelve days later, he, too, was shot while hiding in a Virginia tobacco barn. On his body was found a diary containing the photographs of five women, including his lover during his sojourn in Portland, Helen Western.[84]

Another violent struggle would follow the Civil War: the one to alter the hearts and minds of Americans concerning the rights of newly freed Blacks in the South. Reuben Ruby's youngest sons, George and Horatio, would play key roles in that conflict: not in the North, but in Louisiana, Texas, and Kansas.

CHAPTER 9

Carpetbaggers and Exodusters

The Maine citizen may go to Colorado and California and be welcome. It is no reproach to him that he was born in the East and votes the republican ticket. Let him go to Georgia or Carolina, and carry with him his principles, and his fate is social, personal, political ostracism.

—*New York Herald*, 1876

In January 1864, George Thompson Ruby moved to occupied Louisiana. His brothers, William and Horatio, were still serving there with the Union Army. But George didn't enlist as a soldier or mess cook; he signed on as a teacher. Growing up in Portland and New York, he surely didn't know what he'd find in the South, nor that teaching recently emancipated men and women to read, write, and do arithmetic was as dangerous as soldier's duty on the front lines.

New Orleans had fallen to the Union early on, in 1862. In January 1863, Lincoln issued the Emancipation Proclamation, which freed enslaved persons in ten states—including Louisiana—that had seceded. As a result, Louisiana became prime territory for Lincoln's Reconstruction experiment led by Union general Nathaniel P. Banks. The experiences of George Ruby and his brother Horatio in Louisiana and Texas trace the arc of that experiment.

Intelligent and idealistic, George Ruby was looking for a meaningful vocation; one that might help African Americans realize their potential. Teaching, he thought, was a good start. From the Crescent City, Ruby wrote to *The Liberator* that 35,000 free Blacks lived there, and that the "Government has established some four or five public schools, for the instruction of the lately freed colored children of the city."[1]

As a newcomer arriving in New Orleans from the North, Ruby was considered a "carpetbagger." No more loaded word exists in the English language. Carpetbaggers were, in the largest, most neutral sense, northerners who traveled south during Reconstruction. Some sought public office; some sought economic opportunity; some sought to take advantage of the postwar chaos to grab land, money, and power. Some sought to help freed men and women adjust to a new normal. Ruby wasn't in it for the money, since he pursued teaching positions that paid little or nothing and he struggled to get by.[2] But in the South, all northerners were viewed with suspicion. Republicans, and those who sought to help freed men and women improve their situations—like Ruby—were especially mistrusted.

George had shown intellectual promise from a young age. After Portland reincorporated Black students into regular classrooms, he graduated with high honors from the High School for Boys—the first Black male to do so.[3] He was said to be "an unusually gifted young man."[4] Like his father, he was ambitious, committed to Black equality and civil rights, and anxious to follow that commitment in his life's work. Those tendencies lured him away from Maine to some challenging environments.

Three years out of high school, at age twenty, Ruby moved to Haiti to join a community of free African Americans. In 1804, enslaved Haitians had liberated themselves and their country, defeating Napoleon's army and quashing his ambitions for a French empire in the Americas. In winning the long battle for freedom, Haiti became the first nation on earth to ban slavery and the slave trade. In 1861, Haiti's president, Nicholas Fabre Geffrard, extended a broad invitation to African Americans: "All ye negroes and mulattos who, in the vast continent of America, suffer from the prejudices of caste, the [Haitian] Republic calls you; she invites you to bring your arms and your minds."[5] Many free Blacks were intrigued.

In the States, the leading voice for emigration to Haiti was, oddly, James Redpath, a Scottish immigrant to America, staunch abolitionist, and seasoned journalist. Redpath had worked for the *New-York Tribune* and other newspapers, traveling undercover in the South to interview enslaved individuals and reporting back on what he witnessed. In May 1861, he began publishing the *Pine and Palm* newspaper from Boston to promote migration to Haiti.

Whether it was the words of Geffrard or the encouragement of Redpath, George Ruby was converted. He moved to Haiti and began working as a correspondent for the *Pine and Palm*, encouraging other African Americans to emigrate.

Though George inherited Reuben's passion for social equality, his decision to move to Haiti was at odds with his father's values. Redpath's was a colonization scheme, intended to recruit African Americans to settle in Haiti, a majority-Black nation with a Black-run government, where they would supposedly live free of White prejudice. Reuben and his closest activist associates had strenuously opposed colonization for decades; to them, it undermined the drive for abolition and emancipation at home. Blacks born on American soil had helped build the United States; many had fought in the Revolution and the War of 1812. They believed they were entitled to full U.S. citizenship and were committed to securing it by standing their ground.

But as racial strife came to a head in the 1850s, many African Americans became disillusioned. The Fugitive Slave Law and the *Dred Scott* decision had convinced them that equality could never be achieved on U.S. soil. Some insisted that moving to Black-majority countries would bring them greater personal freedom and a chance to show what they could accomplish unencumbered by prejudice. John Brown Russwurm, Reuben Ruby's friend and the editor of *Freedom's Journal*, was among colonization's most visible advocates. He had written his senior commencement address at Bowdoin College on the prospects for Haiti as a sovereign, Black-run nation, and he later emigrated to Africa to serve as the first Black governor of the West African colony Maryland-in-Africa, created specifically for African American migrants. Henry Highland Garnet, a well-known activist and Presbyterian minister, also supported emigration. Even Frederick Douglass, who advocated that Blacks should fight for their rights at home, planned to visit Haiti in April 1861 at the behest of Redpath and the Haitian government. The outbreak of the Civil War prevented that trip. "I am not an Emigrationist," Douglass declared, but he was clearly intrigued by Haiti's potential.[6]

Just before signing the Emancipation Proclamation, Abraham Lincoln had agreed to use federal funds to transport some 450 newly freed African Americans to Haiti for resettlement. Lincoln had long supported the notion of colonization to relocate freed African Americans outside the United States.[7] In August 1862, Lincoln addressed a delegation of Black men at the White House: "I think your race suffer very greatly, many of them by living among us, while ours suffer from your presence. In a word we suffer on each side. If this is admitted, it affords a reason at least why we should be separated."[8]

The most important influence on George Ruby's Haiti sojourn, how-ever, was Reverend John W. Lewis. "Mr. Lewis, our old and mutual friend from Maine," wrote Ruby, "is the leader of a colony of about 800," near Saint-Marc, Haiti, on the Artibonite River. Lewis had offered Ruby the chance to cultivate cotton with him.[9] Reverend Lewis was a Baptist min-ister and activist from Reuben Ruby's generation. Born in South Berwick, Maine, he had spent time in Portland, where he is said to have started the first temperance society.[10] He was also a member of the New Hampshire Anti-Slavery Society, and he led a Baptist congregation in Boston. Living and working in Boston had brought him into contact with Redpath.[11] In early 1860, Lewis lectured on Haiti and its revolution in churches around Boston, likely to recruit emigrants to accompany him.[12] Later that year he moved to Haiti and founded a Protestant immigrant community at Saint-Marc.[13]

In March 1861, George Ruby sailed to the island and began regularly reporting back on his experiences. His earliest letters were enthusiastic, noting that Haitians had "fought manfully and successfully for liberty, and have risen . . . to a *place* among the Nationalities of the world."[14] Although he had no farming experience, he was anxious to learn cotton cultivation with Reverend Lewis. To Ruby, it was equal parts livelihood and political statement. He predicted that, in five years, Haiti would be "supplying the world with cotton, thereby giving the bugbear King Cotton, in the Confed-erate States, a knock in the head from which he will never recover."[15]

Although Ruby was determined to see Haiti in its best light, trouble followed the settlement scheme. The local government had guaranteed land and housing to the immigrants, but proved ponderously slow in delivering on its promises. And tropical illnesses took a toll on newcom-ers. Lewis fell ill and died in August 1861, only a few months after Ruby arrived. Lewis wasn't the only one: as Ruby admitted in the *Pine and Palm*, a number of recent emigrants to Saint-Marc died that summer. And although he sought to blame many of the deaths on "intemperance, dissipation, &c.," he was clearly concerned.[16]

In August 1862, George Ruby returned to Maine to visit his father, who was ill. He intended to go back to Haiti in October: he was "an adopted citizen of Hayti," stated a notice in the *Pine and Palm*, "and says he could not now endure the prejudices of Americans."[17] But while he was in Maine, both the resettlement scheme and the *Pine and Palm* col-lapsed, leaving him without a job or a purpose in returning.[18]

After filling in at the Portland custom house for his father while Reuben recovered from illness, George was again anxious to leave Maine. In December 1863, eight months after New Orleans surrendered to the Union Army, he set out for the Crescent City. Ruby began teaching at a night school for newly freed men and women in a New Orleans church and then moved on to St. Bernard Parish, southeast of the city. He was praised as a teacher and school organizer.[19]

In March 1865, Congress created the Bureau of Refugees, Freedmen, and Abandoned Lands—or Freedmen's Bureau. Though the bureau had taken over the responsibility for starting schools from the army, it had no budget or funds. Teachers like Ruby were forced to live off whatever meager tuition payments formerly enslaved students could muster. Because money was tight and newly freed persons had barely enough to eat, those payments simply couldn't cover teachers' expenses, to say nothing of books, slates, and other supplies.

George Ruby was cash poor but appreciated. In July 1865, he returned to New Orleans and began teaching at the Frederick Douglass School, where he rapidly rose to head teacher and then principal. Ironically, the school was located at the corner of Esplanade and Moreau (now Chartres), the former site of one of the city's many "slave pens," where free Black Solomon Northup who wrote *Twelve Years a Slave* had been sold after being kidnapped from the North. At the Douglass School, Ruby managed 11 teachers and 793 students who spoke a mixture of English, French, and Creole.[20]

In early 1866, many of the newly established Black schools in New Orleans closed for lack of funds. As a result, Ruby became a traveling agent for the Freedmen's Bureau, charged with starting schools in the interior of the state. The job paid a regular salary, but it was complex and dangerous. It involved helping Black communities find and organize school resources of all kinds: land, buildings, teachers, principals, supplies, and means of paying expenses.[21] And it meant facing down Whites intent upon preventing Blacks from attending school.

Throughout the state, Ruby found that formerly enslaved Blacks were anxious to learn. As Black author and educator Booker T. Washington wrote:

> It was a whole race trying to go to school. . . . As fast as any kind of teachers could be secured, not only were day-schools filled,

but night-schools as well. The great ambition of the older people was to try to learn to read the Bible before they died. . . . Men and women who were fifty and seventy-five years old, would be found in the night-school. . . . Day-school, night-school, Sunday-school, were always crowded, and often many had to be turned away for want of room.[22]

Despite their enthusiasm, Blacks in rural Louisiana encountered significant barriers. In St. Helena Parish, Ruby found most Whites to be "intensely rebel in sentiment, hating all Yankees most heartily." He wrote that they disliked "the trouble of education for themselves and children, resent the idea of schools for freedmen and do all they dare to intimidate and frighten blacks about the matter."[23]

In June, Ruby arrived in Jackson in East Feliciana Parish, about thirty-five miles north of Baton Rouge. There, he "found much prejudice existing in the minds of the whites" against Black education. He was frequently threatened. Nevertheless, he took a room in a local boarding-house and began teaching classes.

One night he was awakened by noise outside the house. The boardinghouse owner "said that there were about a hundred fellows, with their faces blackened, after me. Some of them came up to me, flourishing pistols and calling on me to surrender," Ruby recounted afterward. He was taken, barefoot and scantily clothed, to nearby Thompson Creek, beaten severely, and forced to swim across the creek. "S'pose you thought the United States Government would protect you, did you?'" said one of his attackers. "D—n the United States, we don't care for it; why don't it protect you now?"[24] Terrified, bloody, and exhausted, Ruby was again forced to swim across the creek and told never to return. If he reported the incident, his assailants promised, they would kill him. But Ruby did report the incident, his drive for justice outweighing concern for his own security. And the perpetrators—nine White residents of Jackson—were arrested and taken to jail in New Orleans, with bail set at $20,000.[25]

A few days after testifying against the men in New Orleans, Ruby witnessed another frightening episode: the New Orleans Massacre of 1866. Because elections were on the horizon, Republicans had called for a new Constitutional Convention to be held at Mechanics Hall in New Orleans. Under the old state constitution, Black voting was banned, and without it, Republicans knew they stood no chance of winning locally.

So Black suffrage was front and center on the convention agenda. Lou-isiana's governor, James Madison Wells, was a Republican. But New Orleans was run by staunch Confederate sympathizer John T. Monroe. The local sheriff, Harry T. Hays, was a former Confederate general, and he deputized a large number of ex-Confederates expressly to disrupt the convention.[26]

On the morning of July 30, twenty-five Black Republican delegates began marching toward Mechanics Hall to attend the convention. About two hundred Black veterans of the Union Army accompanied them, carrying flags and banners supporting Black suffrage, civil rights, and the removal of Louisiana's repressive "Black laws." Mayor Mon-roe called for Whites, including Hays's deputized police force, to block their way. Scuffles began, shots were fired, and as the delegates ran into Mechanics Hall for protection, the police began firing into the building and the crowd outside. One man, Reverend Dr. Jotham Horton, shouted to the police, "I beseech you to stop firing; we are noncombatants. If you want to arrest us, make any arrest you please, we are not prepared to defend ourselves." A member of the police force replied, "We don't want any prisoners; you have all got to die."[27] Horton was shot and killed. An image of his murder in the vestibule of Mechanics Institute later ran on the cover of *Harper's Weekly*.[28]

Other delegates tried to surrender but were pursued, beaten, and shot. Absalom Baird, a Union general stationed in New Orleans, described the scene to Secretary of War Edwin Stanton: "The police, aided by the citizens, became the assailants, and . . . exercised great brutality in making their arrests. . . . The people inside the hall gave up some who surrendered, and were attacked afterward and brutally treated."[29] The violence spread, and even Black individuals who weren't involved in the convention were attacked and killed in the streets. Reports of casualties varied widely, depending on who was doing the reporting. But General Baird ordered an army surgeon, Dr. Albert Hartsuff, to go door-to-door to confirm the dead and injured. Hartsuff found that thirty-four Blacks and four Whites had been killed. Of the 146 injured, 119 were Black.[30]

General Philip Sheridan, the Union officer in charge of the military district of New Orleans, was away in Texas during the massacre, and he believed that Mayor Monroe had waited for him to leave to start trou-ble. The massacre was "premeditated," said Sheridan, a planned effort to murder Louisiana Unionists and remove them from the state. He wrote to General Ulysses S. Grant, "It was no riot; it was an absolute massacre by the police. . . . The Mayor and police of the city perpetrated [it] without the shadow of a necessity."[31] Despite the presence of Union soldiers in New Orleans, the Confederates were intent on maintaining control by any means necessary.

Such violent episodes were frighteningly common in Louisiana. A Freedmen's Bureau report details the murders and outrages committed against Black individuals and bureau agents, including George Ruby, between July 5, 1865, and February 20, 1867:

Freedmen killed by whites	70
Freedmen supposed to have been killed at Riot in addition to those reported	10
Freedmen murdered—no clue to perpetrators	6
Freedmen shot at, whipped, stabbed, beaten &c	210
Freedmen supposed to have been wounded at Riot in addition to those reported	20
Freedmen murdered by Freedmen	2
Whites murdered by Freedmen	1

> In no instance in any of the foregoing cases has a white man been punished for killing or ill treating a freedman. In some few cases the guilty parties are in jail awaiting trial but the majority have either been justified by a Coroner's Jury, acquitted or admitted to bail. . . . Of the three freedmen charged with murder, two have been convicted and hung.[32]

THROUGH HIS WORK ON the ground for the Freedmen's Bureau, George Ruby experienced firsthand the horrors that those recently freed from slavery faced. As a result, he decided to leave Louisiana for Texas in September 1866, settling in Galveston, an important port for cotton. Galveston was also the site of the first Juneteenth. Just fifteen months before Ruby arrived, on June 19, 1865, General Gordon Granger and his troops had landed in the city and had declared the Black population free, reading General Order No. 3 at military headquarters, the custom house, and several Black churches.

In October, Ruby secured a teaching job at a Methodist Episcopal church in in the city. While enrollment grew fast under his tutelage, he was forced to live off tuition payments, which didn't cover his expenses.[33] And he found Texas scarcely more secure than Louisiana had been. From Galveston he wrote to the *New Orleans Tribune* calling for greater military presence in all states of the former Confederacy:

> Unionism, black or white, is *not* safe anywhere here beyond the military limit. Is not this too true of Louisiana? We need provisional government for these conquered territories, ousting these rebels who assume in the face of four years of carnage . . . to rule with the venom of slavery. I hope to heaven that Congress may have backbone enough to do justice by the suffering Unionists of this foully ruled State.[34]

The war had changed many things, but not the minds of many southern Whites nor their willingness to use violence to constrain African Americans who sought education and equal rights.

IN THE SPRING OF 1867, Ruby left teaching to earn a regular salary as an agent for the Freedmen's Bureau. "He is an energetic man," Assistant Commissioner Charles Griffin wrote to Bureau Commissioner Otis O. Howard, "and has great influence among his people." Ruby was quickly promoted and charged with evaluating Freedmen's Bureau agents and race relations across the state. He also assessed schools, searched for opportunities to open new ones, and promoted temperance in Black communities, a favorite cause of both his father and Commissioner Howard, the former Union general.[35] Ruby also became active in local politics through the Republican Party and the Union League, a secret organization working to mobilize Black voters in Texas.

As an agent for the bureau, Ruby's reports from the field painted a dire picture. He wrote that, in one community, "terrorism engendered by the brutal and murderous acts of the inhabitants, mostly rebels," had blocked the opening of a school for Blacks. Whites "murder and outrage the freed people with the same indifference displayed in the killing of snakes or other venomous reptiles." In another community, he took it as a positive sign that only one Black had been "taken out and hung within a year." His reports show that Blacks endured most of the violence, but Whites who supported the Republican cause were also "socially ostracized and debarred even from school privileges by their rebel neighbors."[36]

In April 1867, Ruby purchased a passage on the steamship *Morgan* from Galveston to Brashear City—present-day Morgan City, Louisiana. He'd intended to take a cabin with his friend R. K. Smith, a White Republican and former Union Army surgeon, but the ship's purser and the captain denied him cabin accommodations on account of his race. Ruby was given two options: remain on deck or go below in the hold with the cattle. He remained on deck throughout the stormy passage but later sued the Morgan Line for $5,000 in damages, recruiting R. K. Smith as a witness.[37]

The case went to U.S. District Court, where Ruby was awarded $250.[38] But his victory was more substantial than a monetary award. According to the *New Orleans Republican*, "Hereafter passengers who purchase first class tickets on the Morgan line of steamships will be afforded first class accommodations." This new regulation was "adopted in consequence of the suit for damages . . . by . . . George T. Ruby."[39] Word of Ruby's discrimination case was carried widely in newspapers across the United States, and while victories like his eventually gave way to strict segregation and "Whites only" laws of Jim Crow, Ruby had demonstrated what could be accomplished for Blacks in the South through protest and legal action: at least during the early days of Reconstruction. His father must have been proud.

IN SEPTEMBER 1867, THE governor of Texas, Elisha Marshall Pease, a Union loyalist, appointed George Ruby notary public for Galveston County.[40] In December, Ruby was chosen as the Republican delegate from Galveston to the Republican National Convention, to be held in May in Chicago. He was the only African American in the Texas delegation.[41]

Texas's own Republican convention was to be held in Austin on June 15, 1868, and in some circles, Ruby's increasing visibility as a politician was becoming a liability. One local newspaper suggested that he might be appointed president of the "Mongrel Convention." Alluding to his suit against the Morgan Line, the article pondered, "Where will Ruby board? Who shall have the honor of having the President of the Convention at his table, and furnishing the fine linen sheets, between which the great Ruby shall repose and dream of future honors—the Capitol at Washington—the Senatorial dignity—the Presidency of the model Republic?"[42] It was the classic lampooning of a Black man who had the audacity to vote, run for office, and seek to exist on an equal footing with Whites.

Still, Ruby remained on the fast track to political prominence. To reenter the Union and gain representation in Congress, Texas was required to do several things under the Reconstruction Act of 1867. It had to ratify the Thirteenth and Fourteenth Amendments to the U.S. Constitution, which abolished slavery and guaranteed citizenship and equal protection to all born in the United States. And it had to write a new state constitution, winning the approval of a majority of citizens, including African American voters. In electing delegates to the constitutional convention of 1868–69, Black Texans came out in force for George Ruby. He became one of ninety delegates—ten of whom were Black—to the state constitutional convention.[43]

Democrats at the convention sought to retain as many of Texas's pre–Civil War laws as possible. Republicans were split into two factions: conservatives, who, like the Democrats, wanted to retain much of the older constitution and keep the state's borders intact; and radicals, who supported writing a wholly new constitution and dividing the state in two, separating pro-South East Texas from pro-Union West Texas. Ruby was among the radicals.

In early September of 1868, Ruby had a violent falling out with his former friend, R. K. Smith, at a meeting of the Galveston Republican Association, demonstrating just how fraught the constitutional convention was. While details of the disagreement aren't clear, it seems to have erupted after Smith charged that Ruby had betrayed Black voters.[44] Ruby was charged with assaulting Smith; Smith was charged with "carrying concealed weapons, to-wit: a pistol, and drawing the same with intent to use it"; and a third man, a Dr. Haslea, was charged with "carrying concealed weapons, to-wit: a bowie knife, and drawing the same with intent to use it on G. T. Ruby."[45]

Ruby sought to achieve meaningful change at the constitutional convention by proposing an ordinance that prevented voter intimidation by violence, threats, or loss of property and employment.[46] Such a law would be a critical measure for enfranchising Black voters, who were already experiencing violence at the hands of the Ku Klux Klan. Ruby was acutely aware of the terrible cost that voting exacted on African Americans. He'd witnessed as much in New Orleans Massacre in 1866.

In Texas, *a report of the Special Committee on Lawlessness and Violence in Texas*, commissioned by the constitutional convention, noted the utter "insecurity of life in Texas" for those loyal to the Union, but especially for Blacks. It concluded that those "who participated in the rebellion, disappointed and maddened by their defeat, are now intensely embittered against the freedmen on account of their emancipation and enfranchisement, and on account of their devotion to the Republican party." This bitterness resulted in Whites murdering some 373 Blacks in Texas between 1865 and 1868.[47]

Ruby's proposal to prevent voter intimidation was denied by a vote of the delegates. Immediately, he and a number of likeminded delegates signed a protest letter stating that extending voting rights to former Confederates who had become a "public enemy of the United States," was unacceptable. They charged that the majority at the convention had intentionally removed safeguards for voters. R. K. Smith, who also signed the protest letter, noted that such omissions would be "the first step toward a general disfranchisement of the colored race." Ruby agreed, adding that the rights of "loyal blacks and whites are imperiled" and that "the express will of Congress has been ignored."[48] The next day, he resigned from the convention.

The Democrats and conservative Republicans at the convention had managed to engineer a constitution that the radical Republicans saw as a step backward for Black civil rights and the Union. So in early 1869, Ruby and other radical Republicans traveled to Washington, D.C., to try to delay the vote on the new constitution. On April 1, they met with President Grant.[49] Grant was sympathetic to their complaints and is said to have told them that he would put a stop to the violence against Blacks in Texas.

In May, Ruby published a letter in New York's *Evening Post* describing the situation in Texas. He wrote that Texas's draft constitution would prevent African Americans from holding office and that it included no provisions for the security of Texas voters nor for protecting ballots. But his main objection was that the constitution "allows every unrepentant, violent and murderous rebel ruffian in the State, with the disfranchised of other reconstructed Southern States, to vote and be the governing power."[50] Despite Ruby's intense lobbying, Texas's new constitution went forward without the support of the radical Republicans.

Still, Ruby was optimistic about the way forward for Texas, and he believed he could make an important contribution. In 1869, he helped organize the Black vote to deliver the governorship for E. J. Davis, a Republican and champion of Black civil rights.[51] And Ruby himself ran for and won election to the state senate in a predominantly White district. He became one of the first two African Americans elected to the body.[52] Ruby served as senator in the twelfth and thirteenth Texas legislatures. He worked on the incorporation of several railroads and helped to organize the Labor Union of Colored Men at Galveston, where Whites had previously dominated work on the docks. He also worked to end discrimination on public transportation, protect voting rights, and secure a free public school system for all students, Black and White.[53] Sensitive to the ongoing violence that Black communities faced from racial terrorism, he supported an 1870 bill to give the governor authority to order state militias to enforce martial law where needed. That bill ultimately passed the Texas senate in June, but not without controversy. The *Dallas Weekly Herald* wrote that the bill would allow the governor to order "hireling soldiery" to "leer upon your wives and daughters, steal your poultry, burn your rails, invade your cornfields, . . . demoralize and debauch your negro servants and harass you at every turn." Several senators were prevented from voting on the bill, and this, opined the *Herald*, "was done through the influence of the immortal nigger carpetbagger Ruby."[54]

ON SEPTEMBER 20, 1870, twenty-nine-year-old George Ruby took a respite from politics to marry eighteen-year-old Lucy V. Nalle, a dressmaker from Washington, D.C.[55] Her mother Catherine was also a dressmaker, and her father Charles worked as a hack driver and as a domestic and civil servant.[56] Lucy was said to be a beauty, with a light freckled complexion and hair "tinged with red."[57] They may have met while Ruby was in Washington on political business in 1869.

Lucy's father, who had been enslaved in Virginia, was well known in abolitionist circles. In 1860, Charles Nalle, who had escaped his enslaver, a Virginia man named Blucher Hansbrough, had been seized and ordered remanded back to Hansbrough. The events that ensued were undoubtedly traumatic for the entire family, including Lucy, who was then five years old.

While enslaved, Nalle had been permitted to marry another enslaved person named "Kitty," later known as Catherine. The couple had children, and when Catherine was freed upon her enslaver's death, so were they. As free Blacks, they were forced out of Virginia and took up residence in nearby Washington, D.C. But Charles remained in bondage—that is, until he heard that he was to be sold south. At that point, in October 1858, he escaped from Hansbrough.[58]

After traveling north along the Underground Railroad, Nalle made his way to Troy, New York, where he was reunited with his family. In Troy, he worked as a coachman for the mayor, and he and his family lived in relative security.[59] But on April 26, a U.S. marshal arrested him and brought him before the fugitive slave commissioner. Members of the local vigilance committee learned of Charles's arrest and summoned citizens: "An excited crowd of some 1,000 persons . . . gathered about the Commissioner's Office, threatening a rescue," wrote a local paper.[60] Among them was Harriet Tubman, the famed Moses of the Underground Railroad, who happened to be in Troy visiting relatives. She forced her way into the building where Nalle was being held, and as he was being escorted out by law officers, the five-foot-tall Tubman grabbed onto the prisoner and refused to let go. The crowd overwhelmed the officers and helped Tubman wrest Nalle away from them. Nalle managed to escape across the Hudson River on a ferry.

On the opposite shore, Nalle was again taken into custody and, again, a crowd of citizens intervened and managed to free him. "Blows, pistol shots and knockdowns occurred during the affair, but no one was seriously injured," wrote one local newspaper. "Colored people were the most active participants in the rescue. There has been the greatest excitement."[61]

Nalle escaped to Schenectady and then traveled farther north, hiding for months. His employer, Troy's former mayor, Uri Gilbert, managed to raise $650 to purchase Nalle's freedom from Blucher Hansbrough, who, ironically, was Nalle's younger half-brother.[62] Nalle returned to Troy once the war began, and afterward he and his family—including the teenaged Lucy—moved back to Washington, D.C.

Soon after their wedding, George and Lucy Ruby traveled north to attend receptions and visit the Ruby family. On September 22, 1870, "all the combined wealth, intelligence, and refinement of colored New York" met at Cooper Institute to honor the ambassador to Haiti, Ebenezer T. Bassett, the first African American to be appointed by the U.S. government to a foreign post. George and Lucy "occupied a prominent place on the platform," along with Ambassador Bassett; James M. Priest, the former vice president of Liberia; J. J. Spellman, a member of the Mississippi state legislature; Reverend Henry Highland Garnet; and Peter Vogelsang, a former lieutenant in the Union Army's famed all-Black Fifty-fourth Massachusetts Volunteers. Dr. William P. Powell, a surgeon in the Union Army, helped to arrange the event.

Although Ruby was a prominent Texas politician, he and Lucy had a difficult time finding accommodations in New York City. "It was said that Senator Ruby and his bride, who is perfectly white, did not know where they were going to sleep last night," reported a New York paper. Ten hotels, including the New York Hotel and the Astor House, rejected them based on race.[63] Many northerners, it seems, hadn't fully embraced Reconstruction.

Beyond New York, the couple were abused in the press for the mistaken notion that Lucy was White. In Pennsylvania, the *Harrisburg Patriot* called them a "pair of practical amalgamationists" and suggested that was why they'd been refused accommodations in New York City.[64] And in Galveston, one editor even suggested that Ruby had done the Black community a disservice by "passing their sisters in contempt and selecting for his wife . . . the daughter of white folks."[65]

In Portland, the couple found some respite from hostility. They were greeted with fanfare at a reception at the city hall that included the mayor and other local dignitaries as well as Reuben and his third wife, Annie. While Portland's mayor, Benjamin Kingsbury, acknowledged the Rubys' ill-treatment by New York hotels, he also spoke of "the pleasure it gave him to see the prejudice against the colored people so far done away with." Again, however, a local newspaper reporting on the event mistook Lucy Ruby for White: "[She] is white and very attractive." George Ruby himself spoke at the reception "with much fluency and grace of manner." He stated that the political situation in Texas was promising; that polarization was waning; and as proof, showed a gold pocket watch given him by the Democrats of Galveston.[66]

But Ruby had witnessed some disturbing trends in the Lone Star State. He returned to the state senate in 1872 to finish his term, but his party hadn't done well in the elections that year. The federal Amnesty Act of 1872 had allowed most former Confederates to vote and run for office once again, and the Ku Klux Klan was actively suppressing the

Black vote. During the thirteenth legislative session, many of the laws that Ruby had helped to pass were overturned. There would be no centralized control of schools. Instead, local communities would make all decisions, once again leaving Blacks on their own. The state police force was also voted down so that the governor could no longer declare martial law. These setbacks opened the way for unequal education and continued violence against Blacks.

Ruby didn't run for reelection in 1873. Once again, the Klan was actively working to suppress the Black vote, and many Whites had moved into Texas from other southern states. The Democrats won in a landslide.[67]

After stepping away from politics, Ruby started and ran his own newspaper, the *Standard*, in Galveston. But the city already had two well-established Democratic newspapers and a growing Democratic majority that was openly hostile to Republicans, so the *Standard* didn't last long. In 1874, George and Lucy moved back to Louisiana, where George again worked as a journalist: first at the *Louisianan* and later as owner and publisher of the *New Orleans Observer*.

IN 1876, REPUBLICAN RUTHERFORD B. Hayes was narrowly elected president, with contested electoral results in the states of Louisiana, South Carolina, Florida, and Oregon. Small contingents of federal troops still protected the statehouses in South Carolina and Louisiana, but once Hayes took office, he reassigned those troops with a promise from local officials that both Black and White Republicans would be allowed to vote. However, southerners soon reneged and began instituting the hallmarks of Jim Crow—intimidation, fraud, poll taxes, literary tests, and the like—to exclude Black voters.[68]

The backlash against Reconstruction was rapid. By 1879, all of the inclusive governments of the South were gone. Black Republican legislators and those who had held public office after the war were voted out or removed. Black voters were largely disenfranchised; Black schools were underfunded and in disarray; and courts became brazenly biased against Black citizens. But these injustices were merely the tip of the iceberg; many African Americans felt they risked their lives simply by living in southern states.

Before leaving office, President Grant compiled a list of southern Blacks who had been whipped, maimed, or murdered between 1868 and 1876, which he submitted to Congress; the list went on for ninety-eight pages and numbered some 4,000 people. William Murrell, a Black leader in New Orleans, estimated that, between 1866 and 1875, 2,141 Blacks were killed and 2,115 injured in Louisiana for political reasons. General Philip Sheridan, who commanded federal troops in Louisiana, wrote that in 1868 alone 1,884 persons had been killed or assaulted there for their political opinions. "Human life in the state is held so cheaply," Sheridan wrote, "that when men are killed on account of political opinions the murderers are regarded rather as heroes than as criminals in the localities where they reside."[69]

At the Colored Convention in New Orleans in April 1879, George Ruby addressed the crowd. Seeing all the gains he had worked hard to earn for Blacks systematically erased stung bitterly. He described Blacks' fear that slavery was being effectively reinstated across the South, offering what he saw as the only solution: "All rights of freemen denied, and all claims to a just recompense for labor rendered, or honorable dealings between planter and laborer disallowed; justice a mockery and the law a cheat, the very officers of the courts being themselves the mobocrats and violators of the law, the only remedy left the colored citizens in the many parishes of our State to-day is to migrate."

But migrate where? "Kansas with her freedom and broad prairies," Ruby said, "with the memories of John Brown and his heroic struggle, seems naturally the State to seek."[50] Ruby was referring to the militant abolitionist who had led a group of armed men during the Bleeding Kansas crisis of 1856 to steer the territory's path forward as a free rather than slave state.

The most visible spokesman for Blacks' rights, Frederick Douglass, argued that migration wasn't the answer. "The business of this nation is to protect its citizens *where they are*," wrote Douglass, "not to transport them where they will not need protection."[51] In many southern voting districts, Blacks held the majority, and Douglass knew that by migrating, Black citizens would dilute the potential political power they held. Still, as Ruby understood, life in New Orleans, Mobile, Biloxi, or Galveston was a different world entirely from Douglass' Washington.

In March of 1880, Ruby testified before the U.S. Senate Committee on Black Emigration. He estimated that some 3,000 Blacks had already left Louisiana for Kansas and that "discontent was on the increase," suggesting even more departures to come.[72] In all, some 40,000 to 60,000 African Americans would migrate west after the demise of Reconstruction.[73]

Kansas alone would gain some 27,000 new African American residents during the 1870s.[74] Despite advocating for migration away from the South, George Ruby and his family remained in New Orleans where he continued to work as a journalist.

HORATIO RUBY, GEORGE'S YOUNGER brother, was more than just an advocate for migration. He gained notice as a leader of the Black exodus from Texas to Kansas—a group of migrants commonly known as the Exodusters.

After the war ended, Horatio returned to Portland, and in November 1867 he married Angelia Eastman, the eldest of six children from a prominent Portland family. Her father was Charles F. Eastman, who owned a barbershop and was active in the Abyssinian Church and the Underground Railroad.[75] Horatio and Angelia settled down in Portland, and their son Frederic was born there in January 1869.[76] But like his father and his brother George, Horatio was an adventurer. So in September 1869, just eight months after his son was born, he signed on as a cook for a U.S. Navy excursion to the Darién in Colombia, a thickly forested region of the isthmus that joins South and Central America.

President Grant had commissioned the crew to identify a suitable spot for building a canal across the isthmus to connect the Atlantic and Pacific Oceans, which would speed travel between the East and West Coasts of the United States. He had a personal stake in the project. Eighteen years earlier, as a quartermaster, Grant had led the U.S. Army's Fourth Infantry and their families across the isthmus on their way to garrison duty in California. The trip had been disastrous: 150 of the men, women, and children under his charge had died of cholera. "The horrors of the road in the rainy season are beyond description," Grant wrote at the time.[77]

Horatio Ruby sailed aboard the U.S.S. *Nipsic* under Commander Thomas Oliver Selfridge, arriving in Colón on Panama's Atlantic shore in January of 1870. The *Nipsic* returned to the United States in July of that year, as the rainy season intensified. While Selfridge led a second expedition to the isthmus in 1871, Horatio Ruby moved to Galveston, securing a job as a customs inspector, likely through his brother's political influence. It's not clear whether Angelia and son Frederic moved with him. He nearly lost his life when, as an inspector, he was aboard the ship *Virginia Dare*, which sank during the Galveston hurricane.[78]

Horatio was outspoken like the rest of the Rubys. He was also said to be intelligent, witty, and "a man of marked ability and a born leader."[59] Horatio was involved in local Texas politics as long as conditions permitted, and he appeared to have little tolerance for duplicity. At a public event, he challenged a White judge and former slaveowner who was running for office and expounding on the debt that the local Black community owed him for his kindnesses. Ruby stood up and spoke: "He says that we owe him a debt. I think we do and I want to pay it. I propose that we take up a collection here and now and pay the judge and I will start it myself with this five-dollar bill." The audience roared with laughter, while Ruby, stone-faced, walked up and down the aisles gathering donations. He then delivered the money to the humiliated judge, saying, "If that don't wipe out the bill, give me a receipt on account and I'll collect the rest."[80]

Ruby later moved to rural Burleson County, Texas, some three hundred miles inland from Galveston. In July 1879, he attended the state's Colored Convention in Houston, where he was elected as a representative from his Texas congressional district to lead the Black migration effort to Kansas. The meeting addressed the growing Black exodus from the state, and Horatio publicly articulated the reasons:

> It is a well known fact that the old Bourbon element of the southern states has deprived . . . us of all our civil and political rights in order to perpetuate our ignorance and control our labor.
>
> The sentiment of our people is that, having appealed to all of the highest tribunals of the land for assistance, and having had no response, that we go away to ourselves where, under the broad stars and stripes that we helped to defend, we may be secure in the exercise of all our political and civil liberties.[81]

By 1880, Horatio had moved to Kansas, though his wife Angelia and son Frederic were living in Portland with Angelia's parents.[82] That may have been prudent, given the risks. That year, Horatio, like George, testified before the U.S. Senate committee that was investigating the Black exodus from the South. His testimony was summarized in *The New York Times*: "Horatio Ruby, a colored man, . . . testified that he had emigrated to Kansas several months ago. He said the reasons for blacks leaving Texas were to be found in the lack of educational facilities for their children and obnoxious laws upon the statute-books of the State, which were prejudicial to colored men." These "obnoxious laws" were the so-called "Black laws," instigated in many southern states to limit, control, and discourage free Blacks from achieving even a semblance of equality. Blacks who had committed minor offenses, said Ruby, were hired out to planters as forced laborers. One Black woman he knew had been convicted of petty larceny and fined $30; she was then hired out to a planter at one-quarter cent per day, a fine large enough to ensure her bondage for thirty-two years. Ruby also complained that Democrats were determined to cleanse the South of Republicans and that many Republicans had been murdered as a result. He also mentioned "the insecurity of colored women against the insults of white men," noting that "if any colored man should pass [similar] remarks to white women there would soon be a funeral of a negro in that locality."[83] The incidents that Horatio witnessed and described grew to define culture in the South during Jim Crow.

Horatio's candor made him a lightning rod for criticism, and in the South such honesty was dangerous. The *Memphis Daily Appeal* covered his testimony in an April 23 article with the headline "All Men Are Liars, Says the Good Book, But As a Single-Handed, Go-As-You-Please Prevaricator, Mr. Colored Ruby, of Texas, Must Be Allowed to Go Up Road and Stay There." On May 14, a Texas paper, the *Brenham Weekly Banner*, noted that "the north atmosphere of old Burleson, in the matter of regard for the truth, was immensely improved" when Ruby moved to Kansas.[84]

In May 1880, Horatio returned to Portland to speak at the Abyssinian Meeting House about the Black exodus and to take up a collection for the migration project. He also traveled to Bangor to lecture on the matter.[85] But his Kansas experiment was nearly over. Perhaps the atmosphere for Blacks in Kansas wasn't as he had hoped, or perhaps he had received threats for speaking his mind. Whatever the case, he did have a family to support. So by December 1880, he had signed on for another adventure: as a cook with the Atrato Mining Company of Portland, which was embarking on a gold mining expedition in Colombia. He knew the region, having participated in the Darién expedition in 1870, and the example of his father, who succeeded in boosting his personal worth through prospecting for gold at least once no doubt helped motivate him.[86]

Shortly thereafter, tragedy struck the Ruby family again. On October 31, 1882, Horatio's brother George died in New Orleans of malaria at age forty-two. He was the publisher of the *New Orleans Observer* at the time and left behind his wife Lucy and three children. His death merited a small notice in the local *Times-Picayune*, stating only that he was "a colored man" who "came to New Orleans six or seven years ago" and was affiliated with several local newspapers. An obituary in the *Portland Daily Press* was more laudatory. It detailed his political and journalistic careers and described him as "well-educated, an eloquent speaker, [and] an accomplished writer" who was known for his "upright character and his intelligence." [87] In Texas, where he'd played a key role in Reconstruction politics, his death went largely unnoticed in the newspapers.

HORATIO RUBY MADE THREE trips to Colombia during the 1880s. But while at home, he was involved with the Greenback Party in Maine politics, which managed to elect a governor, Harris M. Plaisted, in 1880. The Greenbacks were a minority party, with the Republicans having the majority of registered voters. Still, the Greenbacks and Democrats forged ties and had sufficient numbers to undermine the Republicans' power in Maine. The Panic of 1873 had made paying taxes tough for Mainers, particularly farmers, who had seen crop prices fall dramatically. So many farmers in this predominantly rural state supported the Greenback platform: lower taxes, smaller government, and the printing of more paper money not backed by specie. Such policies, they felt, would help them out of the economic depression.[88]

By aligning with the Greenbacks, Horatio stirred up dust in the media, even in Portland. The Republican *Portland Daily Press* wrote, "Mr. Horatio F. Ruby has not yet been nominated for anything by the Democrats. Is this discrimination against him on account of his color? Almost anybody else, not able to get office in the Republican party, is good enough to be nominated by Democrats."[89] Ruby answered the charge three days later in the same paper, threatening to "pull the nose" of the person who had written the piece. When it came to politics, he was more confrontational than his father or brothers: "I am not the right sort of man to represent the labouring man, for when a disagreeable thing is said to me, I feel like fighting," he wrote. In the same edition, the *Press* responded by calling Ruby "a jewel of a Democrat: one who learned what Democracy is in the South where it is the purest, but he does not understand the Northern ways very well yet." It was as if Horatio were a carpetbagger in his own home town.[90]

By March 1885, Horatio was back in Colombia, once again working with the Atrato Company. He wrote to his brother William from Cartagena: "We had quite a number of accidents. The ship sprang a leak; we had a fire on board the ship in mid-ocean, and came near being shipwrecked at last." In addition to the hazards at sea, the company faced the prospect of armed conflict: "The government is massing troops and all the old forts are again occupied." Just two months later, Gaitán Obeso laid siege to Cartagena with a force of some 3,000 rebels. Fortunately, Horatio had already left for the United States, arriving in New York on March 4, 1886.[91]

But he wasn't done with his South American adventures. That September, Horatio sailed to Colombia on a fourth venture, this time to engage in a sugar-making enterprise on the Atrato River.[92] He likely returned home and made yet another trip, for the 1888 *Portland Directory* lists him as a "steward" living on Anderson Street. He died shortly thereafter in Colombia. "There were conflicting reports concerning the manner and time of his death, but there was no doubt that he died there," wrote the *Portland Sunday Times*. "He did not win the success he dreamed of, and he was not fitted by nature to the slow work of the bench or the counter. He was able, a bit dashing and at his best was a careful man."[93]

GEORGE AND HORATIO RUBY were restless, inquisitive, and ambitious. Like their father, they made no pretense of hiding their opinions or beliefs. Both were drawn away from the relative security they experienced in Maine to the American South during its most turbulent years. There, they worked on behalf of education and voting rights and urged governments to guarantee security for Black citizens as retribution increased. They faced threats and violence in the process, and contributed to many measured, though fleeting, gains on behalf of African Americans.

The backlash against emancipation and equality in the South enabled Whites to reassert their political dominance and find less overt—though equally violent—forms of repression: segregation, Black laws, voter suppression, racial terrorism. Tens of thousands of African Americans were brutalized and killed in the wake of the Civil War for attempting to exercise their rights or simply for being Black. Tens of thousands more fled the South, seeking equality and security in the North, the Midwest, and the West. Despite losing the war, the American South proved resistant to change.

The supposed damage done to the South by carpetbaggers became accepted doctrine in North and South alike. The carpetbagger was many things, none of them good: a newcomer, a Yankee, a radical Republican, a thief, an opportunist, an oppressor, a scoundrel. As early as 1868, northern newspapers adopted the South's interpretation of the villain of Reconstruction. According to the Democratic *New York Herald*, "it is the miserable, whining, hypocritical 'carpetbagger' who creeps into the South, like a thief at midnight into a dwelling, steals all he can lay his hands on, poisons the minds of credulous people, and then crawls away."[94] Other newspapers fell in line: "Every prominent Democratic paper in the country has a corps of correspondents organized for the special purpose of defaming the character of the negro and his friend, the 'carpetbagger,'" wrote a North Carolinian in a letter to the *Portland Daily Press*.[95]

Some transplants from the North did escape the stereotype. As historian Eric Foner has written, "a Northerner, whatever his origins or character, who joined the Democratic Party and believed in white supremacy was a gentleman; one who joined the Republicans and defended the rights of blacks was a carpetbagger."[96] Indeed, the *Portland Daily Press* noted with irony in 1877, "So the Democratic nominee for Senator in Louisiana is a 'carpet-bagger'! He was born in Connecticut. But then he has lived in Louisiana for several years, and has always been of Democratic politics. The latter fact would save him from the name of 'carpetbagger' if he had moved but yesterday."[97]

But no one did more to define the word *carpetbagger* than did Thomas Nast in a cartoon published in *Harper's Weekly* in 1872. The man portrayed in the drawing, Carl Schurz, was a German immigrant, a Union general in the Civil War, a senator from Missouri, and secretary of the interior. To this day, the Nast drawing is almost universally recognizable, having been reprinted in histories and text books throughout the last century and a half. And although few knew the name of Carl Schurz, the unflattering image stuck in the minds of adults and schoolchildren alike, and northerners began to hate the carpetbagger with the vehemence of their southern counterparts. The image came to symbolize Reconstruction itself.

In 1877, one of the nation's most progressive Republican papers, the *Chicago Daily Tribune*, published an obituary:

> *Died—The Carpet-Bagger*. . . . He went south to aid the people of that country in returning to their allegiance. . . . He tried to awaken a friendly spirit among the white people of the South, by keeping them free from the cares and exasperations of office. . . . He endeavored to initiate them into the mysteries of political mechanism by disfranchising his opponents and binding together his friends through the cohesive power of public plunder. . . . He is now *in articulo mortis*. He has at last gone out of politics.[98]

FIGURE 13. Thomas Nast, "The Man with the Carpet Bags," 1872. Library of Congress, Prints and Photographs Division.

If the South didn't win the Civil War outright, it did win the propaganda war, in part by cultivating the image of the monstrous carpetbagger.[99] Individuals like George and Horatio Ruby, no matter how well intentioned, could not effectively fight the battle for the rights of emancipated African Americans with the press and public opinion—North and South alike—against them.

CHAPTER 10

Up in Smoke

The wind blew a perfect gale, and the flames ran like wild horses from point
to point. . . . Families moved their effects four or five times only to have them
destroyed at last.

—New York *Evening Post*, July 13, 1866

As a mess cook, William Ruby hadn't been permitted to prove himself on the battlefield. But after the war, events at home would test his character and his courage. After leaving the Union Army in 1864, he returned to Portland and opened a small grocery in the family's home on Sumner Street.

On July 4, 1866, Portlanders, including William, were enjoying a huge Independence Day celebration. The great war was over, the Union had prevailed, slavery had been abolished, and though Maine had lost nearly 9,000 men in battle and to disease, nearly 64,000 had returned home.[1] Bands played throughout the city; a hot-air balloon struggled to take off near Deering Oaks Park despite strong winds; a hippopotamus and four elephants were displayed on the Eastern Promenade. That evening, citizens could look forward to a huge display of fireworks that would "eclipse any before exhibited east of Boston."[2]

At about 5 p.m. William Ruby was driving his carriage near Commercial and Maple Streets when he noticed a fire in a boat shop. As a youngster in New York City, he'd seen the Great Fire of 1845 consume entire city blocks, so he was immediately alarmed, especially given the stiff wind. He began calling out, "Fire! Maple Street—District Eight!" Word spread, and a nearby church bell began tolling—eight times, then eight more times—alerting Portland's fire company to the location.[3]

With the wind and plenty of tinder to feed it, the fire spread rapidly from the boat shop to Upham's Flour Mill and then to the giant sugar house of J. B. Brown, who had made Portland a leader in the sugar and molasses trade. The imposing eight-story brick building was thought to be fireproof. The July 4 conflagration proved otherwise.

As the blaze grew and spread to the northeast, it completely overwhelmed Portland's fire company with its four steam engines, hook and ladder truck, and eighty-five firemen.[4] Dousing buildings with water was futile, so the firemen turned to pulling down buildings and blowing them up with gunpowder, hoping to create a break that would stop the fire's fury. "Many buildings—perhaps 50," wrote *The New York Times* the next day, "were blown up to check the flames, but the inhabitants could scarcely do more than flee with their families to the upper part of the city, saving such goods as they could carry."[5] Many gathered at the new city hall, also believed to be fireproof.

Calls for help had been telegraphed to towns and cities nearby, but by the time their fire companies arrived, the blaze was unmanageable. "The streets, lanes and alleys [were] roaring like so many furnace flues," recalled Portland writer John Neal.[6] The fire was so enormous that its glare on the horizon could be seen from sixty miles away.[7] "Fed by a gale from the south, [the blaze] marched on, fighting its way through the principal retail business houses of the town to the new City Hall," reported *Harper's Weekly*. "Everything in its path was reduced to smoking ruin."[8] That included the city hall, only three years old and considered to be one of the most beautiful buildings in the Northeast. Only its façade remained standing.

As the fire spread east toward Munjoy Hill, many residents took refuge in the open space of Eastern Cemetery. William Ruby didn't. He climbed onto the roof of the Abyssinian Meeting House—the structure that his father and other African Americans from the community had built—and spread wet blankets over it in an attempt to save the building. Many of the houses on Sumner Street, where the meeting house was located, were destroyed, though it's not clear whether the Ruby's house was damaged. Nearly all the houses on nearby Hampshire Street, where William's aunt Sophia Manuel lived, were burned or heavily damaged, as were those on Abyssinian Court, on the west side of the meeting house. But the Abyssinian itself remained standing.[9]

The Abyssinian was one of the few. Before the fire burned itself out some fifteen hours after it began, eight churches were destroyed, along with seven hotels, all the newspaper offices—there were at least seven of them—banks, and lawyers' offices. Three large schoolhouses and three firehouses were burned, as were many retail establishments and half of the city's manufacturing establishments.[10] Some 1,500 buildings were gutted. According to *Harper's Weekly*, "a space of one and a half miles long, by a quarter of a mile wide appears like a forest of chimneys, with fragments of walls attached to them. . . . No fire which has ever been inflicted upon an American town has been so ruinous."[11]

While it was clear where the fire had started, no one knew its precise cause. Some speculated that a cache of fireworks near Hobson's Wharf

FIGURE 14. Aftermath of the Portland Fire of 1866. Note the tents in the foreground, where displaced residents were living. From a stereoscopic image, New York Public Library Collections.

had been set off by vandals; others, that "a fire-cracker, thrown by a heedless boy, upon a pile of scattered shavings outside of a boat-builder's shop" had caused it; a third theory suggested that it could have been started by ashes from a cigar.[12] Whatever its origin, many thousands were left homeless. General George Shepley, with whom William Ruby had served during the war, set up a tent city near the foot of Munjoy Hill. Yet even after 1,500 tents were pitched, some 6,000 citizens remained without shelter.[13]

Samuel Fessenden's house on India Street and Joshua Gordon's on Smith Street were both leveled. The Gordon widows—Mary, age sixty-five, and her sister Harriet, sixty-six—were fortunate; they lived on Park Place, just west of where the fire started and began to move east, so their home was spared. Still, they undoubtedly felt the heat generated by the enormous conflagration at J. B. Brown's Sugar House, just two blocks away.[14]

Looters and thieves took advantage of the chaos, and the government had to deploy troops to control them. Portland "is filled with pickpockets from Boston and New York," reported *The New York Times*. One man "had his pocket picked in Congress-street this morning of $1,500. A man was bustled and robbed of $400 on Middle-street this forenoon. A fireman was beaten by two roughs last night."[15]

Still, the outpouring of assistance was impressive. Cities including Bangor, Biddeford, Portsmouth, Montreal, Providence, Philadelphia, and New York sent provisions, building materials, and funds. Boston sent five rail cars full of food, which was distributed at Portland's old city hall.[16] Helen Western, the Portland actress who had performed with John Wilkes Booth, gave a benefit performance in Boston for fire victims. "The manager of the Howard Athenaeum has set apart this evening for a benefit for the relief of Portland, Miss Helen Western and the stock company having volunteered for the occasion," reported the *Portland Daily Press*.[17] The charitable response was so great that some sought to take advantage. William Ruby, then the chairman of the Abyssinian Church, was forced to place a notice in the newspapers saying that the meeting house had not been "destroyed or injured by the late fire" and that the congregation had "not authorized any person to solicit or receive contributions" on its behalf.[18]

Once the smoke and debris were cleared, Portland launched a feverous rebuilding effort. By 1868 the city featured a new commercial center with dozens of imposing brick and stone buildings in the Italianate and Second Empire styles. Much of the debris from the fire was dumped into the tidal basin known as Back Cove, creating new buildable land. To ensure a consistent supply of water, the newly founded Portland Water Company laid a pipeline to Sebago Lake, some twenty miles away, and reservoirs were erected at opposite ends of the peninsula. The city also purchased a plot of land in the heart of the business district for a park that could serve as a firebreak. They named it Phoenix Square, after the symbol Portland had adopted when the town was leveled by British naval vessels in 1775. Soon, however, the city changed the name to Lincoln Park in honor of the fallen president.[19]

IN 1867, JUST AFTER the Great Fire, William Ruby built a large new store and ten-room dwelling on Sumner Street, which had been renamed Newbury Street. Previously, he had lived under the same roof with his father Reuben and Reuben's third wife, Annie. And father and son didn't always see eye to eye. The new structure allowed William, now thirty-three years old, to start fresh and establish his independence. "It is one of the neatest and most commodious grocery stores in the city," wrote the *Portland Daily Press*, "and we hear that Mr. Ruby has an extensive patronage."[20]

Then came a streak of bad luck. The store suffered considerable smoke damage when an attached shed burned. "It is supposed the fire was set in the shed," wrote the *Daily Press*, implying arson. Two weeks later, another blaze destroyed Ruby's store, inventory, and home, devastating his prospects. Again, the fire was suspicious: "This is the third time within a few months that this building has been set on fire."[21] Throughout the nineteenth century, African American homes and businesses were often burned in response to various grievances. But this was also the second major fire for which Ruby had sounded the alarm, and once again no culprit was ever identified. All we know is that someone seemed determined to destroy his home and livelihood.[22] The remains of the building were auctioned off in 1869.[23]

To make ends meet, William and his brother Horatio started a carpet-beating business. But that venture was short-lived: Horatio was restless and soon left on the Darién expedition. William then worked as a "truckman" and again started selling provisions out of his father's home.[24]

Briefly, he moved to Boston to work as a tailor, but he soon returned to Reuben's house and took a job as a clothes cleaner. [25] Though he was struggling financially and finding it hard to settle into employment, he, along with many other Portlanders, sent a donation to help the survivors of Chicago's Great Fire of 1871, which was even more devastating than Portland's had been.[26] William's generosity was well known; according to some, it "made him lose money frequently."[27]

In April 1874, following his father's example, William opened an oyster house on the lower level of Portland's Falmouth Hotel.[28] It was the first in a series of restaurants and catering businesses that he would operate. That October, he sued his wife, Madeline Talbot, for divorce, and in 1875 he married Sarah Butler of Portland. [29] In November of 1876, Ruby suffered another small fire while residing at his aunt's former home on Hampshire Street. He collected $15 in damages from insurance.[30]

In 1877, William again demonstrated his daring, this time in helping to save a group of young men who were out in a small boat on Casco Bay. On July 9, five of them had set out in a dinghy from Long Island, intending to row to Hog Island, now called Great Diamond Island. "They had been drinking hard, and were in no condition to get into a boat," wrote the *Portland Daily Press*, "but they were bound to go." Heavy winds capsized their boat, and they struggled to swim to shore. William Ruby and a man named Witham, both of whom were on Long Island at the time, grabbed dinghies and rowed to the rescue. They managed to save four of the swimmers, but a fifth drowned. The *Daily Press* declared that, "but for the assistance" of Ruby and Witham, the young men "would have all drowned." [31]

Despite his heroics, circumstances suggest that Ruby may have contributed to the tragedy. Shortly after the incident, he was charged with dispensing liquor on Long Island, where the young men had been staying. Manufacturing, dispensing, and drinking liquor had been forbidden in Maine since 1851, and it remained a dry state for eighty-two years, until the Twenty-first Amendment repealed national prohibition in 1933.[32] At the time of the rescue and drowning, Ruby was a boarder at a Long Island hotel, where he was caught "dispensing beer to a large number of persons" and had a jug of whiskey nearby. Ruby may very well have provided the liquor that caused the five young men to attempt their ill-fated trip to Hog Island.[33]

Both Ruby and the hotel owner, Ernesto Ponce, were arrested, though Ruby claimed that the liquor was his and that Ponce had known nothing about it. Nevertheless, Portland's municipal court found both men guilty, fined them $100 each, and sentenced them to three months' imprisonment. On appeal in superior court, both were forced to pay $100 and court costs; William narrowly escaped spending time in jail.[34] His scrape with the law undoubtedly made relations with his father even more difficult; Reuben had been committed to temperance his whole life.

Debt was another sore spot in their relationship. That same year, Reuben took William to court over a debt of $229 and won. While William didn't have enough liquid assets to meet the amount, he did have a one-third interest in his aunt Sophia's former home on Hampshire Street, where he was currently living. Upon his father's death, William was to share ownership of the house with his brothers George and Horatio. But after Reuben won the lawsuit, William moved out and apparently forfeited his interest in the property.[35]

Despite his legal troubles, William continued to cater steamer excursions for churches and Sunday schools. For a time, he operated a dining room with its own baseball field on Long Island for clubs and outings. He also ran an eating house on Pearl Street in Portland.[36] "A 25 cent dinner in his place was equal to a 50 cent one in almost any other eating house in New England," wrote a local paper, and "the favoring of his customers rather than himself . . . made him lose money."[37] It's not surprising, then, that in 1885, he was declared "an insolvent debtor."[38] Despite bankruptcy, William managed to hang onto his Pearl Street restaurant—at least for a time—and he later operated dining rooms at two other locations. He continued to be a popular restauranteur, though none of his business enterprises was especially lucrative. In his later years, he was reduced to running a small outdoor food stand near Deering Oaks Park.[39]

Throughout his life, William Ruby was active in Republican politics. Because the party held the majority in Maine, he wasn't a lightning rod for criticism or reprisals as his brother George had been in the South and Horatio had been at home. And while some Whites undoubtedly resented Black voters, no violent gangs sought to terrorize Blacks or prevent them from casting their votes. William represented Portland Republicans at several state conventions and even served on Portland's city committee.[40] But neither he nor any other Black citizen rose to state office as George Ruby had done in Reconstruction Texas; Maine didn't elect its first Black state representative until Gerald Talbot won a seat in the legislature in 1972.

WILLIAM'S TRUE PASSION WAS firefighting, and in that role he found professional, if not financial, success. As soon as his family had returned to Portland from New York in 1849 or 1850, sixteen-year-old William had joined the "hand tubs": engines pumped by hand to shoot streams of water at fires. Later, as a restauranteur, he catered numerous firemen's musters and clearly enjoyed their amiability. And firemen were known to be a hard-drinking bunch, despite the state's prohibition on liquor. As the president of the Portland Veteran Firemen's Association recalled, "we were all temperance men, but there was a principal involved. We had imbibed the idea as firemen . . . that water was to be used principally to extinguish fires, and did not want it used for other purposes."[41] That culture may have contributed to Ruby's scrape with the law.

In 1884, at age fifty, William joined the Portland Fire Department, possibly the first African American in its ranks. Ruby was nominated to serve with Machigonne Engine Company Number 1, the home of Portland's first steam-powered engine.[42] The state of Maine had established the Portland Fire Department in 1831, complete with rules and regulations.

Although Blacks had long been members of private fire companies in the North and South alike, they faced barriers when it came to being appointed to posts in paid, as opposed to all-volunteer, fire departments. The very year that Ruby joined the Portland Fire Department, a Black member of Philadelphia's city council demanded that the fire department hire African Americans. "This is the only department which is closed to the colored man," he stated. The fire commissioner took issue, saying, "When I entered the department, there was a colored man employed in one of the stables." "That is not what we want," replied the Black council member.[43] Black citizens of Cleveland, Ohio, also petitioned to be represented among the city's fire companies. When some suggested that all-Black fire companies be formed to accommodate their wishes, African Americans argued that "other nationalities were not represented in any of the departments in such a manner."[44]

Five years later, an African American man passed the examination for cadetship in the Cleveland Fire Department. The White members of the department declared that "they would not object to a colored company but they don't care to bunk and sleep in the same bed with a colored man."[45] And when the New York City Fire Department hired its first paid Black fireman in 1898, his White colleagues complained. "We do not mind working with him," they said, "but we object to bunking with him. That's too much."[46]

In Portland, things were different. After joining the all-White fire department, Ruby was soon promoted to pipeman—the lead person on the hose—and elected foreman of the fire company. In 1886, he was appointed assistant engineer of Company Machigonne 1. And in 1888, his fire company awarded ex-Captain Ruby an engraved gold watch and chain, a testament to their respect for him.[47] By 1890, however, personnel changes at the fire department forced him to retire.

Still, William remained passionate about firefighting. He joined the Veteran Firemen's Association and often responded to second alarms as a volunteer.[48] In 1891, fire broke out at a ship's chandlery on the Portland waterfront. At the time, the crew of Engine Number 5 were on Long Island, picnicking and playing ball with a fire crew from the city of Auburn. Ruby took charge of the relief men, and he and the substitute crew doused the flames "in very short order."[49]

WILLIAM RUBY FACED CHALLENGES in the postwar North, though it's hard to know the degree to which race, character, or bad luck contributed to those difficulties. We simply don't know who set fire to the store and home he built himself, or what it meant, and speculation reveals no truths. In the aftermath of that devastating fire, Ruby floundered, regained his footing, and at last found modest success and fulfillment as a caterer, restauranteur, and member of the firefighting community. He was sociable and well liked. As a local newspaper declared at his death in 1906, William was "one of the best known and most respected colored residents of Portland."[50]

Being an African American in Portland in the wake of the Civil War was undeniably challenging. But this small northern city was free enough to allow William Ruby to be active in politics, to socialize with people from all backgrounds, to make mistakes and redeem them through spontaneous acts of courage and altruism. And even when relations with his father were strained, William lived by the family's values: social and political engagement and helping others despite risks to self.

CHAPTER II

Family Fortunes

Money often costs too much.

—Ralph Waldo Emerson

During the Gilded Age, when a select few were amassing huge fortunes in oil, railroads, steel, and banking, most Americans were struggling to stay afloat. With 12 million immigrants arriving in the United States between 1870 and 1900,[1] job security for the working classes was non-existent, pensions were unheard of, and family wealth and the kindness of neighbors comprised the whole of the social safety net. Women were in especially precarious positions because they faced limits and prejudice in their professional pursuits. Whether Black or White, a woman's prospects had little to do with ability, education, literacy, or even raising enough children to care for her in her old age. Rather, she depended heavily on having married well, her husband's financial success, and her capacity to rebound from widowhood.

The Gordon women were caught in this bind. Though the men of the family had risked much at sea, especially in trafficking in human beings, the Gordons' fortunes were short-lived. The risks they took cost their families dearly. The early deaths of Morgan, at age fifty-two, Nathaniel II at fifty, and Nathaniel III at thirty-six devastated their survivors' economic prospects, and their crimes tainted the family name.

The fortunes of Mary Gordon, wife of the sea captain and mother of the executed slave trader, took an abrupt turn after her husband's death. The emotional and financial trauma of losing her spouse was compounded by the very public trial and hanging of her son. Mary died twelve years after her son's execution, and her death notice is telling: "Mrs. Nathaniel Gordon . . . was the widow of Capt. Nathaniel Gordon, formerly a wealthy resident of Portland, and she had for several years past been an inmate of the Aged Women's Home."[2] Like so many women of her era, Mary's public identity occupied the space between her husband and son. While the notice mentions her "wealthy" spouse, strikingly absent is any mention of her son, the convicted slave trader. Social mores dictated that difficult topics were avoided. Yet even though her obituary failed to mention that episode, everyone in town knew the story. And Mary lived under that cloud throughout her final years.

Mary Gordon lived for a quarter-century as a widow, facing illness and dwindling financial resources. The family's one-time home, 27 York Street, had been "a very swell affair in its day" and "the scene of some of the most brilliant assemblages Portland has ever beheld."[3] But in the last years of her life, Mary was admitted to Portland's Home for Aged Women, a church-supported facility that provided shelter for indigent women without families or other sources of income. She had suffered "a shock of paralysis," and members of Portland's High Street Church, where she'd long been a member, applied for her to enter the home and set aside money for her expenses. Her son-in-law—husband of her daughter Mary, the only child to survive her—paid her entrance fee. She died at age seventy-six of apoplexy.[4]

Mary's sister, Harriet Gordon, also ended her days at the home. Harriet had lost her husband, merchant William Gordon, when she was in her late twenties and had been a widow for nearly fifty years. For many of those years, she'd depended on her sister Mary and brother-in-law Nathaniel II. After Nathaniel II's death, she lived with Mary and her nephew, Nathaniel III, who was soon to be arrested for piracy. She then lived with her son, George B. Gordon, a livery man with a wife and three children. But "finding herself uncomfortably situated" there, she moved into the Home for Aged Women. According to the home's intake book, Harriet had "in former years moved in the first circles of society," but "at the advanced age of 73 years [she had] become dependent."[5] When she was admitted in June 1872, she was paralyzed on one side. She died at the home in 1873, aged seventy-four.

Frances Gordon, the wife of slave trader Captain Morgan Gordon, died of consumption in January 1860 at age sixty-three. She had suffered with the disease for eight years. While she apparently did not have to depend upon the charity of the community, records show that she owned no property.[6]

Slave trader Nathaniel Gordon III also left behind a young widow, Elizabeth, who was destitute at her husband's death. Because she had no means of support, friends in New York organized charitable fundraisers on her behalf. Shortly thereafter, she married another sea captain, Lewis Warren. That marriage allowed her to live in relative comfort in Queens for the rest of her life.

BLACK WOMEN'S PROSPECTS WERE even more limited. It was much harder for their husbands to succeed in business, and therefore, to leave behind enough for their widows to live on. And acceptable work for Black women comprised only a few occupations: seamstress or dressmaker, laundress, cook, maidservant.

For a brief while, Lucy Ruby had lived a privileged life as the wife of Texas state senator and newspaper publisher George Ruby. But she became a widow at age thirty-one, with three children between the ages of three and ten to care for. Upon George's death, Lucy returned to Washington, D.C. There, she lived in the home of her widowed mother, Catherine Nalle, and worked as a dressmaker: her occupation before being married. It's unlikely that she could have raised her children without the help of extended family. But in the early 1890s, Lucy was fortunate to find steady work as a civil servant, sewing bindings for the U.S. Government Printing Office.[7] She held that position for nearly twenty years, retiring in 1911, when she was sixty years old.[8] Lucy and George's daughter Mabel became a teacher at Shaw Junior High School in the city, and she helped to support her mother until Lucy's death in 1925.[9]

Sophia Ruby, Reuben's youngest sibling, died in 1875. She had lived as a widow for thirty years. But her husband, Christopher Manuel, had been a successful barber, and the couple had purchased their own home. That house was a critical asset for Sophia, who spent much of the succeeding years working as a laundress, likely earning meager wages but living under her own roof. She was forced to take out several mortgages on the property, yet managed to pay them all off. Her brothers Reuben and Isaiah lived nearby during much of her life and likely helped her a great deal. In her will, Sophia stipulated that her home—worth $1,200 at her death—was to go to Reuben and, at his death, be divided among his three surviving sons: William, George, and Horatio. The reason is poignant and speaks volumes about her fortitude: although Sophia had given birth to nine children, she had outlived them all.[10]

Despite these challenges, Sophia was an active member of Portland's abolitionist community, assisting fugitives from slavery who passed through the city. Listed on Portland's Freedom Trail, her gravestone in Eastern Cemetery commemorates her life and her activism.

IN HIS LATER YEARS, Reuben Ruby secured a steady but modestly paid job at the U.S. custom house in Portland. But civil service work was politically controversial. In 1868, a newspaper article titled "The Office Holder's Army" listed all fifty-seven public employees of the custom house by name and salary. Reuben worked as a porter, and at $500 per year, was the lowest paid. Still, according to the *Daily Eastern Argus*, he and his coworkers lived "at the public crib" and numbered "fifty or sixty thousand" across all federal agencies. The article reserved special resentment for the Freedmen's Bureau, which employed "between eight and nine thousand," complaining that "the tax payers have to foot the bill for all."[11]

Reuben had gotten the job through his political affiliations, and he remained active in politics in his later years, despite an increasingly hostile political climate. In the elections of 1869, seventy-one-year-old Reuben ran for councilman from Ward 2 in Portland but received only 30 votes to the winner's 328. It was a humiliating loss in an election that the newspapers called a thorough sweep by conservatives.[12]

Reuben wasn't always embroiled in controversy. As he aged, he spent more time on social activities. He joined the Aged Brotherhood of Portland, an integrated group of old-timers who got together for conversation, meals, and excursions.[13] He was a gardener, and in an 1874 exhibition sponsored by the Maine State Pomological and Portland Horticultural Societies, he showed pears, everbearing strawberries, cactuses, and a vegetable bouquet. That year he also celebrated a decade of marriage to his third wife, Ann Mayo Ruby.[14] He occasionally catered or organized picnics and continued to be active in the community. He rejoined the Abyssinian Church and represented the congregation in the Widows' Wood Society, a church-affiliated charity that made sure that Portland widows had sufficient fuel for heating and cooking.[15]

Reuben continued to be acutely sensitive to injustice. In October 1870, he fell into a sewer on Newbury Street and cracked two ribs. He sued the city of Portland, claiming a defect in the streets and asking for $2,000 as "compensation for injuries received." He recovered $400 in the judgment.[16] And in 1875, just a year before suing his son William for a debt, he renewed his lawsuit against the Abyssinian Church for repairs made decades before.

The Abyssinian was struggling financially, but as Reuben renewed his lawsuit, he had his own fiscal troubles. At seventy-eight, he was facing retirement from the custom house.[17] He suffered increasingly from rheumatism and neuralgia, and because pensions for federal workers didn't exist before 1920, he was likely concerned about his and Annie's financial state after retiring. So in renewing his suit against the Abyssinian, he was, out of necessity, calling in debts that he felt were owed him.

The Abyssinian's fortunes—and its very existence—were closely tied Reuben's. He'd been instrumental in founding the Abyssinian Religious Society, in providing the land on which its meeting house had been built, and in extending credit to the church to keep the building in repair. But he had a changeable relationship with the Abyssinian; at times he played a fatherly role, helping to conceive the institution and looking out for its interests; at others, he seemed like an estranged family member, disillusioned with church members, their failure to keep the building in repair, and their handling of the church's finances.

Despite Ruby's early commitment and assistance, the Abyssinian faced financial woes from the very start. Its small congregation, most of whom worked for painfully low wages, always struggled to secure enough funds to pay a minister and afford regular upkeep. Ironically, some of the Abyssinian's best years had occurred under Reverend Amos Noë Freeman during the 1840s, when Ruby was away in New York. The church had grown under Freeman—from fifty-seven members to more than eighty and up to two hundred worshippers on Sundays.[18] Yet even then the Abyssinian couldn't surmount its financial difficulties. To supplement his meager earnings as minister, Freeman had taught school for Portland's Black community in the basement of the meeting house, earning extra income from tuition payments. His situation grew so dire that neighbors and congregants organized a fundraiser for him and his family. "If sympathy is due to anyone, it must be felt for Mr. Freeman and his Family," wrote Portland's *Christian Mirror* in promoting the event.[19]

It wasn't enough. Four months later, Freeman bid an emotional goodbye to the Abyssinian and left for a position in Brooklyn, New York. According to the *Mirror*, "his labors here are wasting away his health. To supply his lack of salary he has taught school for several years. If he resigns his school, the greater part of his means of living fail."[20] Brooklyn's larger population meant he could reach more worshippers and possibly earn a living wage.

By January 1854, the Abyssinian was sinking, and the tiny flock was forced to request help from the larger family of churches. The congregation was hard-pressed to raise just $150, yet the cost of hiring a pastor and maintaining the building came to more than $500 annually. "We have been without a regular Pastor for one year and eight months, and in consequence have suffered severely in all our spiritual interests," wrote Deacon John Parrs to the local conference of churches. "We feel the necessity of speedy relief, or what little vitality is left in us will be extinguished." It was a desperate plea for help. But more than money, wrote Parrs, the community needed spiritual leadership: a pastor "who will live among us, visit us in our homes, counsel and advise us in our difficulties, console us in our hours of distress, comfort us in our afflictions, and bury our dead."[21] For several years afterward, the small congregation was buoyed by a series of pastors, including Amos Beman, a prominent abolitionist; Eben Ruby, Reuben's nephew; and, for a brief time, J. W. C. Pennington, a former fugitive from slavery, well-known abolitionist, and author.[22]

Although the Abyssinian Meeting House survived the Great Fire of 1866, it closed for repairs in the spring of 1870. Throughout the subsequent decade, newspaper notices announced numerous fundraisers for the church: some authorized, some not. When Reuben renewed his lawsuit in October 1875, members asked if he would settle out of court, in which case they'd promise to pay him.[23] It's unclear from the records whether or how the matter was resolved, but it's doubtful that either side gained much satisfaction.

For the Abyssinian, Ruby's lawsuit was one in a series of fatal blows. By the 1880s, the congregation was half the size it had been during the 1840s. Lack of resources made it hard for the church to attract and keep ministers. Some worshippers left for the Mountfort Street Methodist Church, which would eventually become Portland's Green Memorial African Methodist Episcopal Zion Church. With a dwindling congregation and no stable pastoral leader, the Abyssinian foundered.[24]

Then, on a frigid night in November of 1898, a tragedy occurred that affected the entire city, but especially the Abyssinian. The steamship *Portland*, a luxurious symbol of the Gilded Age, was caught in a storm. The 291-foot wooden-hulled *Portland*, with 167 cherry-paneled staterooms, regularly carried passengers between Portland and Boston.[25] It left Boston on the Saturday evening after Thanksgiving despite the approach of bad weather. Off Gloucester, Massachusetts, the steamer encountered gale-force winds, driving snow, and rough seas—a once-in-a-generation storm now known as the Portland Gale. It was the proverbial perfect storm: two low-pressure systems collided in the Atlantic to produce a spectacular weather event.

In the late evening, a fisherman saw the steamer struggling off Cape Ann; its high sidewheels and shallow draft—which allowed it to accommodate many passengers—caused the ship to struggle in the heavy seas. The next morning, the *Portland* was nowhere to be found.[26] *The New York Times* surmised that "the Portland, with its side paddlewheels and large exposure of hull, must have been smashed by the seas and rolled by the mad waves, and at last foundered in the height of the gale Sunday morning."[27] The *Portland* wasn't alone. Nearly two hundred ships were wrecked along the New England coast, sunk or driven ashore as a result of the winds and high seas.[28]

The whereabouts of the *Portland* weren't known until bodies and pieces of the vessel began to wash ashore on Cape Cod. "The back side of Cape Cod . . . is strewn with wreckage," wrote one newspaper. "Bodies have been washing ashore with life belts on marked with the steamer's name"; their stopped watches all marking the moment of sinking at 9:30.[29] Nearly two hundred passengers and crew were lost, though the exact number is unknown, since the passenger list went down with the ship. In the wake of the tragedy, ships began leaving copies of their manifests ashore.[30]

"The Abyssinian church has been a great loser by the loss of the steamer Portland," wrote the *Portland Daily Press*. "[It] suffered more loss than any other congregation in the city, having lost 19 of its parishioners."[31] And the church's troubles continued. Two years later, at century's end, the Abyssinian's pastor Theobold Smyth resigned his post, and "rumor gained currency that the church had ceased its existence."

Nonetheless, the tiny congregation declared that they were committed to continuing.[32]

Dramatic changes in Portland's demography—and its character—during the last half of the century propelled the Abyssinian's decline. Between 1860 and 1900, the city's population nearly doubled, from 26,023 to 50,146. At the same time, its Black population declined from 318 to 291. Losing twenty-seven individuals might not seem like many, but as a percentage of total population, it meant that Portland's Black population had declined by more than half: from 1.2 percent to 0.58 percent.[33]

The influx of immigrants and competition for jobs were key factors in this decline. Beginning in the early 1840s, Irish immigrants flooded into American cities fleeing the Great Famine. By 1860, two-thirds of Portland's immigrant population was Irish, and they gradually took over Black residents' main source of employment: dock work.[34] By the 1880s, Portland's longshoremen's union was predominantly Irish, and the union successfully forced African Americans out of the business. The 1881 and 1883 bylaws of Portland's Longshoremen's Benevolent Society stated that "no colored person shall at any time be admitted as a member of this society."[35]

Throughout Maine, job prospects for African Americans were shrinking. Though Blacks continued to work as cooks and stewards on a burgeoning number of steamships, immigrants were increasingly filling their positions as sailors. Although Maine witnessed growth in manufacturing at its many textile mills and shoe factories, those jobs were largely filled by immigrants from Quebec.[36] Pushed out of their traditional jobs at home, many of Maine's African Americans left, seeking work in larger American cities.

The Abyssinian Church faltered in the early years of the twentieth century, and finally, in 1917, it was dissolved by an act of the Maine legislature. For several years, the building lay vacant. Eventually, it was sold. The new owners covered the clapboard siding with shingles, divided the open sanctuary into small apartments on three floors, replaced its large windows with smaller ones, and removed the pews and wainscoting. Throughout much of the century, it served as an unremarkable, and often rundown, tenement. In 1991, the city of Portland condemned the building and seized it for back taxes.[37]

REUBEN RUBY DIED ON July 3, 1878, at the age of seventy-nine. He'd been in poor health, confined to his home—his sister's former home—for a year, with his wife Annie, then sixty-seven, as his nurse and companion. At his death, Annie became both resident and part-owner of the house on Hampshire Street.[38]

Reuben had lived a remarkable life. He'd witnessed three-quarters of the nineteenth century, persistently advocated for equal rights for Blacks, watched as court decisions and constitutional amendments denied and confirmed his equality and humanity by turns, risked jail by assisting those who'd escaped from slavery, endured a great civil war, saw slavery abolished and the vote extended to African American men throughout the United States, and then watched as those gains were systematically erased by Jim Crow laws.

Like most individuals, Ruby was complex. He was litigious: suing the Abyssinian several times, the city of Portland for a hole in the street, and his own son for debts he didn't repay. But those lawsuits can be seen in light of his values; they reflect, not merely a desire for compensation, but a strong drive for justice. The truth is, whenever Ruby wasn't struggling to support his family, he was working energetically on behalf of others: widows in his home town, fugitives from slavery, enslaved people he'd never met. And in some cases, he seemed to feel, others took advantage of his altruism.

In Portland, two brief death notices announced Reuben Ruby's passing. The *Portland Daily Press* referred to him as "venerable" and "our respected colored citizen." The *Daily Eastern Argus* called him "a well-known colored citizen" and one of two "prominent hackmen in town."[39] His neighbors' respect for him emerges clearly. But neither description does justice to his life and his character. They offer no hint of his adventurous nature: of a Black man from rural Maine launching a restaurant in New York City or venturing to the California gold fields through unknown lands and places hostile to non-Whites. Nor do they mention his most important legacies: his role in founding the Abyssinian Religious Society and building its meeting house, his contributions to Portland's Underground Railroad, his prominence in local politics and the national Colored Convention movement, his outspoken advocacy for immediate emancipation when it was an incendiary concept, and his behind-the-scenes support for Black persons in trouble.

THE LEGACIES OF BOTH the Rubys and the Gordons were quickly forgotten in their hometown. After the Civil War and for most of the following century, few citizens had an appetite for discussing Maine's treatment of abolitionists, the role of its maritime and sugar industries in sustaining slavery, or its native son who was hanged for slave trading. Mainers did celebrate winning the Civil War, but they were silent about the role that Black citizens had played in that victory. And while the South became increasingly determined to reestablish its old ways, the North was tired of fighting. "Everybody is sick of this eternal reconstruction," declared the *Daily Eastern Argus* just five years after the war ended.[40] The statement might have served as the credo for the Gilded Age.

BUT EVEN IF LEGACIES don't live on in the public consciousness, they often live on in families. In 1898, the sinking of the battleship *Maine* in Havana Harbor drew the United States into the conflict between Spain and Cuba, which was fighting for its independence. The government mustered African American units into the U.S. Army and Navy, and Black soldiers served in predominantly White units, too. William W. Ruby, Jr., son of the fireman and grandson of Reuben, served with Company A of the First Maine Infantry as an "artificer," repairing the unit's equipment.[41]

In June, Ruby was stationed at Chickamauga Park, Georgia, a large army training encampment for soldiers headed to the Spanish-American War. There, with two of his Maine comrades, Ruby attempted to cross the line of the Second Kentucky Volunteer Infantry. The Kentucky soldiers forbade them to cross. Like the rest of his family, William Ruby wasn't inclined to take such slights quietly. An argument ensued, and soldiers of the Second Kentucky, not used to seeing a Black man stand his ground before Whites, grabbed a rope, tied it to a tree, and surrounded Ruby, chanting, "Hang him, hang him." Within minutes, an officer arrived and ordered the soldiers to attention. The Kentuckians obeyed, allowing soldiers from the First Maine to whisk Ruby and his companions away to the regimental guardhouse.[42]

Ruby wrote an account of the incident for the *Portland Daily Press*. He recounted that he had been seized by the soldiers about a hundred yards from the Kentucky guard line. "Of course I made a kick and you can guess how mad I was," Ruby wrote. "I was hustled up to their regimental headquarters and I told the crowd what I thought of them." Although the Kentuckians were calling for him to be hanged, Ruby wrote, "strange as it may seem I did not feel any fear."[43]

The incident speaks to the racial violence that Blacks endured in the Jim Crow South after Reconstruction. Young William Ruby narrowly escaped becoming one of the 4,084 African Americans lynched in the South between 1877 and 1950 for infractions including seeking to vote, failing to yield the sidewalk to Whites, and challenging White authority.[44] But it also speaks to traits that were part of the Ruby family: audacity, defiance, and an acute sensitivity to injustice based on race.

William Ruby Jr. survived the incident and received a commission as lieutenant in one of the Army's African American regiments.[45] After mustering out in October 1898, he returned to Portland, where he found employment at Portland's Union Station.[46]

NATHANIEL GORDON IV, THE son of slave trader Nathaniel Gordon III, was five years old when his father was executed. Afterward, he lived with his mother Elizabeth, his stepfather Lewis Warren, and four half-brothers and sisters in Queens, New York. Curiously, census records from several different years list the child's birthplace as Illinois and Green Bay, Wisconsin, though Maine's vital records show he was born in Cape Elizabeth, across the Fore River from Portland, in 1857. In the 1880 census, taken when he was twenty-three years old, he is listed as Nathaniel Warren. Were these simply mistakes on the part of census takers or an intentional attempt to disassociate him from his father and his family name?[47]

The slave captain's criminal exploits, as well as his very public execution, were covered in the national press, leaving a legacy of shame and humiliation that must have dogged his son. Newspapers wrote that Nathaniel III's offenses were "painfully and degradingly expiated on the public scaffold."[48] Just before the execution, Elizabeth Gordon composed a poem for First Lady Mary Todd Lincoln, begging her "to rescue from a life of shame, / The wife and child who bear his name." And on the eve of his death, the slave trader himself "spoke of his child, and hoped that the stigma of his parent's shameful death might not rest upon its innocent head."[49] It was a heavy burden for the younger Gordon to carry.

On the surface, at least, Nathaniel IV seems to have overcome his troubled start in life. He followed the sea as his father and uncles had done, not as a ship captain but as a marine diver. And in 1882, he returned to Maine, where his extended family was well known.[50] There, he again went by the name Nathaniel Gordon.

Gordon attracted local attention as a diver. He took on salvage operations and underwater repairs and inspections, and he recovered bodies after drownings. He also operated a confectionary store and billiard hall in South Portland.[51] And he did well for himself, owning a "handsome steam yacht," the *Nadine*, and living in a "fine residence."[52] The *Portland Daily Press* even mentioned him as a potential Republican candidate for Portland alderman in 1901: "Mr. Gordon would be thoroughly awake to all questions affecting the vital interests of this city. He is that kind of man."[53]

On the outside, at least, Nathaniel Gordon IV had managed to make his own way, emerging from the long shadow cast by his infamous father. He was a trusted professional, notable but not notorious. Although the nation at large failed to fully appreciate the lessons of the slave trader's execution, his son was forced to take those lessons to heart.

FAMILIES CONVEY BOTH TRAITS and values, sometimes across many generations. But as Nathaniel Gordon IV shows, none of us is bound to follow the paths that our predecessors lay out. And culture changes over time. What was considered respectable in the decades before the Civil War changed dramatically in its aftermath. Slavery, once accepted as an economic necessity, became the nation's greatest moral transgression—at least in the North. The war's enormous toll—death, bloodshed, and destruction—helped to erase the notion that slavery was in any way a benign institution.

But such convictions didn't last. By the early twentieth century, nostalgia for the Old South had set in. Robert E. Lee and his Confederate soldiers were worshipped and deified, and slavery was recast as a paternalistic but benevolent institution—a natural extension of family bonds and responsibilities. The cult of the Lost Cause was born.

Despite the Civil War and its aftermath, the United States has never fully resolved the complex questions of social, economic, and racial equality. The pursuit of freedom and civil rights for all was never a regional matter nor a question of northern versus southern values. Rather, it was a struggle that defined the American character—and our large blended family—from the beginning. For as long as we've been a nation, we've argued over who deserves full rights as citizens, whose economic interests should predominate, what happens when one person's rights impede another's, and to whom the phrase "all men are created equal" pertains.

Even today, American schoolchildren are taught that slavery and emancipation were regional struggles that divided the agricultural South from the industrial North via a neatly demarcated Mason-Dixon Line. And most continue to believe it as adults. But the struggle was equally a local one: a test of Americans' foundational beliefs that played out in neighborhoods, communities, and families in the North and South alike. The experiences of the Rubys and Gordons demonstrate that clearly, whether they resided in New York, California, Louisiana, Texas, or Portland, Maine.

Does that mean that the notion of a "free state" was a myth? As long as slavery continued in the South, northern states never managed to eradicate its influence over their economies, institutions, and ways of life. And even though Blacks in the North were not viewed as chattel, they were not full citizens either. Free states and municipalities enacted their own Black laws that restricted African Americans' right to vote, to live and work in all sectors, to attend schools with White students, to travel by train, ship, streetcar, or taxi.

For all of Maine's flaws and the compromises made by its politicians, its institutions, its inhabitants, and its maritime trade, the state was among the freest in the nation for those of African heritage. In the wake of the 1850 Fugitive Slave Act, Maine, along with seven other states, enacted personal liberty laws to prevent African Americans from being seized and remanded to slavery.[54] Fugitives could not be held in Maine jails, their cases could not be tried in municipal courts, and county attorneys had to provide for their defense. In New York, two such bills, introduced in 1857 and 1859, failed to pass.[55] The Rhode Island General Assembly passed personal liberty laws in 1848 and 1854 but repealed them in 1861 as a concession to southern states intended to prevent full-scale civil war.[56]

Maine's state legislature never abridged Black men's right to vote as so many states, even in the North, did. It encouraged and assisted its Black citizens in establishing their own institutions, including the Abyssinian Religious Society. And the state unwaveringly stood by its African American inhabitants as citizens, even when the nation did not; Maine's Supreme Court declared African American residents to be full citizens when the U.S. Supreme Court's *Dred Scott* decision proclaimed otherwise. Perhaps that's why the Rubys, who traveled widely, returned again and again; perhaps it was more than the comfort of familiar faces, sights, sounds, and smells that called them home.

Maine's African American population was always among the smallest in the nation—peaking at 0.56 percent of its total population in 1790 and declining to 0.18 percent in 1890.[57] Yet the individuals behind those statistics impacted the state and the nation in significant ways. Black Mainers played important roles in local culture and politics, the national maritime trade, the abolition and colonization movements, the Colored Convention movement, the Civil War, and in Reconstruction in Texas and Louisiana. Like most states in the far North, Maine was never the center of the American racial struggle: the proverbial eye of the storm. Rather, it was the leading edge. As a free state in the nineteenth century, Maine was far from blameless with regard to slavery and racial discrimination, but in a few crucially important ways, it showed the way toward a more perfect union. In those ways, Maine and its citizens succeeded in living by the motto they adopted upon statehood in 1820: *Dirigo*—I lead.

Lost and Found

Facts are stubborn things; *and whatever may be our wishes, our inclinations, or the dictates of our passions, they cannot alter the state of facts and evidence.*

—President John Adams

Our collective memory sometimes fails us. History is vital a tool for keeping us mindful of the lessons of the past when memory fades. But history can also be used to bury the past. And what we choose to forget is in many ways more telling than what we remember.

The Rubys and Gordons were prominent during their lifetimes, but their prominence faded. That fact speaks volumes about history's role in helping us to remember *and* to forget. For at least two generations, northerners' uneasiness about their role in the slave trade encouraged writers, historians, teachers, and others to avoid the topic altogether, dismissing both those who engaged in the trade and those who worked to end it.

In 1860, Timothy Meaher had the slave ship *Clotilda* burned and scuttled in the Mobile River under cover of night; he ordered her captives hidden in canebrakes. By doing so, he was controlling the historical narrative. Even as he boasted that he had brought the last shipload of captive Africans into the United States in defiance of the 1820 piracy law, he sought to hide all evidence of the fact, just as Nathaniel Gordon III had done with the *Juliet*, the *Camargo*, and the *Ottawa*, but failed to do with the *Erie*. Better, of course, to be a character of legend than a convicted pirate swinging from the gallows.

Those whom Meaher helped smuggle into the country were largely forgotten; they endured five years of slavery and spent the rest of their lives in obscurity in Alabama. In 1931, Zora Neale Hurston sought to add their perspectives to history by writing *Barracoon*, the personal account of Oluale Kossola, or Cudjo Lewis, one of those carried aboard the *Clotilda* and enslaved by the Meaher family. But publishers repeatedly rejected Hurston's manuscript.[1] In the 1930s, White Americans weren't prepared to view a formerly enslaved person's perspective with an open mind. Jim Crow laws remained in force throughout the South; housing, employment, and other forms of discrimination were rife in the North. Schools and universities taught students that the Civil War had been a battle over states' rights, that the sacrifices made by White northerners had ended slavery, and that Reconstruction was an abysmal failure because African Americans had proven that they were unfit to vote or govern. This view of Reconstruction, promulgated by Columbia University history professor William Archibald Dunning and others, was used to justify the continued suppression of equal rights.

A few of Dunning's contemporaries, most notably W. E. B. DuBois, bravely challenged these notions. "One cannot study Reconstruction without first frankly facing the facts of universal lying," DuBois wrote in *Black Reconstruction in America, 1860–1880* (1935).[2] His book was a bold beginning, but it did not change hearts and minds overnight.

At midcentury, a new generation of Americans provoked change in the streets, in Congress, and in the academy. During the civil rights era, Americans fought doggedly to overturn Jim Crow laws and the prevailing notion that Blacks were unworthy of full citizenship. When activists demanded that schools desegregate and African Americans be given full voting rights, they faced violence from mobs and the police, just as their abolitionist forebears had. But this time, the rest of the country couldn't turn away. The struggle played out on television and in newspapers day after day, compelling even those who were not directly involved to grapple with issues of race, equal rights, and justice.

Despite the violence, civil rights activists persisted in their struggle to build a more equitable society on the foundation that their predecessors had assembled: the Thirteenth, Fourteenth, and Fifteenth Amendments to the U.S. Constitution. This generation of activists insisted that those amendments, which dozens of Black codes had circumvented in the South, be fully enforced. And they made significant gains in the courts, Congress, and public opinion. The 1954 Supreme Court decision *Brown v. Board of Education* prohibited segregating public schools by race; the 1964 Civil Rights Act forbade discrimination in public places; and the 1965 Voting Rights Act nullified local laws that kept African Americans from voting.

Civil rights activists addressed the deceptions of the Dunning school head-on. "White historians had for a century crudely distorted the Negro's role in the Reconstruction years," said Martin Luther King, Jr., in 1968. "One generation after another of Americans were assiduously taught these falsehoods and the collective mind of America became poisoned with racism and stunted with myths."[3] Tired of living under the burden of untruths, the civil rights generation asserted its own view of slavery, the Civil War, Reconstruction, and the turbulent nineteenth century.

But even though the nation has made progress, inequalities persist. In the twenty-first century, the tragic and graphic on-camera killings of individuals including Philando Castile, Eric Garner, Ahmaud Arbery, and George Floyd inspired the Black Lives Matter movement. It focused attention on the nation's stubborn failure to guarantee equal justice. Like the civil rights movement, it, too, urged a reassessment of history. In the wake of Floyd's brutal death at the hands of Minneapolis police officers in 2020, 168 statues and symbols celebrating Confederate heroes were removed from public squares across the United States.[4] Yet the movement also aroused a backlash. PEN America, an advocacy group that promotes free expression, found that, between 2015 and 2019, state legislatures introduced 116 bills seeking to limit citizens' right to protest guaranteed under the First Amendment.[5]

Members of the civil rights and Black Lives Matter movements honored their forebears, not merely by acknowledging their bravery and sacrifice, but by taking up the unfinished business that previous generations had left behind. They offered new appraisals of historical events—perspectives accepted by some and rejected by others. But rather than distorting or erasing history, as some have charged, these new perspectives enlarge and enrich the historical narrative, offering an increasingly inclusive and ever-evolving story of the nation.

"Facts are stubborn things," President John Adams once said. And as relics and artifacts from the past continue to resurface, their tangible reality compels us to confront history and adjust our perspectives. In 1991, the remains of 419 individuals of African heritage were found in lower Manhattan during construction of a new federal building. These graves—along with the stories of the people buried there—had been hidden beneath structures and landfill for two centuries, a striking example of erasing history. Rediscovering the African Burial Ground—thought to contain as many as 20,000 Black individuals—provided irrefutable evidence that enslaved persons played a key role in the founding and growth of the nation's largest metropolis, even if they did not share in its prosperity.[6]

A decade later, in 2003, construction workers discovered the coffins of eight enslaved persons from the colonial period beneath a street in downtown Portsmouth, New Hampshire. In the early 1800s, Portsmouth's African Burial Ground disappeared from maps, replaced by houses. Once again, the memory of those buried there—who had lived and died in bondage—had been suppressed.[7]

Portland's Eastern Cemetery contains an impressive monument to Alonzo Stinson, the first resident of the city to die in the Civil War. Although Stinson was White, the monument, erected in 1808, was placed in the Black section of the already-full cemetery, and the remains of several Black Portlanders were removed to make way for it.[8] The Stinson memorial symbolizes the sacrifices of Maine soldiers who fought in the war. Yet it also illustrates the human tendency to embrace one historical narrative at the expense of another.

Cultural artifacts from the slavery era continue to resurface, forcing us to acknowledge slavery's full legacy. In 2008, the U.S. National Archives publicly displayed original documents showing that enslaved laborers built our nation's most iconic structures: the U.S. Capitol and the White House. That same year, the Slave Voyages Database (https://www.slave-voyages.com) became an open-access website, offering details on the massive scope of the transatlantic trade that cannot be denied or overlooked. In 2016, scholars, students, and genealogists affiliated with Georgetown University uncovered documents showing that, in 1838, Jesuits in charge of the school sold 272 enslaved individuals to ensure the school's future. The closer we look, the more evidence we find that slavery has been fundamental to American society as a whole. Such facts force us to abandon the argument that slavery was confined to the American South.

In 2018, eighty-seven years after it was written, *Barracoon* finally made it into print. Writer Zora Neale Hurston had died fifty-eight years earlier; but a new generation, raised on a steady diet of racial activism and awareness, declared itself ready to hear the story of a kidnapped African who never saw his homeland again. That man, Oluale Kossola, along with slave captain William Foster and slaveholders James and Timothy Meaher, are forever chained together: their experiences contribute equally to the historical narrative of the United States.

The following year, the *Clotilda* itself was discovered in the mud of the Mobile River, helping to bring the story of capture, enslavement, and deception back into the public consciousness. This time, the author of the scheme, Timothy Meaher, was seen as neither hero nor legend. The protagonists were the scientists and divers who discovered the wreck and brought its existence to light, the descendants of the Africans brought to the United States in 1860 who kept their history alive among themselves, and the captives like Kossola, who survived the brutal Middle Passage and slavery in a strange land to build their home-away-from-home: Africatown in Mobile, Alabama.

EARLIER, IN 2002, EXPLORERS found and identified another wreck, this one in the waters of the Gulf of Maine, some 1,300 miles north of Mobile. They had located the steamship *Portland*, lying largely intact along Stellwagen Bank, where it had sunk in the Portland Gale of 1898. While the story of the tragic shipwreck had never been completely forgotten, its discovery reilluminated a moment in history: when African Americans played a substantial role in Maine's and the nation's maritime industry. Fully half of the *Portland*'s crewmembers were Black.

The disappearance of the steamer and the loss of nineteen members of Portland's Black community contributed to the eventual demise of Portland's Abyssinian Religious Society and Meeting House. For eighty years, the building—once a hub and symbol of the city's African American community—was unseen and unheralded. But at the end of the twentieth century, a new generation of Portlanders, raised during the civil rights era, began to look more closely at their multiracial past and to excavate facts, artifacts, and stories of people long buried. In 1994, Shoshana Hoose released the film *Anchor of the Soul*, a documentary about the Abyssinian Meeting House and Portland's Black history. A cascade of efforts followed. In 1998, the Committee to Restore the Abyssinian purchased the building, which had lain vacant for several years.

In 2006, a group of local writers, journalists, and historians put together a volume titled *Maine's Visible Black History*, the first effort to comprehensively document the history of African Americans in the state. In 2007, Portland's Freedom Trail was established, highlighting landmarks and sites throughout the city connected with the Underground Railroad, including the Abyssinian Meeting House, the Fessenden and Thomas homes, and Reuben Ruby's hack stand.

In 2014, Ron Soodalter published *Hanging Captain Gordon*, an examination of Nathaniel Gordon III's life, trial, and execution as a slave captain. And in 2023, divers in the waters off Brazil discovered the remains of a ship believed to be the *Camargo*, the Maine-built vessel that Gordon had used to bring the last kidnapped Africans to Brazil to be sold into slavery.[9]

FIGURE 15. Front façade of the Abyssinian Meeting House, under renovation, 2001. Courtesy of the Portland Public Library, *Portland Press Herald* Still-Film Negatives Collection. Used with permission.

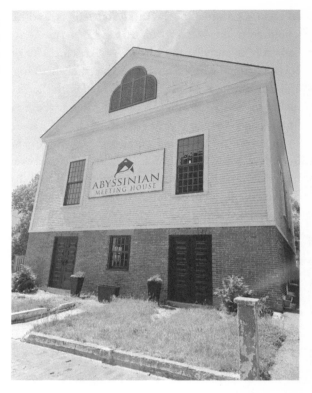

Each of these acts of historical recovery and remembering was conse-
quential, and most were long overdue because the community had kept
silent on these matters for decades. As late as 1992, Roger F. Duncan, in
Coastal Maine: A Maritime History, dedicated a single paragraph to the
trial and hanging of Nathaniel Gordon while writing that "there seems
little evidence that Maine people engaged in the slave trade to any great
extent."[10] Portland's well-known nineteenth-century historian William
Willis said nothing about Gordon in his *History of Portland from 1632
to 1864*, though he was a Gordon family friend. In that book, Willis
didn't mention the word *slavery* and only passingly acknowledged Portland's "colored" residents and the Abyssinian. William Goold's *Portland
in the Past* (1886) didn't mention Gordon, nor did William Armstrong
Fairburn's encyclopedic *Merchant Sail* (1945–55) or William Hutchinson Rowe's *Maritime History of Maine* (1948). These writers' conscious
decisions to avoid discussing Gordon and the slave trade was typical of

Americans' reticence on uncomfortable topics, particularly in the wake of the Civil War. Maine did celebrate its soldiers and their many courageous contributions to the Union victory. But for at least two generations, its citizens buried the less savory parts of the story: its divided populace; the violence suffered by abolitionists, Black and White; and its contribution to the slave trade through its shipbuilding, maritime trade, and its sea captains, who brought thousands of Africans to the Americas in violation of U.S. law.[11]

I should know. I was raised in Maine during the twentieth century, the product of twelve years of education in Portland public schools and eight years of higher education in the Northeast and the Mid-Atlantic. My great-grandfather fought for the Union. But no one—teachers, professors, or family members—discussed the North's notorious slave traders, its complicity in our great national transgression, or its Black communities. Researching the events and characters of my hometown in the nineteenth century was, for me, like finding a cache of old photographs that enliven and narrate family episodes never spoken of.

My original motive in researching the Rubys and Gordons was to fill in the long-neglected gaps in my own education: to achieve a deeper understanding of the region I call home. But in retelling their stories, I was compelled to stray beyond region and race. The Rubys' and Gordons' experiences resist the confines of regional history, Black history, and White history. Together, their stories offer a portrait of our diverse and extended American family: one that reveals glimpses of us all.

Notes

A NOTE ON LANGUAGE

1 John Daniszewski, "The Decision to Capitalize Black," Associated Press, June 19, 2020, https://blog.ap.org.

2 Nancy Coleman, "Why We're Capitalizing Black," *New York Times*, July 5, 2020.

3 National Association of Black Journalists, "NABJ Statement on Capitalizing Black and Other Racial Identifiers," June 11, 2020, https://nabjonline.org.

4 Kristen Mack and John Palfrey, "Capitalizing Black and White: Grammatical Justice and Equity," MacArthur Foundation, August 26, 2020, https://www.macfound.org.

5 Ann Thuy Nguyen and Maya Pendleton, "Recognizing Race in Language: Why We Capitalize 'Black' and 'White,'" Center for the Study of Social Policy, March 23, 2020, https://cssp.org.

PROLOGUE: FAMILY PORTRAITS IN BLACK AND WHITE

1 Jason Finkelstein, "The Governor's Gallows: Joshua Chamberlain and the Clifton Harris Case," *Maine History* 45, no. 2 (2010): 178.

2 W. E. B. DuBois, *Black Reconstruction in America, 1860–1880* (1935; reprint, New York: Free Press, 1998), 190.

3 Thomas Jefferson, "Notes of Proceedings in Congress," July 2, 1776, in the Library of Congress exhibit "Creating the Declaration of Independence," https://www.loc.gov.

CHAPTER 1: FREE STATE

1 Commonwealth of Massachusetts, *Massachusetts Soldiers and Sailors of the Revolutionary War*, vol. 6, 1896–1908 (Boston: Wright and Potter, 1896), 638.

2 Marriage record of Boston Ruby and Zeruiah Lewis, December 6, 1783, Maine marriage records, 1713–1922, Maine State Archives, Augusta. Boston Ruby's name variously appears in public records as "Boston Ruby," "Boston Ruben," and "Boston

Black." Charles P. M. Outwin wrote that "Boston Black" may have been a personal servant of Reverend John Wiswall of Saint Paul's Anglican parish in Falmouth and that he was freed sometime around 1775 ("An Index of Named Slaves at Falmouth in Casco Bay [Portland] and in Lower Cumberland County, Maine, c. 1760-'75," unpublished manuscript, 2006, Maine Historical Society, Portland). However, Outwin cites no sources for this theory, and I have found no records to confirm it.

3 Randolph Stakeman, "The Black Population of Maine, 1764–1900," *New England Journal of Black Studies* 8 (1989): 25.

4 According to historian Joanne Pope Melish, census statistics listed a few enslaved people in Rhode Island as late as 1840 ("Rhode Island, Slavery, and the Slave Trade," *EnCompass*, https://encompass.rihs.org.)

5 New-York Historical Society, "NYC: Facts: When Did Slavery End in New York State?," https://www.nyhistory.org.

6 Commonwealth of Massachusetts, *Massachusetts Constitution*, part 1, "A Declaration of the Rights of the Inhabitants of the Commonwealth of Massachusetts," art. 1.

7 Commonwealth of Massachusetts, "Massachusetts Constitution and the Abolition of Slavery," https://www.mass.gov; Robert M. Spector, "The Quock Walker Cases (1781–83): Slavery, Its Abolition, and Negro Citizenship in Early Massachusetts," *Journal of Negro History* 53, no. 1 (1968): 12.

8 U.S. Census Bureau, "Schedule of the Whole Number of Persons within the Several Districts of the United States" (1790), https://www2.census.gov.

9 Leonard P. Curry, *The Free Black in Urban America, 1800–1850: The Shadow of the Dream* (Chicago: University of Chicago Press, 1981), 85; *A Volume of Records Relating to the Early History of Boston Containing Minutes of the Selectmen's Meetings, 1799 to, and Including, 1810* (Boston: 1904), 77.

10 Commonwealth of Massachusetts, "An Act to Prevent the Slave Trade, and for Granting Relief to the Families of Such Unhappy Persons as May Be Kidnapped or Decoyed Away from This Commonwealth," March 26, 1788, in *The Laws of the Commonwealth of Massachusetts from November 28, 1780 to February 28, 1807* (Boston, 1807), 1:408.

11 *Jenks' Portland Gazette*, September 20, 1802, 4.

12 U.S. Census Bureau, census for New Gloucester, ME (1790), https://www2.census.gov.

13 I am indebted to Bob Greene for information on Phebe Ruby.

14 In Portland's *Daily Eastern Argus* (September 2, 1869, 3), Reuben Ruby is listed as a member of the "Aged Brotherhood of Portland" and cites the year and location of his birth as December 28, 1798 in Gray. See also D. C. Colesworthy, *School Is Out* (Boston: Barry and Colesworthy, 1876), 381, which provides a brief bio of Ruby.

15 U.S. Census Bureau, census for Gray, ME (1800), https://www2.census.gov.

16 Maine Bureau of Parks and Lands, "The Mayall Mills, 1791–1902," https://www.maine.gov; New England Historical Society, "How Maine's Samuel Mayall Brought America Its First Woolen Mill," https://www.newenglandhistoricalsociety.com.

17 Marriage record of John Lake and Zeruiah Lewis, December 1, 1804, and marriage record of John Lake and Hannah Lake, August 10, 1793, Maine marriage records, 1713–1922, Maine State Archives, Augusta.

18 In the 1800 census, Lake is listed as the head of a household of four people, all of

whom are designated as "white" (U.S. Census Bureau, census for New Gloucester, ME [1800], https://www2.census.gov.

19 Amber D. Moulton, *The Fight for Interracial Marriage Rights in Antebellum Massachusetts* (Cambridge, MA: Harvard University Press, 2015). Bob Greene has done extensive research on Blacks in Maine and has found numerous cases in which Blacks and Whites married one another (personal communication, June 11, 2021).

20 Samuel Freeman, letter to Thomas Jefferson, May 1, 1793, https://founders.archives.gov.

21 The 1821 law declared that "all marriages between any white person and any Negro, Indian, or Mulatto shall be absolutely void" (State of Maine, "An Act for Regulating Marriage," in *Laws of the State of Maine; to which are prefixed The Constitution of the U. States and of Said State with an Appendix* [Hallowell, ME: Spaulding, 1822], sec. 2, 276).

22 Portland didn't segregate its schools until 1836 (Edward Henry Elwell, "The Schools of Portland, from the Earliest Times to the Centennial Year of the Town, 1886," in *City of Portland Mayor's Address and Annual Report for the Financial Year 1887–88* [Portland, 1888], 105, 106).

23 William Gordon was born a year before Reuben Ruby; his brother Nathaniel, eleven months after. The notion of separate schools for Black and White children didn't take hold in New England until the 1820s and 1830s, when Reuben was an adult (Joanne Pope Melish, *Disowning Slavery: Gradual Emancipation and "Race" in New England, 1780–1860* [Ithaca, NY: Cornell University Press, 2016], 188). For a while, Portland girls attended school with boys, but eventually the schools shifted to all-boy classes (Elwell, "The Schools of Portland," 88, 90).

24 Carl Patrick Burrowes, "A Child of the Atlantic: The Maine Years of John Brown Russwurm," *Maine History* 47, no. 2 (2013): 170.

25 Elwell, "The Schools of Portland," 105.

26 "John Brown Russwurm," Bowdoin College Library, George J. Mitchell Department of Special Collections and Archives, Africana Studies Resources, https://library.bowdoin.edu.

27 The 1850 census lists Isaiah Ruby as a mariner in Portland (U.S. Census Bureau, census for Portland, ME [1850], https://www2.census.gov.)

28 Nathaniel C. Jewett, *Portland Directory and Register* (Portland, 1823), 35, 49.

29 *Portland Transcript*, November 21, 1874, 6.

30 Bob Greene, "Reuben Ruby: Hackman, Activist," https://www.mainememory.net.

31 Jacqueline Jones, *American Work: Four Centuries of Black and White Labor* (New York: Norton, 1998), 261.

32 David C. Young, comp., *Royal River Valley Families (Old North Yarmouth, Cumberland Co, Maine Families)*, 1997, http://files.usgwarchives.net; "Record of Baptisms, at the First Church, North Yarmouth," *Old Times: A Magazine Dedicated to the Preservation and Publication of Documents Relating to the Early History of North Yarmouth, Maine*, January 1, 1883, 981.

33 *Weekly Eastern Argus*, October 13, 1808, 4.

34 Marriage of Nathaniel Gordon and Althea Mitchell, January 22, 1809, Maine marriage records, 1713–1922, Maine State Archives, Augusta.

35 Death notice for Nathaniel Gordon I, *Columbian Centinel* (Boston), July 4, 1818, 2. According to the *New England Palladium and Commercial Advertiser* (July 3, 1818,

2), "[Nathaniel Gordon I] took passage last January in a vessel at Plymouth bound to Kennebunk, but being driven off in a gale, they put into St. Barts." This suggests that Gordon was not a mariner but a passenger.

36 See ship arrivals in *Boston Commercial Gazette*, October 24, 1822, 2, which show the *Orono*, which Nathaniel Gordon captained, arriving in Portland from Saint Domingo.

37 Jean F. Hankins, "Settling Oxford County: Maine's Revolutionary War Bounty Myth," *Maine History* 42 (2005), no. 3: 141; MassHumanities, "March 15, 1820: Massachusetts Loses Maine," www.massmoments.org/. For population statistics, see U.S. Census Bureau, censuses for Massachusetts and the District of Maine (1790, 1820), https://www2.census.gov.

38 Irwin Gratz, "How Maine Became a State 200 Years Ago, and What That Had to Do with Slavery," *Maine Public*, July 31, 2019, https://www.mainepublic.org.

39 Illinois was admitted in December 1818 and Alabama in December 1819.

40 The five who opposed the Missouri Compromise were Martin Kinsley, Joshua Cushman, Ezekiel Whitman, Enoch Lincoln, and James Parker (*Eastern Argus*, March 14, 1820, 3).

41 Thomas Jefferson, letter to John Holmes, April 22, 1820, Library of Congress, https://www.loc.gov.

42 *Eastern Argus*, March 14, 1820, 3.

43 According to Matthew Mason, "The most pressing slavery" that statehood advocates observed "was that of the District [of Maine] to its Federalist overlords in Boston" ("The Maine and Missouri Crisis: Competing Priorities and Northern Slavery Politics in the Early Republic," *Journal of the Early Republic*, 33, no. 4 [Winter 2013]: 683).

44 Richard C. Rohrs, "Exercising Their Right: African American Voter Turnout in Antebellum Newport, Rhode Island," *New England Quarterly*, 84, no. 3 (2011): 402.

45 Charles E. Nash, *The Debates and Journal of the Constitutional Convention of the State of Maine, 1819–'20* (Augusta, ME, 1894), 125–26.

46 Mason, "The Maine and Missouri Crisis," 680.

47 *Portland Weekly Advertiser*, April 12, 1836, 4; April 4, 1837, 3; April 10, 1838, 1.

48 Mason, "The Maine and Missouri Crisis," 694–95.

49 U.S. Congress, "An Act to Continue in Force 'An Act to Protect the Commerce of the United States, and Punish the Crime of Piracy,' and also to Make Further Provisions for Punishing the Crime of Piracy," 1820, 16th Cong., sess. 1, chap. 113, stat. 1, sec. 4.

50 John Harris, *The Last Slave Ships: New York and the End of the Middle Passage* (New Haven, CT: Yale University Press, 2020), 3, 17; Randy J. Sparks, "Blind Justice: The United States' Failure to Curb the Illegal Slave Trade," *Law and History Review* 35, no. 1 (2017): 53, 56–57.

CHAPTER 2: FREE TRADE

1 William Hutchinson Rowe, *The Maritime History of Maine: Three Centuries of Shipbuilding and Seafaring* (1948; reprint, Gardiner, ME: Harpswell Press, c. 1989), 115, 116.

2 David Carey, Jr., "Comunidad Escondida: Latin American Influences in

Nineteenth- and Twentieth-Century Portland," in *Creating Portland: History and Place in Northern New England*, ed. Joseph A. Conforti (Durham: University of New Hampshire Press, 2005), 95.

3 W. Jeffrey Bolster, *Black Jacks: African American Seamen in the Age of Sail* (Cambridge, MA: Harvard University Press, 1997), 2.

4 *The Portland Directory* (Portland, ME: Coleman, 1830); Earle G. Shettleworth, Jr., and William David Barry, *Mr. Goodhue Remembers Portland: Scenes from the Mid-19th Century* (Augusta: Maine Historic Preservation Commission, 1981), 12.

5 "Collection of the Revenue in Portland and the Site of the New Custom House," *Portland Daily Press*, April 13, 1872, 1.

6 Some estimates of the number of impressed American sailors run as high as 10,000 (William Armstrong Fairburn, *Merchant Sail* [Center Lovell, ME: Fairburn Marine Educational Foundation, 1945–55], 1:621).

7 Kelley Bouchard, "Resonating in Maine History: The War of 1812," *Portland Press Herald*, June 17, 2012; "Impressment of Seamen," *Portland Gazette*, May 13, 1811.

8 W. Jeffrey Bolster, "Letters by African American Sailors, 1799–1814," *William and Mary Quarterly*, 3rd ser., 64, no. 1 (2007): 179, 177.

9 Fairburn, *Merchant Sail*, 1:615.

10 *Newburyport Herald* (MA), July 15, 1808, 3.

11 Charles E. Hill, "James Madison," in *American Secretaries of State and their Diplomacy*, ed. Samuel F. Bemis (New York: Knopf, 1927), 3:135.

12 Rowe, *Maritime History of Maine*, 84.

13 "From the Impartial Observer," *Portland Gazette and Maine Advertiser*, November 21, 1808, 1.

14 Louis Clinton Hatch, ed., *Maine, a History* (New York: American Historical Society, 1919), 1:72.

15 Jeffrey Bolster, "'To Feel Like a Man': Black Seamen in the Northern States, 1800–1860," *Journal of American History* 76 (March 1990): 1184.

16 William Goold, *Portland in the Past with Historical Notes of Old Falmouth* (Portland, ME, 1886), 423–24.

17 Harvey Strum, "Smuggling in Maine during the Embargo and the War of 1812," *Colby Library Quarterly* 19, no. 2 (1983): 90.

18 *Freeman's Friend* (Saco, ME), June 4, 1808, 3.

19 According to John Quincy Adams, the governors of the West Indian islands wrote proclamations during the embargo stating that they would accept U.S. ships without regular papers, thus encouraging smuggling (Frank Lee Benns, "The American Struggle for the British West India Carrying-Trade, 1815–1830," *Indiana University Studies* 10 [March 1923]: 26; John Quincy Adams, *Memoirs of John Quincy Adams, Comprising Portions of His Diary from 1795 to 1848*, ed. Charles Francis Adams [Philadelphia: Lippincott, 1874–77], 3:393).

20 Strum, "Smuggling in Maine," 93.

21 "The Embargo, on New Principles," *Portland Gazette*, January 11, 1808, 1, reprinted from the *Columbian Centinel* (Boston).

22 Kelley Bouchard, "Resonating in Maine History: The War of 1812," *Portland Press Herald*, June 17, 2012.

23 Henry Adams, *The History of the United States of America during the Second Administration of Thomas Jefferson* (New York: Scribner, 1890), 4:277.

24 Paul A. Gilje, "'Free Trade and Sailors' Rights': The Rhetoric of the War of 1812," *Journal of the Early Republic* 30, no. 1 (2010): 14–15.

25 *Berkshire Reporter* (Pittsfield, MA), October 14, 1813, 3.

26 Strum, "Smuggling in Maine," 96.

27 Maine Bureau of Corporations, Elections, and Commissions, "The War of 1812: America's 'Second War for Independence' (1812–1815)," https://www.maine.gov. It's important to note that Caleb Strong, the governor of Massachusetts (and the District of Maine), was against the war and had refused the federal government's offer of troops.

28 Nathaniel G. Jewett, *Portland Directory and Register* (Portland, ME: Todd and Smith, 1823), 22.

29 U.S. Census Bureau, census for Portland, ME (1830), https://www2.census.gov.

30 At trial in the United States, Joshua, Nathaniel, and Paul—all of whom were ultimately embroiled in the case—argued that the insurance covered loss by shipwreck and other natural hazards only, not losses due to piracy. A court ruled for the plaintiff. But in appeal, the verdict was set aside and a new trial called for. What happened at that trial, or whether it was settled out of court, isn't certain. See *Levy et al. v. Merrill et al.*, in Simon Greenleaf, *Cases Argued and Determined in the Supreme Judicial Court in the State of Maine* (Boston: Little, Brown, 1852), 4:156–65.

31 James A. Wombwell, *The Long War against Piracy: Historical Trends* (Fort Leavenworth, KS: Combat Studies Institute Press, 2010), 37.

32 "Particulars of the Massacre of Captain Hilton and Crew," *Bangor Weekly Register*, March 3, 1825, 3.

33 "Pirates," *Aurora and Franklin Gazette* (Philadelphia), August 18, 1824, 2.

34 The Gordons recovered funds for a partial loss only. See *William Gordon v. Massachusetts Fire and Insurance Company*, in Octavius Pickering, *Reports of Cases Argued and Determined in the Supreme Judicial Court of Massachusetts* (Boston: Harrison Gray, 1826), 2:249–55.

35 Jewett, *Portland Directory and Register*, 1823. Although I've located no birth record for Harriet and William's son George, his marriage record, April 1, 1861, lists both of their names (Massachusetts marriage records, 1840–1915, New England Historic Genealogical Society, Boston).

36 Isaac Hull to Samuel Southard, December 21, 1825, in U.S. Navy, *Annual Report of the Secretary of the Navy, 1826*, 19th Cong., 2nd sess., no. 319, 735, https://www.history.navy.mil.

37 Hull to Southard, 735.

38 "A list of merchant vessels boarded by the United States frigate United States, Isaac Hull, commander, during the period from March 30, 1824, to December, 1825," in Hull to Southard, 739.

39 U.S.S. *United States* logbooks, 1823–1827, ms. 1190, J. Y. Joyner Library, East Carolina University, https://digital.lib.ecu.edu.

40 *Richmond Enquirer* (VA), May 29, 1827, 4.

41 Hunter Miller, ed., *Treaties and Other International Acts of the United States of America* (Washington, DC: Government Printing Office, 1933), 3:499.

42 Miller, *Treaties*, 3:487.

43 U.S. Congress, "An Act for the Relief of a Part of the Crew of the Brig *Sarah George*," June 30, 1834, 23rd Cong., sess. 1, chap. 253, stat. J.

44 U.S. House of Representatives, Committee of Ways and Means, report 149, January 8, 1834, 23rd Cong., 1st sess., 2, vol. 260, U.S. Congressional Series (Washington, DC: Government Printing Office, 1834). In these records, Merrill is mistakenly referred to as "Therrill" and is listed as a resident of New York. However, the owner was Eli Merrill of Portland, who may have been a relative of Gordon's brother-in-law, Paul Merrill.

CHAPTER 3: TOWNS DIVIDED

1 William J. Brown, *The Life of William J. Brown of Providence, R.I., with Personal Recollections of Incidents in Rhode Island* (1883; reprint, Durham: University of New Hampshire Press, 2006), 50, 74. For further information on the riot, see Irving H. Bartlett, "The Free Negro in Providence, Rhode Island," *Negro History Bulletin* 14, no. 3 (1950): 52.

2 Douglas Edelstein, "Cincinnati Riots of 1829," *Black Past*, December 4, 2017, https://www.blackpast.org.

3 Stuart C. Henry, "The Lane Rebels: A Twentieth-Century Look," *Journal of Presbyterian History* 49, no. 1 (1978):1.

4 Douglas Edelstein, "Cincinnati Race Riots (1836)," *Black Past*, March 1, 2018, https://www.blackpast.org.

5 Leonard Curry, *The Free Black in Urban America, 1800–1850* (Chicago: University of Chicago Press, 1981), 106.

6 Beverly C. Tomek, "Pennsylvania Hall," *The Encyclopedia of Greater Philadelphia*, https://philadelphiaencyclopedia.org; "People and Events: Pennsylvania Hall, 1838," *Africans in America*, part 4, *Judgment Day*, https://www.pbs.org.

7 Benjamin Quarles, *Black Abolitionists* (New York: Oxford University Press, 1969), 58; Hilary Moss, "'Cast Down on Every Side': The Ill-Fated Campaign to Found an 'African College' in New Haven," in *African American Connecticut Explored*, ed. Elizabeth J. Normen, Katherine J. Harris, Stacey K. Close, William Frank Mitchell, and Olivia White (Middletown, CT: Wesleyan University Press, 2014), 148–54.

8 "Noyes Academy," *Herald of Freedom* (Concord, NH), August 22, 1835.

9 Brown, *Life of William J. Brown*, 25.

10 Michael C. Connolly, "Black Fades to Green: Irish Labor Replaces African-American Labor along a Major New England Waterfront, Portland, Maine, in the Mid-Nineteenth Century," *Colby Quarterly* 37, no.4 (2001): 363.

11 Interview in *Portland Sunday Telegram*, October 18, 1903, reprinted in H. H. Price and Gerald E. Talbot, eds., *Maine's Visible Black History: The First Chronicle of Its People* (Gardiner, ME: Tilbury House, 2006), 147.

12 Marriage record for Reuben Ruby and Jeannette C. Pear [Pierre], October 23, 1821, Maine marriage records, 1713–1922, Maine State Archives, Augusta; Price and Talbot, *Maine's Visible Black History*, 117.

13 *Gazette of Maine* (Portland), September 19, 1826, 2. This letter also appeared in other newspapers. The other co-signers were John Siggs, Caleb Johnson, Clement Thomson, and Job Wentworth.

14 John Neal, "The Abyssinian," *Yankee* (Portland, ME), July 2, 1828, 215.

15 Ephraim Small, "1828 Petition by Ephraim Small to Incorporate the Abyssinian Religious Society" (1828), https://digitalmaine.com.

16 Arron Sturgis, personal communication, September 9, 2021. Sturgis, a specialist in timber-frame construction, worked on restoring the Abyssinian Meeting House.

17 The Abyssinian Meeting House was added to the National Register of Historic Places on February 3, 2006 (U.S. Department of the Interior, National Park Service, National Register Information System ID no. 05001612). See also Julie Larry and Gabrielle Daniello, "History of Portland's India Street Neighborhood," *Portland Brick*, https://www.portlandbrick.org.

18 Death record for William A. Ruby, October 29, 1828, Maine Death Records, 1761–1922, Maine State Archives, Augusta.

19 Randolph Stakeman, "The Black Population of Maine, 1764–1900," *New England Journal of Black Studies*, no. 8 (1989): 29.

20 *The Portland Directory* (Portland, ME: Coleman, 1830), 70.

21 *Portland Weekly Advertiser*, October 29, 1832, 2.

22 "1832 Presidential General Election Results—Maine," *Dave Leip's Atlas of U.S. Elections*, https://uselectionatlas.org.

23 *Weekly Eastern Argus*, November 13, 1832, 4; Van Gosse, *The First Reconstruction: Black Politics in America from the Revolution to the Civil War* (Chapel Hill: University of North Carolina Press, 2021), 207–8.

24 Amos Gerry Beman, "Letter to Rev. James W. C. Pennington," *Colored American* (NY), November 7, 1840.

25 *Portland Daily Advertiser*, July 24, 1834, 2; "List of City Officers," *Portland Weekly Advertiser*, April 12, 1836, 4; April 4, 1837, 3; April 10, 1838, 1.

26 *The Liberator* (Boston), October 20, 1832, 166.

27 Austin Willey, *History of the Antislavery Cause in State and Nation* (Portland, ME: Brown, Thurston and Hoyt; Fogg and Donham, 1886), 45–50.

28 George Thompson to William Lloyd Garrison, October 28, 1834, in *Letters and Addresses by George Thompson during His Mission in the United States* (Boston: Knapp, 1837), 12–14; Willey, *History of the Antislavery Cause in State and Nation*, 53.

29 Willey, *History of the Antislavery Cause in State and Nation*, 58.

30 George Thompson to William Lloyd Garrison, October 27, 1834, in *Letters and Addresses*, 11–16.

31 Ruby was present at the Maine Anti-Slavery Convention ("Maine Anti-Slavery Convention," *The Liberator*, November 1, 1834, 173).

32 Sarah H. Southwick, *Reminiscences of Early Anti-Slavery Days* (Cambridge, MA: Riverside, 1893), 12.

33 Southwick, *Reminiscences*, 13.

34 Lydia Maria Child to Mrs. Ellis Gray Loring, August 15, 1835, in *Letters of Lydia Maria Child with a Biographical Introduction by John G. Whittier and an Appendix by Wendell Phillips* (Boston: Houghton Mifflin, 1883), 15.

35 "The Fanatic Anniversary," *The New York Courier and Enquirer*, May 13, 1835, reprinted in *The Liberator*, May 30, 1835, 85.

36 *Hampshire Republican*, reprinted in *The Liberator*, June 6, 1835, 90.

37 *New Hampshire Gazette*, September 22, 1835, 1.

38 *Liberator*, June 6, 1835, October 24, 1835, December 5, 1835.

39 For an account of Phelps's visit to Portland, see Amos Augustus Phelps to Charlotte Phelps, December 7, 1834, *Digital Commonwealth*, https://www.digitalcommonwealth.org.

40 *The Liberator*, June 13, 1835, 95.

41 *The Liberator*, May 24, 1835, 83; June 13, 1835, 95.

42 *Minutes of the Fifth Annual Convention for the Improvement of the Free People of Colour in the United States Held by Adjournments, in the Wesley Church, Philadelphia, from the First to the Fifth of June, Inclusive, 1835* (Philadelphia: Gibbons, 1835), 8, 2, 11, 14–15, 17–18.

43 *The Liberator*, August 8, 1835, 128.

44 *The Minutes and Proceedings of the First Annual Meeting of the American Moral Reform Society, Held at Philadelphia in the Presbyterian Church in Seventh Street, below Shippen, from the 14th to the 19th of August, 1837* (Philadelphia: Merrihew and Gunn, 1837).

45 *The Colored American*, August 26, 1837, March 29, 1838.

46 *The Liberator*, September 29, 1837, 159.

47 *Eastern Argus*, August 25, 1835, 2.

48 *Portland Daily Advertiser*, August 13, 1835, 2.

49 Louis Clinton Hatch, ed., *Maine: A History* (New York: American Historical Society, 1919), 1:288.

50 *Portland Daily Advertiser*, August 20, 1835, 2.

51 The *Haverhill Gazette* (MA) carried a notice about the mob, but local Portland papers did not (September 24, 1836, 2).

52 John L. Myers, "The Antislavery Agency System in Maine, 1836–1838," *Maine History Journal* 23, no. 2 (1983): 62, 64.

53 "Report of the Maine Anti-Slavery Society Regarding Asking the Mayor of Portland for Protection during an Upcoming Meeting," October 27, 1836, https://www .mainememory.net; Hatch, *Maine*, 1:289.

54 Reuben Ruby to Amos Augustus Phelps, September 29, 1836, *Digital Commonwealth*, https://www.digitalcommonwealth.org. I am grateful to Mary Tibbetts Freeman for noting the existence of this letter during a lecture at the Maine Historical Society, July 22, 2021. See also Mary Tibbetts Freeman, "The Politics of Correspondence: Letter Writing in the Campaign against Slavery in the United States" (PhD diss., Columbia University, 2018).

55 *New-Bedford Mercury*, October 7, 1836, 1; *Weekly Messenger* (Boston), October 5, 1836, 1.

56 On Rogers as a moderator, see Abyssinian Religious Society Records, May 12, 1840, Congregational Library and Archives, https://www.congregational library.org. Jeremiah Rogers appears on the list of attendees of the 1841 Maine State Convention of Colored Citizens, held in Portland ("Minutes of the First Colored Convention, Held in the City of Portland, October 6, 1841," Colored Conventions Project, Digital Records, https://omeka.coloredconventions .org/items/show/1178.

CHAPTER 4: METROPOLIS OF LIBERTY

1 Gordon appears in *Longworth's New York City Directory* for 1838–39 (New York: Longworth, 1839), 277. His indictment, *U.S. v. Nathaniel Gordon* (G. 14, August 1, 1838, Southern District of New York), also describes him as "Nathaniel Gordon of the City and County of New York."

2 Samuel Rezneck, "The Social History of an American Depression, 1837–1843," *American Historical Review* 40, no. 4 (1935): 664.

3 In 1830, Gordon partnered with a New York merchant named Noble K. Walcott to operate a trading business in Manhattan while still living in Portland. *Longworth's American Almanack, New York Register, and City Directory* lists "Wolcott & Gordon, merchants," at 107 Broad Street ([New York: Longworth, 1835], 722). Wolcott's residence was listed at the same address. In 1836, Gordon parted from Wolcott and went into business for himself. On the dissolution of the partnership, see advertisement, *New York Journal of Commerce*, November 3, 1836, 3.

4 *Longworth's American Almanack, New York Register, and City Directory* (New York: Longworth, 1838–39), 277; advertisement, *Northern Journal* (Lowville, NY), July 5, 1838.

5 According to the June 25, 1838, issue of the *Evening Post*, the molasses was intended for the firm of Dunlap and Jewett in Portland.

6 *Mirror of Liberty* (NY), January 1, 1839, 4. In discussions of the *Dunlap* case, several historians have mistaken Gordon II for his son, but the latter was only twelve years old when the *Dunlap* was seized in 1838.

7 *Evening Post*, July 17, 1838, 3; *U.S. v. Nathaniel Gordon*, August 1, 1838.

8 *Evening Post*, July 28, 1838, 4.

9 The other members of the committee were William Johnston, Robert Brown, George R. Barker, and J. W. Higgins (New York Committee of Vigilance, *The First Annual Report of the New York Committee of Vigilance: For the Year 1837, Together with Important Facts Relative to Their Proceedings* . . . [New York: Piercy and Reed, 1837], 3).

10 New York Committee of Vigilance, *First Annual Report*, 3.

11 Slaveholders were permitted to bring enslaved individuals into New York for nine months; once they overstayed the limit, those individuals were legally free. The nine-month limit was repealed in 1841.

12 Steven H. Jaffe, "David Ruggles' Committee of Vigilance," *Lapham's Quarterly*, May 21, 2018, https://www.laphamsquarterly.org.

13 New York Committee of Vigilance, *First Annual Report*, 8.

14 *Mirror of Liberty*, January 1, 1839, 26–28.

15 "Overdoing a Business: Kidnapping a Brig and Captain," *New York Express*, August 8, 1838, reprinted in *The Mirror of Liberty*, January 1, 1839, 26–28.

16 "Slave Case," *Mirror of Liberty*, August, 1, 1838, 12; *Columbian Centinel*, August 4, 1838, 4.

17 *Mirror of Liberty*, August 1, 1838, 12.

18 *American and Commercial Daily Advertiser* (Baltimore), December 22, 1836, 2.

19 Graham Russell Gao Hodges, *David Ruggles: A Radical Black Abolitionist and the Underground Railroad in New York City* (Chapel Hill: University of North Carolina Press, 2010), 98.

20 *New York Herald*, February 20, 1837, 2.

21 "United States Court, Aug. 22. Charge of Kidnapping Africans," *New York Morning Herald*, August 24, 1838.

22 Joanne Pope Melish, *Disowning Slavery: Gradual Emancipation and "Race" in New England, 1780–1860* (Ithaca, NY: Cornell University Press, 1998), 102.

23 *Evening Post*, September 5, 1838, 2.

24 "The Kidnapping Case," *Commercial Advertiser* (NY), September 5, 1838, 2; "The Kidnapping Case," *Liberty Advocate* (MS), October 25, 1838.

25 U.S. Congress, "An Act in Amendment of the Acts for the Punishment of Offences against the United States" (1835), 23rd Cong., sess. 2, chap. 40, stat. 2, sec. 3.

26 *New York Morning Herald*, November 18, 1837, 2.

27 *New York Morning Herald*, November 18, 1837, 2.

28 *New York Morning Herald*, July 22, 1839, 3.

29 *Lincoln Telegraph* (Bath, ME), August 15, 1839, 2.

30 "Report of the Secretary of the Navy to the President of the United States, December, 1842," *Alexandria Gazette and Virginia Advertiser*, December 13, 1842, 2.

31 *North Carolina Standard* (Raleigh, NC), September 7, 1842, 4.

32 "Murder in Africa," *Baltimore Sun*, reprinted in *New York Daily Tribune*, August 24, 1842, 3.

33 *Vermont Telegraph*, August 31, 1842, 199.

34 "From Africa," *New York Herald*, October 12, 1842, 3.

35 Matthew C. Perry to Abel P. Upshur, August 3, 1843, in U.S. Senate, *Public Documents*, 28th Cong., 2nd sess., no. 150, 10, https://www.govinfo.gov.

36 "Extract from a Letter," *Washington Globe*, March 14, 1844, 3; Harry Allanson Ellsworth, *One Hundred Eighty Landings of United States Marines* (Washington, DC: U.S. Marine Corps, History and Museums Division, 1974), 5–7.

37 The 1840 federal census places Gordon II back in Portland, and Portland city directories show Nathaniel as a steady presence throughout the 1840s (U.S. Census Bureau, census for Portland, ME [1840], https://www2.census.gov; Harlow Harris, *Portland Directory for the Year 1841* [Portland, 1841], 40; S. B. Beckett, *Portland Reference Book and City Directory for 1847–8* [Portland, 1847], 57).

38 John Harris discusses the influx of Spanish and Portuguese slave-trade investors into New York during the 1850s (*The Last Slave Ships* [New Haven, CT: Yale University Press, 2020], 47, 91).

39 *National Advocate* (NY), July 14, 1826, 2.

40 Jeffrey Bolster, *Black Jacks: African American Seamen in the Age of Sail* (Cambridge, MA: Harvard University Press, 1997), 183, 185; Leslie M. Harris, *In the Shadow of Slavery: African Americans in New York City, 1626–1863* (Chicago: University of Chicago Press, 2003), 238.

41 *Weekly Anglo-African* (NY), September 17, 1859, 2.

42 Frederick Douglass, *Narrative of the Life of Frederick Douglass, an American Slave* (1845; reprint, New York: Penguin, 2014), 101–3.

43 *The Portland Directory* for 1837 lists Ruby as "hack driver" on Federal Street ([Portland, Maine: Shirley, 1837], 65).

44 Randolph P. Dominic, Jr., "Down from the Balcony: The Abyssinian Congregational Church of Portland, Maine" (PhD diss., University of Maine, 1982), 11. Niles, however, was able to recover the property in 1839 (real property records, Cumberland County, Maine Registry of Deeds , bk. 00166, 2).

45 *Reuben Ruby v. Abyssinian Religious Society of Portland*, April 1839, Maine Supreme Judicial Court, 15 Me. 306, https://cite.case.law.

46 *Reuben Ruby v. Abyssinian Religious Society of Portland*.

47 Cindy R. Lobel, "'Out to Eat': The Emergence and Evolution of the Restaurant in

Nineteenth-Century New York City," *Winterthur Portfolio*, 44 (Summer–Autumn 2010): 214.

48 William Grimes, *Appetite City: A Culinary History of New York*, (New York: North Point, 2009), 62.

49 "Adventures of a Gentleman in Search of a Dinner," *Broadway Journal*, June 21, 1845, 387.

50 "Downing's Oyster House," *Mapping the African American Past*, http://maap.columbia.edu.

51 Thomas Longworth, *Longworth's American Almanac, New-York Register, and City Directory* (New York, 1822–23), 172.

52 Francis Lam, "How Thomas Downing Became the Black Oyster King of New York," *The Splendid Table*, March 14, 2018, https://www.splendidtable.org.

53 While Black male New Yorkers could vote if they owned property, the property requirement was more stringent for Blacks than for whites, allowing only a few individuals to vote.

54 *Emancipator* (NY), June 3, 1841, 19.

55 *The Colored American* (NY), August 12, 1837, 3.

56 *Emancipator*, June 3, 1841, 19; *New-York Observer*, July 11, 1840, 5.

57 Benjamin Quarles, *Black Abolitionists* (New York: Oxford University Press, 1969), 100.

58 *The Colored American*, February 6, 1841, 2.

59 Eric Foner, *Gateway to Freedom: The Hidden History of the Underground Railroad* (New York: Norton, 2015), xiv; David F. White, "Reliving Walt Whitman's New York," *The New York Times*, September 10, 1976.

60 Foner, *Gateway to Freedom*, 89.

61 Leonard P. Curry, *The Free Black in Urban America, 1800–1850: The Shadow of the Dream* (Chicago: University of Chicago Press, 1981), 218. For a Black population estimate, see Carla L. Peterson, "Answers about Black Life in 19th-Century New York, Part II," *New York Times*, February 11, 2021.

62 *Colored American*, November 21, 1840, 3.

63 Rhoda Golden Freeman, *The Free Negro in New York City in the Era before the Civil War* (New York: Garland, 1994), 101; Henry Highland Garnet, "Reception of Petitions," *Colored American*, February 13, 1841, 1.

64 *Colored American*, July 25, 1840, 3; *The Liberator*, May 1, 1841, 122.

65 *The Liberator*, April 9, 1841, 59.

66 Leslie M. Harris, *In the Shadow of Slavery: African Americans in New York City, 1626–1863* (Chicago: University of Chicago Press, 2003), 75.

67 Hodges, *David Ruggles*, 43, 60.

68 Harriet Jacobs, *Incidents in the Life of a Slave Girl* (Boston, 1861), 287.

69 *The Emancipator*, March 2, 1837, 175.

70 Freeman, *The Free Negro in New York City*, 53; *Emancipator*, November 2, 1837, 104.

71 David Ruggles, "A Boy Kidnapped," *Colored American*, September 16, 1837, 3.

72 "A Northern freeman enslaved by northern hands," *American Anti-Slavery Almanac for 1838* (New York, 1838), 19.

73 "Kidnapping," *Mirror of Liberty*, August 1, 1838, 10.

74 Solomon Northup, *Twelve Years a Slave, Narrative of Solomon Northup, a Citizen of New-York, Kidnapped in Washington City in 1841, and Rescued in 1853, from a Cotton Plantation Near the Red River, in Louisiana* (Auburn, NY, 1853).

75 *New York Spectator*, July 31, 1837, 3.

76 *The Colored American*, November 2, 1839, 3.

77 *The Colored American*, May 20, 1837, 3.

78 Hodges, *David Ruggles*, 87–88.

79 "Self Interest," *Freedom's Journal*, November 7, 1828, 259.

80 *Charleston Courier* (SC), July 7, 1840, 3.

81 *Charleston Courier* (SC), May 20, 1842, 2.

82 "A Member of the Bar," *Colored American*, July 3, 1841, 3.

83 U.S. Census Bureau, census for New York City, Ward 2 (1840), https://www.census.gov.

84 Foner, *Gateway to Freedom*, 45–46.

85 Carl Moneyhon, *George T. Ruby, Champion of Equal Rights in Reconstruction Texas* (Fort Worth: Texas Christian University Press, 2020), 8; U.S. Census Bureau, census for Portland, ME (1850), https://www.census.gov.

86 "Loss of the Steamer Atlantic," *Portland Transcript*, December 5, 1846, 7.

87 *Doggett's New York City Directory for 1842 and 1843* (New York, 1842), 278; *Doggett's New York City Directory for 1843 and 1844* (New York, 1843), 293; *Doggett's New York City Directory for 1846 and 1847* (New York, 1846), 339.

88 *New York Herald*, July 20, 1845, 3.

89 Stefan C. Schatzki, "Cholera," *American Journal of Roentgenology* 204 (March 2015): 685–86.

CHAPTER 5: GOLD RUSH

1 While most nineteenth-century mariners and investors believed that a single slave ship could make a man's fortune, Robert Paul Thomas and Richard Nelson Bean contend that there was "zero *average* economic profit for the British slave-trading industry as a whole" ("The Fishers of Men: The Profits of the Slave Trade," *Journal of Economic History* 34, no. 4 [1974]: 897).

2 William Willis, *History of Portland*, 2nd ed. (Portland: Bailey and Noyes, 1865), 731.

3 Ralph Waldo Emerson, "Address on the Anniversary of Emancipation in the British West Indies, 1844," in *The Portable Emerson*, ed. Jeffrey S. Cramer (New York: Penguin, 2014), 462.

4 The duplex still stands at 126 and 128 Danforth Street.

5 "The Slaver Spitfire," *African Repository and Colonial Journal* 21, no. 7 (1845): 203–4.

6 Bruce L. Mouser, "Women Slavers of Guinea-Conakry," in *Women and Slavery in Africa*, ed. Claire C. Robertson and Martin A. Klein (Portsmouth, NH: Heinemann, 1997), 330. According to Mouser, Mary Faber was likely born of Black parents from Freetown, Nova Scotia (329).

7 *Niles' National Register* (Baltimore), September 20, 1845, 40.

8 "The Slaver Spitfire," 204.

9 "A Slaver Captured," *The Liberator*, May 23, 1845.

10 John Newton, *Thoughts upon the African Slave Trade* (London, 1788), 17–18.

11 "The Slaver Spitfire," 204.

12 "The Slaver Spitfire," 204.

13 "The Slaver Spitfire," 203; *Decisions of Hon. Peleg Sprague, in Admiralty and Maritime*

Causes in the District Court of the United States for the District of Massachusetts (Philadelphia: Johnson, 1861) 1:110–11.

14 "Capture of a Slaver," *Corrector* (Sag Harbor, NY), May 21, 1845, 2; "Seized on Suspicion of Being Intended for the Slave Trade," *Brooklyn Daily Eagle and Kings County Democrat*, September 13, 1844, 2.

15 "Case of the Spitfire," *Daily Union* (Washington, DC), June 6, 1845, 2, reprinted from the *Boston Morning Post*.

16 "The Slaver Spitfire," 202.

17 "Capture of a Slaver," *Evansville Journal* (IN), May 29, 1845, 3; "A Slaver Captured," *The Liberator*, May 23, 1845, 83.

18 "The Slaver Spitfire," 199–200, 203.

19 "The Slaver Spitfire," 202.

20 *Niles' National Register*, September 20, 1845, 40.

21 "Case of Flowery," in *The Law Reporter*, ed. Peleg W. Chandler (Boston: Weeks, Jordan, 1846), 8:141.

22 Mouser, "Women Slavers of Guinea-Conakry," 332.

23 *Daily Atlas* (Boston), April 9, 1845, 2.

24 Leonardo Marques, *The United States and the Transatlantic Slave Trade to the Americas, 1776–1867* (New Haven, CT: Yale University Press, 2016), 204; Thomas Savage to T. H. Hatch, "list of vessels transferred at Havana, 1857," August 7, 1857, in U.S. House of Representatives, *African Slave Trade, Message from the President of the United States*, 36th Cong., 2nd sess., exec. doc. 7, 72, https://www.govinfo.gov. The ships were the *Minnetonka*, the *J. H. Record*, the *R. B. Lawton*, the *Niagara*, and the *Braman*.

25 U.K. House of Commons, *Accounts and Papers of the House of Commons*, vol. 61, *3 Dec. 1857–2 Aug. 1858* (London: Harrison, 1858), 39.

26 Thomas Savage, "List of vessels, which, under American colors, are known or believed to have engaged in or been fitted out for the slave trade," report to U.S. State Department, dispatch no. 51, August 7, 1857, in U.S. House of Representatives, *Executive Documents*, 36th Cong., 2nd sess. (Washington, DC: Government Printing Office, 1861), 9:201–2.

27 Marques, *The United States and the Transatlantic Slave Trade*, 204.

28 Marques, *The United States and the Transatlantic Slave Trade*, 143.

29 William Armstrong Fairburn, *Merchant Sail* (Center Lovell, ME: Fairburn Marine Educational Foundation 1945–55), 2:936; Nathan Lipfert, "Two Centuries of Maine Shipbuilding," lecture, Tate House Museum, Portland, ME, September 14, 2022.

30 U.S. Census Bureau, "State of Maine: Table No. 1—Population by Age and Sex" (1860), http://www2.census.gov.

31 *Niles' National Register*, August 9, 1845, 362.

32 Fairburn, *Merchant Sail*, 2:923.

33 *Daily Argus*, December 18, 1847, 2. The account also appeared in the *Boston Post* (December 21, 1847) and the *New York Herald* (December 23, 1847).

34 *New York Herald*, December 13, 1861, 1.

35 *The New York Times*, February 22, 1862, 8.

36 James A. Rawley, *London: Metropolis of the Slave Trade* (Columbia: University of Missouri Press, 2003), 154–55.

37 Gorham Parks to David Tod, January 29, 1850, in U.S. Senate, *Executive Documents*, vol. 2, *Executive Document no. 6B*, 31st Cong., sess. 2 (Washington, DC: Union Office, 1851), 35, 32.

38 James K. Polk, "Fourth Annual Message to Congress," December 5, 1848, The American Presidency Project, University of California Santa Barbara, https://www .presidency.ucsb.edu/documents/fourth-annual-message-6.

39 Polk, "Fourth Annual Message."

40 Rudolph M. Lapp argues that the sea route was the most secure for black gold seekers (*Blacks in Gold Rush California* [New Haven, CT: Yale University Press, 1977], 38).

41 John Haskell Kemble, "The Genesis of the Pacific Mail Steamship Company," *California Historical Society Quarterly* 13, no. 3 (1934): 249.

42 Although the list of passengers for February 2, 1849, doesn't include Ruby's name ("Ho! for California," *New York Herald*, February 2, 1849, 2), he was interviewed for a story in the *New-York Daily Tribune* that states he "left here in the steamer Falcon on the 1st of February last" (August 17, 1849, 4).

43 W. Jeffrey Bolster, *Black Jacks: African American Seamen in the Age of Sail* (Cambridge, MA: Harvard University Press, 1997), 194, 199; *The Negro Law of South Carolina, Collected and Digested by John Belton O'Neall* (Columbia, SC, 1848), 2nd sec. 7, stat. 471, sec. 59, 15.

44 Charles A. Ranlett to Robert C. Winthrop, August 29, 1850, in U.S. Congress, *Appendix to the Congressional Globe*, 31st Cong., 1st sess. (Washington, DC: Rivers, 1850), vol. 22, part 2, 1654–55.

45 Bayard Taylor, *Eldorado: Or, Adventures in the Path of Empire* (New York: Putnam, 1882), 4–5.

46 *Green-Mountain Freeman* (Montpelier, VT), January 4, 1849.

47 *New York Herald*, January 28, 1849, 3.

48 Charles R. Schultz, "The Gold Rush Voyage of the Ship *Pacific*: A Study in Ship Management," *American Neptune* 53 (Summer 1993): 195.

49 Augustus Campbell and Colin D. Campbell, "Crossing the Isthmus of Panama, 1849: The Letters of Dr. Augustus Campbell," *California History* 78, no. 4 (1999–2000): 230.

50 Henry Tracy to M. O. Roberts, February 24, 1851, in John Haskell Kemble, "The Gold Rush by Panama, 1848–1851," *Pacific Historical Review* 18, no. 1 (1949): 51, 50.

51 Kemble, "The Gold Rush by Panama," 51.

52 Taylor, *Eldorado*, 14.

53 Kemble, "The Gold Rush by Panama," 51.

54 Campbell, "Crossing the Isthmus," 232.

55 Campbell, "Crossing the Isthmus," 235.

56 Campbell, "Crossing the Isthmus," 235.

57 Campbell, "Crossing the Isthmus," 236, 235.

58 Taylor, *Eldorado*, 32.

59 J. H. Carson, *Early Recollections of the Mines, and a Description of the Great Tulare Valley*, published to accompany the steamer edition of the *San Joaquim Republican* (Stockton, CA: 1852), 8.

60 Theodore Taylor Johnson, *Sights in the Gold Region, and Scenes by the Way* (New York: Baker and Scribner, 1849), 109–10.

61 Theodore Henry Hittel, *History of California* (San Francisco: Stone, 1897) 3:118–19.

62 [S. Shufelt], *A Letter from a Gold Miner: Placerville, California, October, 1850*, intro. by Robert Glass Cleland (San Marino, CA: Friends of the Huntington Library, 1944), http://www.loc.gov.

63 [Shufelt], *A Letter.*
64 *Alta California,* August 1, 1850, 6. The riot took place on July 15, 1849.
65 "Foreign Miners' Tax Documents, 1850–1867," MS 3481, Archives of California, http://www.oac.cdlib.org.
66 "California Gold," *New-York Daily Tribune,* August 17, 1849, 4.
67 *New-York Daily Tribune,* November 21, 1849, 1.
68 Samuel L. Davis, letter to the editor, dated December 30, 1849, *Liberator,* February 15, 1850.
69 *Portland Daily Advertiser,* November 27, 1849, 2, reprinted from the *Bangor Whig* (ME).
70 U.S. Census Bureau, census for Portland, ME (1850), https://www2.census.gov.
71 *Daily Crescent* (New Orleans), March 23, 1849, 2; John C. Pinheiro, "James K. Polk: Life after the Presidency," UVA Miller Center, https://millercenter.org; James K. Polk, diary entry, June 1, 1849, in *The Diary of James K. Polk during His Presidency, 1845 to 1849,* ed. Milo Milton Quaife (Chicago: McClurg, 1910), 4:439.
72 Historians have posited that Taylor died of heat stroke, gastroenteritis, or poisoning, but cholera remains a plausible cause (Scott Bomboy, "Zachary Taylor's Shocking Death amid the Slavery Expansion Crisis," *Constitution Daily,* October 2, 2014, https://constitutioncenter.org).
73 Joseph P. Byrne, ed., *Encyclopedia of Pestilence, Pandemics, and Plagues* (Westport, CT: Greenwood, 2008), 1:100, 101; G. F. Pyle, "Diffusion of Cholera in the United States in the Nineteenth Century," *Geographical Analysis* 1, no. 1 (1969): 65, 67.
74 *Gloucester Telegraph* (MA), June 9, 1849, 2; *Maine Democrat,* July 3, 1849, 3.

CHAPTER 6: FUGITIVES

1 Nathaniel Gordon, transfer of property to Nathaniel Gordon, Jr., March 31, 1849, real property records, Cumberland County, bk. 00216, 14, Maine Registry of Deeds; Nathaniel Gordon, Jr., transfer of property to Mary Gordon, April 2, 1849, real property records, Cumberland County, bk. 00216, 17, Maine Registry of Deeds.
2 "The Case of the Slave Captain Nathaniel Gordon—A Sketch of His Life—Feeling in Portland about His Execution, Etc.," *New York Herald,* December 13, 1861, 1. On Gordon III's departure to California, see *Portland Transcript,* June 23, 1849, 6.
3 Mary Gordon, transfer of property to James M. Tufts, December 3, 1850, real property records, Cumberland County, bk. 00227, 53, Maine Registry of Deeds; Nathaniel Gordon to Charles Q. Clapp, foreclosure notice, June 14, 1854, real property records, Cumberland County, bk. 00250, 507, Maine Registry of Deeds.
4 *Daily Alta California,* June 3, 1851, 3.
5 "Ship Registers of the District of Newburyport, 1789–1870, Compiled from the Newburyport Custom House Records Now in Possession of the Essex Institute," *Historical Collections of the Essex Institute, 1934–04* 70, no. 2 (1934): 194; Ebenezer Mack Treman and Murray E. Poole, *The History of the Treman, Tremain, Trueman Family in America* (Ithaca, NY: Press of the *Ithaca Democrat,* 1901), 1:423–24; Ron Soodalter, *Hanging Captain Gordon: The Life and Trial of an American Slave Trader* (New York: Washington Square Press, 2004), 193–94.

6 The *Camargo* arrived in Río de Janeiro from California on November 20, 1851 *(New York Herald*, January 10, 1852, 8).

7 Brazil outlawed the trade in kidnapped Africans in 1831, but that law was often flouted. In 1850, the Eusébio de Queiroz Law strengthened penalties against the trade. Brazil did not outlaw slavery itself until 1888.

8 Robert Schenk to Daniel Webster, April 26, 1852, in U.S. Senate, Executive Document 47, 33rd Cong., 1st sess., item 45, 10–11, https://www.govinfo.gov.

9 Leonardo Marques, "The Contraband Slave Trade to Brazil and the Dynamics of US Participation, 1831–1856," *Journal of Latin American Studies* 47, no. 4 (2015): 680.

10 "Congo Slavers," *Nautical Magazine and Naval Chronicle for 1853* (January): 55. Jonathan W. White argues that there is no proof that Oaksmith was seeking to transport and enslave Africans on this voyage (*Shipwrecked: A True Civil War Story of Mutinies, Jailbreaks, Blockade-Running, and the Slave Trade* [Lanham, MD: Rowman and Littlefield, 2023], 42–43). Still, Henry Southern's letter, as quoted in the text (and cited above), suggests otherwise.

11 U.K. House of Commons, *Report from the Select Committee on Slave Trade Treaties: Together with the Proceedings of the Committee, Great Britain, Parliament, House of Commons, Select Committee on Treaties and Engagements between Great Britain, Spain and Portugal Respecting the Slave Trade* (London, c. 1853), 209–10.

12 Carlos Haag, "Made in U.S.A.: Trafficking, the Search for the 'Camargo,' One of the Many American Slave Ships That Came to Brazil," *Revista Pesquisa* 156 (February 2009), https://revistapesquisa.fapesp.br.

13 Paulino Jose Soares de Souza to Robert Schenk, February 1, 1853, in U.S. Senate, Executive Document 47, 33rd Cong., 1st sess., item B45, 12, https://www.govinfo.gov.

14 Robert Schenk to Edward Everett, January 14, 1853, in U.S. Senate, Executive Document 47, 33rd Cong., 1st sess., item 45, 11, https://www.govinfo.gov.

15 Leonardo Marques, *The United States and the Transatlantic Slave Trade to the Americas, 1776–1867* (New Haven, CT: Yale University Press, 2016), 182.

16 Marques, *The United States and the Transatlantic Slave Trade*, 196.

17 Marriage record of Nathaniel Gordon and Elizabeth Kinnay, March 28, 1855, Massachusetts Vital Records, 1840–1911, New England Historic Genealogical Society, Boston.

18 Birth record of Nathaniel E. Gordon, April 28, 1857, Cape Elizabeth, Maine Birth Records, 1715–1922, Maine State Archives, Augusta.

19 *New York Herald*, February 18, 1859, 5; *Daily Southern Reveille* (Port Gibson, MS), February 25, 1859, 2.

20 "Names of Vessels Escaping from the Congo River between April, 1859 and February, 1860," *African Repository* 36 (1860): 337.

21 Soodalter, *Hanging Captain Gordon*, 18–19.

22 See, for example, Benjamin Schneider, "It Happened Here: A History of Slavery in California," *SF Weekly*, February 4, 2021; and Kevin Waite, "The Slave South in the Far West: California, the Pacific, and Proslavery Visions of Empire" (PhD diss., University of Pennsylvania, 2016).

23 U.S. Constitution, art. 4, sec. 2, http://www.constitutioncenter.org. This clause is now obsolete.

24 U.S. Congress, [Compromise of 1850], *An Act to amend, and supplementary to, the Act entitled "An Act respecting Fugitives from Justice, and Persons escaping from the*

Service of their Masters," approved February twelfth, one thousand seven hundred and ninety-three, secs 5, 7, https://www.archives.gov.

25 U.S. Congress, [Compromise of 1850], sec. 6.

26 Carol Wilson, *Freedom at Risk: The Kidnapping of Free Blacks in America, 1780–1865* (Lexington: University Press of Kentucky, 1994), 7, 54.

27 Daniel Webster, speech, March 7, 1850, U.S. Senate, http://www.ushistory.org.

28 Theodore Parker, "Discourse Occasioned by the Death of Daniel Webster," in *The Collected Works of Theodore Parker*, ed. Frances Power Cobbe (London: Trubner, 1865), 11:98; Horace Mann, *The Life and Works of Horace Mann by his Wife*, ed. Mary Mann (Boston: Fuller, 1865–68), 1:293.

29 Ralph Waldo Emerson, "Address to the Citizens of Concord," May 3, 1851 in R.W. Emerson, "The Fugitive Slave Law," *Miscellanies*, http://www.emersoncentral .com; "1850, Rev. Jermain Wesley Loguen, 'I Won't Obey the Fugitive Slave Law,'" *Black Past*, January 24, 2007, http://www.blackpast.org; *Frederick Douglass' Paper* (Rochester, NY), April 6, 1855, 1.

30 Joanne Pope Melish, *Disowning Slavery: Gradual Emancipation and "Race" in New England, 1780–1860* (Ithaca: Cornell University Press, 1998), 267; Martin Robison Delany, *The Condition, Elevation, Emigration, and Destiny of the Colored People of the United States, Politically Considered* (Philadelphia, 1852), 155.

31 "Fugitive Slave Law," *Portland Weekly Advertiser*, October 15, 1850, 2.

32 "Meeting in Portland," *Liberator*, November 1, 1850, 176.

33 "Meeting in Portland," 176.

34 Barbara McCaskill, introduction, in *Running a Thousand Miles for Freedom*, by William Craft and Ellen Craft (1860; reprint, Athens: Brown Thrasher and University of Georgia Press, 1999), xi.

35 Craft and Craft, *Running a Thousand Miles for Freedom*, 62.

36 S. T. Pickard to Wilbur H. Siebert, November 18, 1893, Wilbur H. Siebert Underground Railroad Collection, Ohio History Collection, http://www.ohiomemory .org. According to Siebert, "Mrs. [Lydia Neal] Dennett harbored runaway slaves, as did also Nathan Winslow and General Samuel Fessenden." Nathan's wife, Comfort Winslow, was equally involved in these activities (Wilbur H. Siebert, *The Underground Railroad from Slavery to Freedom* [New York: Macmillan, 1898], 133–34). Charlotte Thomas, in an interview, later recalled that Lydia Neal Dennett had brought the Crafts to the Thomas family home in Portland and that her mother, Elizabeth Widgery Thomas, and General Samuel Fessenden had put them on board a Grand Trunk Railway train to Canada (L.C. Bateman, "Portland and the Anti-Slavery Movement," in *A Distant War Comes Home: Maine in the Civil War Era*, ed. Donald A. Beattie, Rodney Cole, and Charles Waugh [Camden, ME: Downeast Books, 1996], 13). However, the Crafts' book suggests that "Daniel Oliver" harbored them and put them on a ship to Nova Scotia, not onto a train.

37 Obituary of Lydia Neal Dennett, *Portland Daily Press*, June 7, 1881, 3.

38 Frederick Douglass, *The Frederick Douglass Papers*, ser. 3, *Correspondence, 1853–1865* (New Haven, CT: Yale University Press, 2018), 2:211.

39 Sue McNelly, "Biographical Sketch of Lydia Louisa Neal Dennett," *Alexander Street*, https://documents.alexanderstreet.com.

40 *Eastern Times* (Bath, ME), November 28, 1850, 3.

41 William Andrews, "'12 Years' Gets Story Right but Context, Some Details May Be Off," *All Things Considered*, December 23, 2013.

42 Public Broadcasting System, "People and Ideas: Civil War and Reconstruction," in "God in America," *American Experience*, https://www.pbs.org.

43 John Andrew Jackson, *The Experience of a Slave in South Carolina* (London: Passmore and Alabaster, 1862), 32; Susanna Ashton, "A Genuine Article," *Common Place* 13 (Summer 2013): 4.

44 Bob Greene, "On the Record: A Look at Early Portland and a First Family," in *Maine's Visible Black History: The First Chronicle of Its People*, ed. H. H. Price and Gerald E. Talbot (Gardiner, ME: Tilbury House, 2006), 44.

45 "The Underground Railroad," in *Maine's Visible Black History*, 255; *Portland Daily Press*, August 18, 1880.

46 "The Underground Railroad," *Maine's Visible Black History*, 256.

47 Sarah H. Southwick, *Reminiscences of Early Anti-Slavery Days* (Cambridge, MA: Riverside, 1893), 6.

48 Austin Willey, *The History of the Antislavery Cause in State and Nation* (Portland, ME: Brown, Thurston, and Hoyt, Fogg and Donham, 1886), 58–59.

49 Context suggests that the fugitive arrived at Ropes's home sometime during the 1830s. In 1830, Ruby was living on Preble Street (*The Portland Directory* [Portland: Coleman,1830], 70). By 1837, Ruby was living on Beaver Street between Congress and Free Streets (*The Portland Directory* [Portland: Shirley, 1837], 65).

50 See Maine Freedom Trail marker "Home of Deacon Brown Thurston," located at 32 Union Street in Portland, erected in 2007 by Maine Freedom Trails.

51 Neal Dow, *Reminiscences of Neal Dow: Recollections of Eighty Years* (Portland, ME: *Evening Express* Publishing Company, 1898), 22–23.

52 Dow, *Reminiscences*, 306.

53 "The Underground Railroad," *Maine's Visible Black History*, 255. The stowaway arrived on the *Albion Cooper* in 1857.

54 Bateman, "Portland and the Anti-Slavery Movement," 13–14.

55 Willey, *History of the Anti-Slavery Cause*, 80.

56 Bateman, "Portland and the Anti-Slavery Movement," 13.

57 Southwick, *Reminiscences*, 39.

58 Ruby stated on October 10, 1854, that his domicile was Butte County, California. He appeared before a justice of the peace in Butte County to sign documents giving Charles Pierre power of attorney to sell a house on Sumner (now Newbury) Street (real property records, Cumberland County, bk. 00258, 143, bk. 00256, 410, Maine Registry of Deeds).

59 George C. Mansfield, *Butte, the Story of a California County* (Oroville, CA: *Oroville Register*, 1919), 14.

60 For Ruby's return to Maine, see Reuben Ruby to Joel Allen, January 29, 1857, real property records, Cumberland County, bk. 00277, 382, Maine Registry of Deeds. An advertisement in the *Portland Weekly Advertiser* (March 23, 1858) shows that he was working in a Portland restaurant. On Ruby's mortgage, see Reuben Ruby to Joel Allen, October 10, 1854, real property records, Cumberland County, bk. 00256, 410, Maine Registry of Deeds. A note in the margin confirms that the mortgage was paid off in September 1858.

61 "The Supreme Court of the United States," *Evening Post* (NY), March 7, 1857, 2.

62 "Dred Scott's Fight for Freedom, 1846–1857," *Africans in America*, part 4, https://www.pbs.org.

63 J. H. Van Evrie, *The Dred Scott Decision: Opinion of Chief Justice Taney* (New York: Van Evrie, Horton, and Company, 1860), 17, 19.

64 *New-York Daily Tribune*, March 7, 1857, 6, 5.

65 *National Era* (Washington, DC), March 12, 1857, 42.

66 *Baltimore Sun*, March 9, 1857, 2.

67 *Richmond Enquirer*, March 10, 1857, 3; March 13, 1857, 3.

68 Abraham Lincoln, speech in Springfield, IL, June 26, 1857, in "Abraham Lincoln, the *Dred Scott* Decision, and Slavery," March 15, 2012, *BlackPast*, https://www.blackpast.org.

69 *Liberator*, August 27, 1858, 183.

70 *The Principia* (NY), March 24, 1860, 147; *Douglass Monthly* (April 1860): 251.

71 Maine Senate, *Report of the Committee on Slavery*, 37th leg. (Augusta, 1858), 1.

72 Jerry R. Desmond, "The Attempt to Repeal Maine's Personal Liberty Laws," *Maine History*, 37, no. 4 (1998): 201.

73 *Union and Eastern Journal*, August 21, 1857, 3.

74 Frederick Douglass to Lydia Neal Dennett, April 17, 1857, in *The Frederick Douglass Papers Project*, vol. 2, *Correspondence*, https://frederickdouglasspapersproject.com.

75 Frederick Douglass, "Speech on the Dred Scott Decision" (May 1857), *Teaching American History*, https://teachingamericanhistory.org.

CHAPTER 7: FREEBOOTERS

1 *Weekly Trinity Journal* (Weaverville, CA), March 29, 1862, 4.

2 "The Case of the Slave Captain Nathaniel Gordon—A Sketch of His Life—Feeling in Portland about His Execution, Etc.," *New York Herald*, December 13, 1861, 1.

3 *New York Herald*, April 20, 1860, 8.

4 *New York Herald*, November 11, 1861, 2.

5 "The Case of Gordon," *New York Times*, February 21, 1862, 5.

6 John Seys to R. R. Gurley, August 28, 1860, *African Repository*, 26, no. 11 (1860): 321–22.

7 John Seys to Jacob Thompson, October 31, 1860, and John Seys to Isaac Toucey, October 26, 1860, in U.S. House of Representatives, Executive Document 28, 37th Cong., 3rd sess., 2–3, 3–4, https://www.govinfo.gov.

8 Seys to Toucey, 4.

9 "Execution of Captain Gordon," *Evening Post* (NY), February 21, 1862, 3.

10 John Harris, *The Last Slave Ships: New York and the End of the Middle Passage* (New Haven, CT: Yale University Press, 2020), 22; Leonardo Marques, *The United States and the Transatlantic Slave Trade to the Americas, 1776–1867* (New Haven, CT: Yale University Press, 2016), 204, 246.

11 *The New York Times*, February 21, 1862, 5.

12 Charles Dickens, *American Notes for General Circulation*, ed. David Price (London: Chapman and Hall, 1913), 67.

13 New York City Correction History Society, "A Tale of the Tombs," http://www.correctionhistory.org; "Doom of the Old Tombs," *New York Times*, July 4, 1896, 9.

14 "Execution of Captain Gordon," *Evening Post* (NY), February 21, 1862, 3.

15 Ron Soodalter, *Hanging Captain Gordon: The Life and Trial of an American Slave Trader* (New York: Washington Square Press, 2006), 92.

16 *The Portland Directory* of 1834 lists David Woodside as a "mariner" living on Danforth Street, the same street where Gordon II had built his house ([Portland, ME: Shirley, 1834], 118). The 1850 federal census also places Woodside and his family in Portland (U.S. Census Bureau, census for Portland, ME [1850], https://www2 .census.gov).

17 While I've relied largely on newspaper accounts of the proceedings for both of Gordon's trials, I owe a huge debt to Ron Soodalter's *Hanging Captain Gordon*, which recounts the events in detail.

18 *The New York Times*, June 19, 1861, 3.

19 "Trial of Captain Nathaniel Gordon for Piracy," *New York Herald*, June 20, 1861, 2.

20 *The New York Times*, June 19, 1861, 3.

21 *The New York Times*, June 19, 1861, 3.

22 *Evening Post* (NY), June 21, 1861, 5.

23 *The New York Times*, June 22, 1861, 3.

24 *Evening Post* (NY), June 21, 1861, 3.

25 *New-York Daily Tribune*, June 22, 1861, 4.

26 Soodalter, *Hanging Captain Gordon*, 120.

27 Soodalter, *Hanging Captain Gordon*, 118.

28 *New York Herald*, November 11, 1861, 2.

29 In 1854, a New York jury convicted James Smith, captain of the Maine-built *Julia Moulton*, of piracy. But after his conviction, the judge declared a mistrial on a technicality. Smith was then sentenced under a lesser charge and pardoned in 1857 (Warren S. Howard, *American Slavers and the Federal Law, 1837–1862* [Berkeley: University of California Press, 1963], 192–95).

30 *New York Herald*, December 1, 1861, 2.

31 *Union Journal*, December 20, 1861, 2–3.

32 *Portland Daily Advertiser*, December 5, 1861, 2. The other Portland newspapers in 1861 were *the Christian Mirror*, the *Weekly Eastern Argus*, the *Daily Eastern Argus*, the *Weekly Advertiser*, and the *Portland Price-Current*.

33 Gilbert Dean to Abraham Lincoln, February 18, 1862; William H. Seward to Abraham Lincoln, February 3, 1862; both in *Abraham Lincoln Papers*, ser. 1, General Correspondence, Library of Congress, http://www.loc.gov.

34 J. W. Chickering to Abraham Lincoln, December 20, 1861, box 2, folder 11, Lincoln Collection, Lincoln Miscellaneous Manuscripts, 1587–1924, University of Chicago Library.

35 Mary Gordon, petition to Abraham Lincoln, January 1862, Abraham Lincoln Collection, 1861–65, New-York Historical Society Museum and Library, http:// www.digitalcollections.nyhistory.org.

36 Ron Soodalter, "The Limits of Lincoln's Mercy," *The New York Times*, February 23, 2012.

37 Rhoda White, petition to Abraham Lincoln, February 17, 1862, *Abraham Lincoln Papers*, ser. 1, General Correspondence, Library of Congress, http://www.loc.gov.

38 Citizens of Portland, ME, petition to Abraham Lincoln, December 1861, RG 204, entry PI-87 1-A, box 12, Office of the Pardon Attorney, U.S. National Archives. Portland had a population of about 26,000 in 1861, so some of the petitioners likely

lived in nearby towns. See also *New-York Tribune*, January 28, 1862, 8; and *Brooklyn Daily Eagle*, February 21, 1862, 2.

39 *New-York Tribune*, January 28, 1862, 8; *Brooklyn Daily Eagle*, February 21, 1862, 2.

40 *New York Herald*, February 20, 1862, 4.

41 Charles Sumner, "Final Suppression of the Slave-Trade," speech in the U.S. Senate, April 24, 1862, in *Charles Sumner; His Complete Works, with Introduction by Hon. George Frisbie Hoar* (Boston: Lee and Shepherd, 1900), 8:337; Michael Burlingame, *The Inner World of Abraham Lincoln* (Urbana: University of Illinois Press, 1994), 23; *Brooklyn Eagle*, March 17, 1862, 1.

42 "The Slave Trade, and Gordon the Slave Trader," *Union and Journal*, February 21, 1862, 3.

43 "Pardon for Gordon the Slave-Trader," *The New York Times*, January 28, 1862, 4.

44 Abraham Lincoln, "Lincoln on the Execution of a Slave Trader, 1862," Gilder Lehrman Institute of American History, https://www.gilderlehrman.org.

45 Burlingame, *Inner World of Abraham Lincoln*, 23.

46 "Execution of Nathaniel Gordon," *Sunday Dispatch* (NY), February 23, 1862, 9.

47 *Evening Post* (NY), February 21, 1862, 3.

48 *Minnesota Pioneer*, March 7, 1862, 6; *Brooklyn Daily Eagle*, February 22, 1862, 2.

49 *Evening Post* (NY), February 24, 1862, 2.

50 *New York Herald*, February 22, 1862, 9.

51 *Brooklyn Eagle*, February 21, 1862, 2.

52 "A Death Blow at the Slave-Trade," *New-York Tribune*, February 22, 1862, 4.

53 *Evening Post* (NY), February 21, 3.

54 On the sentences given to Gordon's mates on the *Erie*, see Soodalter, *Hanging Captain Gordon*, 239–40.

55 *New York Herald*, February 28, 1862, 8.

56 See U.S. Census Bureau, census for Astoria, Queens, NY (1870), https://www2 .census.gov.

57 *New-York Tribune*, February 2, 1862, 4; *Portland Weekly Advertiser*, March 1, 1862, 1; "The First and the Last," *Atlantic Monthly*, December 1868, 752.

58 "Notable Slave Case—Appleton Oaksmith," *San Francisco Bulletin*, December 21, 1861, 1.

59 Jonathan W. White argues that Oaksmith likely wasn't seeking human cargo when he ran aground in the Congo River (*Shipwrecked: A True Civil War Story of Mutinies, Jailbreaks, Blockade-Running, and the Slave Trade* [Lanham, MD: Rowman and Littlefield, 2023], 42–43). But Henry Southern, the British minister to Brazil, suspected that he was, like Gordon, working with George Marsden, a known facilitator between Brazilian slave interests and American sea captains (Leonardo Marques, "The Contraband Slave Trade to Brazil and the Dynamics of US Participation, 1831–1856," *Journal of Latin American Studies* 47, no. 4 (2015): 680). Moreover, the *Nautical Magazine and Naval Chronicle for 1853: A Journal of Papers on Subjects Connected with Maritime Affairs* reported the *Mary Adeline* incident under the headline "Congo Slavers" while mentioning no other ships ([London, 1853], 55).

60 "Appleton Oaksmith Again in Court," *Boston Morning Journal*, January 6, 1862, 4.

61 White, *Shipwrecked*, 146.

62 *Boston Daily Advertiser*, June 19, 1862, 1.

63 *Whaleman's Shipping List* (New Bedford, MA), June 24, 1862, 2; "The Margaret Scott Case," *New Bedford Evening Standard* (MA), June 19, 1862, 2.

64 "Escape from Jail of Appleton Oaksmith," *Boston Evening Transcript*, September 12, 1862, 4.

65 John J. TePaske, "Appleton Oaksmith, Filibuster Agent," *North Carolina Historical Review* 35, no. 4 (1958): 430; Ruth P. Barbour, "Appleton Oaksmith, a Doomed Dreamer," *State* 52 (April 1985): 21; "An Outlaw's Career—a Portland Romance," *Oxford Democrat* (ME), September 9, 1870, 1. On Edward Oaksmith's arrest, see *Boston Herald*, October 18, 1862, 4.

66 See, for example, *Boston Post*, September 18, 1862, 2.

67 "An Outlaw's Career," *Oxford Democrat*, 1; TePaske, "Appleton Oaksmith," 430; Barbour, "Appleton Oaksmith," 21. Jonathan White contends that Oaksmith didn't escape to Portland but went almost immediately to Havana (*Shipwrecked*, 171).

68 Sylviane A. Diouf, "From the Holds of the *Clotilda* to Africatown," *UNESCO Courier* 4 (October–December 2019): 42–45. For this description of the Clotilda affair, I am indebted to the work of Diouf, both in this article and in *Dreams of Africa in Alabama: The Slave Ship "Clotilda" and the Story of the Last Africans Brought to America* (New York: Oxford, 2007).

69 Meagan Flynn, "America's Last Slave Ship," *The Washington Post*, May 23, 2019.

70 "Last Cargo of Slaves," *Globe-Democrat* (St. Louis), November 30, 1890.

71 Diouf, *Dreams of Africa*, 11, 24, 27–28, 62.

72 Diouf, *Dreams of Africa*, 69, 72–73.

73 "Last Cargo of Slaves," *Globe-Democrat*.

74 See, for example, *Alexandria Gazette* (VA), July 11, 1860, 3; and *Daily Exchange* (Baltimore), July 11, 1860, 1.

75 "Last Cargo of Slaves," *Globe-Democrat*.

76 Diouf, *Dreams of Africa*, 86, 87.

77 Sylviane A. Diouf, "Africatown," December 6, 2007, *Encyclopedia of Alabama*, https://encyclopediaofalabama.org.

78 Diouf, *Dreams of Africa*, 76.

79 John Newton, *An Authentic Narrative of Some Remarkable and Interesting Particulars in the Life of John Newton*, 3rd ed. (London: Drapier, Hitch, and Hill, 1765), 154–55.

80 John Newton, *Journal of a Slave Trader, 1750–1754* (London: Epworth, 1962), 81.

81 Marques, *The United States and the Transatlantic Slave Trade*, 3.

82 "The Execution of Gordon; Scenes Incident to His Last Moments," *New York Times*, February 22, 1862, 8.

83 *Reveille Port Gibson* (MS), April 6, 1894, 4.

84 Diouf quotes an account by Noah, a man enslaved by the Meahers, who overheard this conversation between Timothy and Mary Meaher (*Dreams of Africa*, 79).

85 TePaske, "Appleton Oaksmith," 432.

86 John J. TePaske, "The Life of Appleton Oaksmith: Its Latin-American Aspects" (master's thesis, Duke University, 1953), 25.

87 TePaske, "Appleton Oaksmith," 431, 432.

88 TePaske, "Appleton Oaksmith," 431; Diouf, *Dreams of Africa*, 16. I have added Buchanan and Polk to Diouf's list. Polk pardoned Peter Flowery, and Buchanan pardoned James Smith. See Robert Ralph Davis, Jr., "James Buchanan and the

Suppression of the Slave Trade, 1858–1861," *Pennsylvania History*, 33, no. 4 (1966): 447.

89 Diouf, "Africatown."

90 Zora Neale Hurston, *Barracoon: The Story of the Last "Black Cargo,"* ed. Deborah G. Plant (New York: Amistad, 2018), 56–57.

91 *Huntsville Gazette* (AL), March 12, 1892, 2; "Death of a Noted Man," *Alexandria Gazette*, March 10, 1892, 3; "The Last Slave Dealer," *Clarksville Evening Tobacco Leaf–Chronical* (TN), March 5, 1892, 2.

CHAPTER 8: THE WAR WITHIN THE STATES

1   Greg Kesich, "He Heard It from Those Who Heard It from Those Who Were There," *Portland Press Herald*, April 13, 2011.

2   Obituary of Helen Western, *New York Herald*, December 12, 1868, 5.

3   Obituary of Helen Western, *Memphis Daily Appeal*, December 6, 1868, 1.

4   *Portland Advertiser*, April 29, 1862, 2.

5   Peter Hess, "1861: Lincoln and John Wilkes Booth in Albany," *New York Almanack*, December 19, 2019, http://www.newyorkalmanack.com.

6   A note in the margin of the original mortgage certifies it was fully paid off: Reuben Ruby to Joel Allen, October 10, 1854, real property records, Cumberland County, bk. 00256, 410, Maine Registry of Deeds.

7   U.S. Census Bureau, census for Yarmouth, Maine (1860), https://www2.census.gov.

8   "Secession of Maine," *Hallowell Gazette*, December 20, 1861, 3.

9   According to *The New York Times*, the Maine Senate was entirely Republican, and the House had 127 Republicans and 26 Democrats (January, 3, 1851, 5).

10 Abraham Lincoln to Horace Greeley, reprinted in *Morning Express Buffalo* (NY), August 25, 1862, 1, and *Weekly National Intelligencer* (Washington, DC), August 23, 1862, 2.

11 Benjamin F. Butler, *Butler's Book: A Review of His Legal, Political, and Military Career* (Boston: Thayer, 1892), 295–98.

12 William Wells Brown, *The Negro in the American Rebellion* (Boston: Lee and Shepherd, 1867), 55.

13 Frederick Douglass, "Fighting Rebels with Only One Hand," *Douglass' Monthly* (September 1861), http://www.frederick-douglass-heritage.org.

14 W. E. B. Du Bois, *Black Reconstruction in America, 1860–1880*, (1835; reprint, New York: Free Press, 1998), 96.

15 Francis Fessenden, *Life and Public Service of William Pitt Fessenden in Two Volumes* (Boston: Houghton Mifflin, 1907), 1:256.

16 John T. Hubbel, "Abraham Lincoln and the Recruitment of Black Soldiers," *Journal of the Abraham Lincoln Association* 2, no. 1 (1980): 6–21.

17 Abraham Lincoln and William H. Seward, Emancipation Proclamation, January 1, 1863, online exhibit, U.S. National Archives, https://www.archives.gov. The proclamation did not free all enslaved persons in the South; those in nonbelligerent border states or counties and parishes under Union occupation were excepted.

18 Draft registration records for George Ruby and Horatio Ruby, Portland, Maine, July 1, 1863, U.S. Civil War Draft Registration Records, 1863-65, U.S. National Archives.

19 U.S. Congress, "An Act for Enrolling and Calling Out the National Forces, and for Other Purposes," March 3, 1863, 37th Cong., sess. 3, chap. 75.

20 Albon P. Mann, Jr., "The Irish in New York in the Early Eighteen Sixties," *Irish Historical Studies* 7, no. 26 (1950): 90.

21 Alan Pusey, "July 13, 1863: Draft Lottery Sparks NYC Riots," *ABA Journal*, July 1, 2018.

22 *Brooklyn Daily Eagle*, July 14, 1863, 2.

23 Plaque marking the home of Amos Noë and Christiana Williams Freeman, Freedom Trail, Portland, ME.

24 Shannon Luders-Manuel, "Race and Labor in the 1863 New York City Draft Riots," *JStor Daily*, May 4, 2017.

25 Nalleli Guillen, "Lessons Learned? Considering the Draft Riots of 1863 for Today," blog, Brooklyn Public Library, July 16, 2020, https://www.bklynlibrary.org/blog/2020/07/16/lesson-learned.

26 *The New York Times*, July 15, 1863, 4.

27 *Report of the Committee of Merchants for the Relief of Colored People, Suffering from the Late Riots in the City of New York* (New York: Whitehorn, 1863), 22.

28 Leslie M. Harris, *In the Shadow of Slavery: African Americans in New York City, 1626–1863* (Chicago: University of Chicago Press, 2003), 288.

29 *Report of the Committee of Merchants for the Relief of Colored People*, 7.

30 Nalleli Guillen, "Lessons Learned?"

31 "Ovation to Black Troops," *The New York Times*, March 6, 1864, 8.

32 "Ovation to Black Troops," *The New York Times*, 8.

33 H. H. Price and Gerald E. Talbot, eds., "Appendix 11: Some Black Civil War Veterans in Maine," in *Maine's Visible Black History: The First Chronicle of Its People* (Gardiner, ME: Tilbury House, 2006), 374.

34 *Portland Soldiers and Sailors in the War of the Rebellion, a Brief Sketch* (Portland, ME: Thurston, 1884), 15.

35 Maine Memory Network, "12th Maine Regiment in Louisiana," http://www.mainememory.net.

36 August V. Kautz, *Customs of Service for Non-Commissioned Officers and Soldiers as Derived from Law and Regulations and Practised in the Army of the United States: Being a Handbook for the Rank and File of the Army* (Philadelphia: Lippincott, 1864), 41–42, 90.

37 *L'Union* (New Orleans), January 23, 1864, 1. The newspaper notes that a "W. W. Ruby" was involved in "une grande assemblée de citoyens de couleur de la Novelle-Orléans." Ruby would have been there with the Twelfth Maine at the time, and no other W. W. Ruby appears in census or directory records for New Orleans during this period.

38 *Proceedings of the National Convention of Colored Men, Syracuse, New York, October 4–7, 1864* (Boston: Rock and Ruffin, 1864), 8.

39 *Proceedings of the National Convention of Colored Men*, 33–34.

40 Edwin S. Redkey, ed., *A Grand Army of Black Men: Letters from African-American Soldiers in the Union Army, 1861–1865* (New York: Cambridge University Press, 1992), 214.

41 Hannah Johnson to Abraham Lincoln, July 31, 1863, in *Freedom: A Documentary History of Emancipation, 1861–1867*, ser. 2, ed. Ira Berlin, Thavolia Glymph, Steven F. Miller, Joseph P. Reidy, Leslie S. Rowland, and Julie Saville (New York: Cambridge University Press, 1982), 582–83.

42 "George Ruby," *Portland Daily Press*, April 14, 1864, 2.

43 Redkey, *A Grand Army of Black Men*, 137–38.

44 "George Ruby," *Portland Daily Press*, April 14, 1864, 2.

45 Draft registration records for Charles and George Gordon, Portland, ME, July 1, 1863, U.S. Civil War Draft Registration Records, 1863–65, U.S. National Archives.

46 Carter Stevens, "When the Confederates Terrorized Maine: The Battle of Portland Harbor" (honors thesis, Colby College, 2013), 17.

47 Stevens, "When the Confederates Terrorized Maine," 15–16, 19, 21.

48 "The Tacony Affair," *Portland Daily Press*, June 30, 1870, 4. The 1870 federal census places Charles Gordon in Portland's Ward 7 and lists him as the only Charles Gordon in the city (U.S. Census Bureau, census for Portland, ME [1870], https://www2.census.gov).

49 "Moody's Marine Observatory," *Portland Daily Press*, July 14, 1862, 2.

50 Stevens, "When the Confederates Terrorized Maine," 33.

51 Albert Bibber, deposition, *Portland Daily Press*, July 13, 1863, 1.

52 "Capture and Destruction of the Revenue Cutter Caleb Cushing," *Portland Daily Press*, June 29, 1863, 2; Maine Memory Network, "Rebels at the Door," https://www.mainememory.net.

53 "Capture and Destruction," 2.

54 "Capture and Destruction," 2.

55 *Daily Eastern Argus*, March 31, 1864, 3; *Journal of Commerce* (NY), March 25, 1864, 2. George I. Gordon, occupation "captain," appears on the draft registration rolls of Portland, Maine, in 1863 (see note above). After the war, George no longer appears in Maine records or directories, which is consistent with his moving elsewhere.

56 Marcus Price, "Ships That Tested the Blockade of the Carolina Ports, 1861–65," *American Neptune* 8 (1948): 202.

57 *Official Records of the Union and Confederate Navies*, ser. 1 (Washington, DC: Government Printing Office, 1898), 7:464.

58 Thelma Peters, "Blockade Running in the Bahamas during the Civil War," paper presented at the Historical Association of South Florida, May 5, 1943, 26; Price, "Ships That Tested the Blockade," 213.

59 Price, "Ships That Tested the Blockade," 213.

60 Jonathan W. White, *Shipwrecked: A True Civil War Story of Mutinies, Jailbreaks, Blockade-Running, and the Slave Trade* (Lanham, MD: Rowman and Littlefield, 2023), 196–99; John J. TePaske, "Appleton Oaksmith, Filibuster Agent," *North Carolina Historical Review* 35, no. 4 (1958): 430; Ruth P. Barbour, "Appleton Oaksmith, a Doomed Dreamer," *The State* (NC) 52, no. 11 (1985): 21.

61 Sylviane A. Diouf, *Dreams of Africa in Alabama: The Slave Ship "Clotilda" and the Last Africans Brought to America* (New York: Oxford University Press, 2007), 83.

62 Diouf, *Dreams of Africa*, 78, 120, 122.

63 U.S. Supreme Court, *Gray Jacket*, 72 U.S., 347 (1866), https://supreme.justia.com.

64 U.S. Supreme Court, *Gray Jacket*.

65 Daniel Sharfstein, "The Namesake of Howard University Spent Years Kicking Native Americans Off Their Land," *Smithsonian Magazine*, May 23, 2017.

66 Andrew J. DeRoche, "Maine Civil War Soldiers' Attitudes about Slavery and African Americans," *UCLA Historical Journal* 16 (1996): 31.

67 Diane Munroe Smith, *Fanny and Joshua: The Enigmatic Lives of Francis Caroline Adams and Joshua Lawrence Chamberlain* (Lebanon, NH: University Press of New England, 2013), 199, 200; Patrick Rael, "The Chamberlain You Thought You Knew: Joshua Lawrence Chamberlain, Masculinity, and the Memory of the Civil War," lecture, Bowdoin College Faculty Seminar, October 2002; Alice Rains Trulock, *In the Hands of Providence: Joshua L. Chamberlain and the American Civil War* (Chapel Hill: University of North Carolina Press, 1992), 353.

68 While many scholars quote a figure closer to 70,000, the U.S. National Park Service's Soldiers and Sailors Database lists 83,265 (https://www.nps.gov).

69 DeRoche, "Maine Civil War Soldiers' Attitudes," 35; James McPherson, *For Cause and Comrades: Why Men Fought in the Civil War* (New York: Oxford University Press, 1997), 117.

70 Gardner L. Hatch to his mother, November 5, 1864, *in* "Maine Voices from the Civil War," item 93.53.5, Maine State Museum, https://mainestatemuseum.org.

71 John Monroe Dillingham to his mother, March 1, 1863, Dillingham Family Papers, coll. 135, Maine Historical Society, https://www.mainememory.net.

72 Laura Towne, *The Letters and Diary of Laura M. Towne, Written from the Sea Islands of South Carolina, 1862–1884,* ed. Rupert Sargent Holland (Cambridge, MA: Riverside, 1912), 8.

73 James J. Heslin, "A Yankee Soldier in a New York Regiment," *New-York Historical Society Quarterly*, 50, no. 2 (1966): 115.

74 Nathe Austin to Moses Lakeman, December 10, 1861, in "Maine Voices from the Civil War," item 68.9, Maine State Museum, https://mainestatemuseum.org.

75 L. C. Bateman, "Portland and the Anti-Slavery Movement," in *A Distant War Comes Home: Maine in the Civil War Era*, ed. Donald A, Beattie, Rodney Cole, and Charles G. Waugh (Camden, ME: Down East Books, 1996), 15.

76 Brian Swartz, "Some Mainers Broke Racial Barriers in 'White' State Regiments," *Bangor Daily News*, March 20, 2014.

77 U.S. National Park Service, Soldiers and Sailors Database. Although he was Black, Aaron Williams of Industry, Maine, joined the predominantly White First Maine Heavy Artillery Regiment and died in 1865 after being wounded. Three other African Americans—Lemuel Carter and Franklin Fremont from Bath and George Freeman from Brunswick—also joined the First Maine. Eight members of the regiment were Native Americans. Anthony Williams, an African American from Norridgewock, joined Company D of the Thirtieth Maine Infantry Regiment on November 23, 1863.

78 "Colored Troops, 1863–65," http://www.digitalmaine.com; U.S. National Park Service, Soldiers and Sailors Database.

79 Isaiah H. Welch, "An African-American Soldier Fights 'In Defense of My Race and Country,'" https://shec.ashp.cuny.edu.

80 Morgan W. Carter to John Carter, December 3, 1864, in "Black Soldier's Letter Offers Rare View of Civil War," by Diana Penner, *USA Today*, March 5, 2013. Carter was with Company G of the Twenty-eighth U.S. Colored Troops at City Point, VA.

81 Redkey, *A Grand Army of Black Men*, 153–54.

82 U.S. National Archives, "Black Soldiers in the U.S. Military During the Civil War," https://www.archives.gov.

83 Du Bois, *Black Reconstruction in America*, 100.

84 Ford's Theater, "Material Evidence: What Booth Carried," https://www.fords.org.

CHAPTER 9: CARPETBAGGERS AND EXODUSTERS

1 George T. Ruby, "Letter from New Orleans," *Liberator*, February 26, 1864, 36.

2 Barry A. Crouch, "A Political Education: George T. Ruby and the Texas Freedmen's Bureau," *Houston Review* 18 no. 2 (1996): 146.

3 "George Ruby," *Portland Daily Press*, April 14, 1864.

4 "Reception of Hon. G. T. Ruby," *Portland Daily Press*, October 8, 1870.

5 William Seraille, "Afro-American Emigration to Haiti during the American Civil War," *Americas* 35, no. 2 (October 1978): 186.

6 Seraille, "Afro-American Emigration," 191; John R. McKivigan, ed., *The Frederick Douglass Papers*, ser. 4, *Journalism and Other Writings* (New Haven, CT: Yale University Press, 2021), 1:86.

7 Michael Vorenberg, "Abraham Lincoln and the Politics of Black Colonization," *Journal of the Abraham Lincoln Association* 14, no. 2 (1980): 22–45; Sydney Trent, "Abraham Lincoln's Disastrous Effort to Get Black People to Leave the U.S.," *Washington Post*, February 19, 2023.

8 Abraham Lincoln, "Address on Colonization to a Deputation of Negroes," August 14, 1862, in *The Collected Works of Abraham Lincoln*, 8 vols., ed. Roy P. Basler (New Brunswick, NJ: Rutgers University Press, 1953), 5:371–76.

9 G. T. Ruby, "Letters from Haiti," *Pine and Palm*, September 7, 1861. Some historians have confused Robert Benjamin Lewis, an African American from Gardiner, Maine, who wrote *Light and Truth*, with John W. Lewis. But Robert Lewis died in 1858, whereas John Lewis emigrated with the help of the American Missionary Association. See "Haiti," in *Fifteenth Annual Report of the American Missionary Association* (New York: American Missionary Association), 3; and G. T. Ruby, "Notes from Emigrants in Haiti," *Pine and Palm*, November 9, 1861, which mentions John W. Lewis by his full name.

10 Amos Gerry Beman, "Letter to Rev. James W. C. Pennington," *Colored American* (NY), November 7, 1840.

11 "Emigration to Hayti," *Christian Era* (Boston), January 11, 1861, 5; Van Gosse, *The First Reconstruction: Black Politics in America from the Revolution to the Civil War* (Chapel Hill: University of North Carolina Press, 2021), 211.

12 Benjamin Quarles, *Black Abolitionists* (New York: Oxford University Press, 1969), 46–47. For Lewis's lectures, see letter to the editor, *New Bedford Evening Standard* (MA), April 26, 1860, 2; and notices for Lewis's lectures, *New Bedford Evening Standard*, April 24, 1860, 2, and April 25, 1860, 2.

13 On Lewis's residence in Portland, see U.S. Census Bureau, census for Portland, ME (1840), https://www2.census.gov; and Sylvester Breakmore Beckett, *The Portland Reference Book and City Directory, 1847* (Portland, 1847). By 1859, Lewis was in Boston, where he married Jane Toomey on October 15 (Massachusetts marriage records, 1840–1915, New England Historic Genealogical Society, Boston). That marriage record also indicates that he was born in South Berwick, Maine, in about 1809. The 1860 federal census also places Lewis in Boston and confirms his vocation as "Bap.

Clergyman" (U.S. Census Bureau, census for Boston [1840], https://www2.census
.gov). See a note about his emigration to Haiti as a missionary in the Portland-
based *Christian Mirror*, July 2, 1861, 4.

14 G. T. Ruby, "Letter from Haiti," *Pine and Palm*, May 25, 1861.

15 *Pine and Palm*, November 9, 1861.

16 G. T. Ruby, "Letter from a Maine Emigrant," *Pine and Palm*, November 9, 1861.

17 *Pine and Palm*, August 28, 1862.

18 Seraille, "Afro-American Emigration," 200.

19 Carl H. Moneyhon, *George T. Ruby: Champion of Equal Rights in Reconstruction
Texas* (Fort Worth: Texas Christian University Press, 2020), 60.

20 Barry A. Crouch, "Black Education in Civil War and Reconstruction Louisiana:
George T. Ruby, the Army, and the Freedmen's Bureau," *Louisiana History* 38, no. 3
(1997): 293–95. The site is commemorated with a historical marker.

21 Crouch, "Black Education," 302.

22 Booker T. Washington, *Up from Slavery: An Autobiography* (Garden City, NY:
Doubleday, 1900), 30.

23 Moneyhon, *George T. Ruby*, 67.

24 *Troy Daily Times* (NY), August 7, 1866, 1; *New Orleans Daily Crescent*, July 19, 1866,
1; Crouch, "Black Education," 307.

25 *Troy Daily Times*, August 7, 1866, 1; *Elmira Daily Advertiser* (NY), August 2, 1866,
2.

26 Rich Condon, "'An Absolute Massacre'—The New Orleans Slaughter of July 30,
1866," https://www.nps.gov.

27 W. E. B. Du Bois, *Black Reconstruction in America, 1860–1880* (1935; reprint, New
York: Free Press, 1998), 465.

28 *Harper's Weekly*, August 25, 1866.

29 Condon, "'An Absolute Massacre.'"

30 Gilles Vandal, *The New Orleans Riot of 1866: The Anatomy of a Tragedy* (PhD diss.,
College of William and Mary, 1978), 223.

31 Daniel Alexander Payne Murray, *The New-Orleans Riot: Its Official History: The
Dispatches of Gens. Sheridan, Grant, and Baird—The President Answered* (1866),
Daniel Murray Pamphlet Collection, Library of Congress, https://www.loc.gov.

32 Freedmen's Bureau, "Miscellaneous Reports and Lists Relating to Murders and
Outrages, Mar. 1867—Nov. 1868," Records of the Assistant Commissioner for the
State of Louisiana, Bureau of Refugees, Freedmen, and Abandoned Lands, 1865–69,
National Archives Microfilm, M1027, roll 34, http://freedmensbureau.com.

33 Barry A. Crouch, "A Political Education," 147.

34 *New Orleans Tribune*, December 20, 1866, 4.

35 Crouch, "A Political Education," 147, 151.

36 Crouch, "A Political Education," 152–53; Moneyhon, *George T. Ruby*, 90.

37 "The Steamship Morgan in Court," *New Orleans Times-Picayune*, April 30, 1868, 2.

38 "The Ruby Admiralty Case," *Flake's Bulletin*, June 23, 1868, 8.

39 *New Orleans Republican*, August 21, 1868, 3.

40 *San Antonio Express*, September 13, 1867, 2.

41 "A Portland Man in the Texas Convention," *Portland Daily Press*, February 20,
1868, 3.

42 "Why Not Ruby?," *Tri-Weekly State Gazette* (Austin, TX), May 4, 1868, 2.

43 Claude Elliot, "Constitutional Convention of 1868–69" (1952), in *Handbook of Texas*, https://www.tshaonline.org.

44 Moneyhon, *George T. Ruby*, 144–48.

45 "Arrests," *Flake's Bulletin*, September 10, 1868, 5.

46 "An ordinance to prevent the intimidation of voters," in *Journal of the Reconstruction Convention: Which Met at Austin, Texas Dec. 7, A.D. 1868*, 2nd sess. (Austin, TX: Tracy, Siemering, 1870), 2:510–11.

47 *Report of Special Committee on Lawlessness and Violence in Texas* (Austin, 1868), 9, 5.

48 "Petition to Hon. E. J. Davis, President of the convention," in *Journal of the Reconstruction Convention*, 2:518–20.

49 *Daily National Republican* (Washington, DC), April 2, 1869, 2.

50 "The Condition of Texas," *National Anti-Slavery Standard* (NY), May 1, 1869, 1.

51 Du Bois, *Black Reconstruction*, 560.

52 Matthew Gaines was the other Black state senator for Texas. Many former Confederates did not vote in the election.

53 James Smallwood, "G. T. Ruby: Galveston's Black Carpetbagger in Reconstruction Texas," *Houston Review* 5, no. 1 (1983): 30.

54 "The Militia Bill," *Dallas Weekly Herald*, July 2, 1870, 2.

55 *Daily Morning Chronicle* (Washington, DC), September 21, 1870, 2.

56 U.S. Census Bureau, census for Washington, DC, Ward 1 (1870), https://www2.census.gov. For Charles Nalle's employment, see records for Charles Nalle, August 15, 1870, Registers of Signatures of Depositors in Branches of the Freedman's Savings and Trust Company, 1865–74, ARC identifier 566522, Freedman's Bank Records, U.S. National Archives; records for Charles Nalle, RG 101, Records of the Office of the Comptroller of the Currency, 1863–2006, Ancestry.com; records for Charles Nalle, September 30, 1871, U.S. Register of Civil, Military, and Naval Service, 1863–1959, U.S. National Archives.

57 *New Orleans Republican*, October 16, 1870, 7, reprinted from the *Troy Whig* (NY).

58 Suzanne Spellen, "Walkabout: The Rescue of Charles Nalle—A Troy Story," *Brownstoner*, https://www.brownstoner.com.

59 U.S. Census Bureau, census for Troy, NY (1860), https://www2.census.gov. Nalle is also listed, though not by name, in the 1850 federal census slave schedule for Culpeper, Virginia, under Blucher W. Hansbrough (https://www2.census.gov).

60 "Fugitive Slave Case in Troy," *Oxford Times* (NY), May 2, 1860, 2.

61 *Oxford Times*, May 2, 1860. On Tubman's participation in the rescue, see Historical Marker Database, "The Rescue of Charles Nalle, April 27, 1860," http://www.hmdb.org.

62 Historical Marker Database, "The Rescue of Charles Nalle."

63 "Brilliant Assemblage of New York's Colored Elite at Cooper Institute," *New York World*, September 23, 1870, 8. See U.S. Census Bureau, census for New Orleans (1880) and Washington, DC (1900), https://www2.census.gov. Both list Lucy's race as "mulatto."

64 *Harrisburg Patriot* (PA), September 26, 1870, 2. For a description of Lucy's appearance, see *New Orleans Republican*, October 16, 1870, 7.

65 "Going Back on His Friends," *Galveston Daily News*, October 6, 1870, 2.

66 "Reception of Hon. G. T. Ruby," *Portland Daily Press*, October 8, 1870, 4.

67 James Smallwood, "G. T. Ruby: Galveston's Black Carpetbagger," 32.

68 Sheila Blackford, "Disputed Election of 1876: The Death Knell of the Republican Dream," https://millercenter.org; Heather Cox Richardson, "Letters from an American," March 2, 2023, https://heathercoxrichardson.substack.com.

69 John G. Van Deusen, "The Exodus of 1879," *Journal of Negro History* 21, no. 2 (1936): 112–14.

70 George T. Ruby, address to the Colored Convention, New Orleans, April 21, 1879, *Weekly Louisianan*, April 24, 1879, 2.

71 Frederick Douglass, *The Life and Times of Frederick Douglass, Written by Himself* (Hartford, CT: Park, 1881), 441.

72 "The Negro Exodus," *Nebraska Advertiser*, March 25, 1880, 5.

73 "Exodusters and Western Expansion," African American Heritage, U.S. National Archives, https://www.archives.gov.

74 B. T. Arrington, "Southern Exodusters Movement," in *Encyclopedia of American Social Movements*, ed. Immanuel Ness (New York: Routledge, 2015), 776.

75 Marriage record for Horatio Ruby and Angelia Eastman, November 18, 1867, Maine marriage records, 1713–1922, Maine State Archives, Augusta; Stephen R. Ellis, "The Eastmans," in *Maine's Visible Black History: The First Chronicle of Its People*, ed. H. H. Price and Gerald Talbot (Gardiner, ME: Tilbury House, 2006), 46–50.

76 See death record of Frederic Ruby, January 11, 1917, which lists his birthdate as January 10, 1869 (Maine Death Records, 1761–1922, Maine State Archives, Augusta).

77 David McCullough, *The Path between the Seas* (New York: Simon and Schuster, 1977), 37–38.

78 Moneyhon, *George T. Ruby*, 247, 258; "The Storm at Galveston," *New Orleans Republican*, June 8, 1871, 1.

79 "Powerful Figure in Old Greenback Days in Portland: Horatio F. Ruby Remembered in Portland," *Portland Sunday Times*, January 24, 1909, 10.

80 "Powerful Figure," 10.

81 "The Colored Conference," *Galveston Daily News*, July 4, 1879, https://omeka.coloredconventions.org.

82 U.S. Census Bureau, census for Portland, ME (1880), https://www2.census.gov.

83 "The Wrongs of the Blacks," *New York Times*, April 23, 1880, 5.

84 *Memphis Daily Appeal*, April 23, 1880, 1; *Brenham Weekly Banner* (TX), May 14, 1880, 3.

85 *Portland Daily Press*, May 10, 1880, 4.

86 *Portland Daily Press*, December 29, 1880, 3, and September 5, 1882, 4.

87 *New Orleans Times-Picayune*, November 1, 1882, 3; *Portland Daily Press*, November 1, 1882, 4.

88 Everett L. Meader, "The Greenback Party in Maine, 1876–1884" (master's thesis, University of Maine, 1950), 32–33.

89 *Portland Daily Press*, February 22, 1884, 3.

90 *Portland Daily Press*, February 25, 1884, 3.

91 "An Eventful Passage," *Portland Daily Press*, March 21, 1885, 5. For his arrival back in the United States, see entry on March 4, 1886, Passenger Lists of Vessels Arriving at New York, New York, 1820–1897, Records of the U.S. Customs Service, U.S. National Archives; and *Portland Daily Press*, March 8, 1886, 5.

92 *Portland Daily Press*, September 23, 1886, 5.

93 "Powerful Figure," 10.

94 "The Peaceable Condition of the South," *New York Herald*, June 22, 1868, 4.

95 "An Appeal from North Carolina," *Portland Daily Press*, August 14, 1868, 3.

96 Eric Foner, "What It Meant to Be Called 'Carpetbagger,'" *New York Times*, September 30, 1988, 34.

97 *Portland Daily Press*, April 28, 1877, 1.

98 "Died—The Carpet-Bagger," *Chicago Daily Tribune*, April 23, 1877, 4.

99 Ted Tunnell, "Creating 'the Propaganda of History': Southern Editors and the Origins of 'Carpetbagger' and 'Scalawag,'" *Journal of Southern History* 72, no. 4 (2006): 792. Tunnell argues convincingly that the derogatory term *carpetbagger* was almost immediately picked up and widely used by the northern press and effectively undermined Radical Reconstruction.

CHAPTER 10: UP IN SMOKE

1 Candace Kanes, "For the Union: Civil War Deaths," http://www.mainememory.net.

2 Randy Billings, "The Night Portland Burned," *The Great Fire*, https://specialprojects.pressherald.com; advertisement, *Portland Daily Press*, July 3, 1866, 1.

3 Billings, "The Night Portland Burned." While Ruby's obituary in the *Daily Eastern Argus* (March 3, 1906) states that he discovered the fire, the newspaper accounts in the fire's immediate aftermath don't mention him.

4 John Neal, *Account of the Great Conflagration in Portland, July 4th & 5th, 1866* (Portland: Starbird and Twitchell, 1866), 22–23.

5 "Great Fire in Portland," *The New York Times*, July 5, 1866, 1.

6 Neal, *Account*, 5, 7.

7 *The New York Times*, July 10, 1866, 2.

8 "The Portland Fire," *Harper's Weekly* (NY), July 28, 1866, 478.

9 Neal, *Account*, 17. Neal lists the streets where buildings were leveled.

10 Neal, *Account*, 5.

11 "The Portland Fire, Extent of the Losses," *The New York Times*, July 10, 1866, 2; "The Portland Fire, *Harper's Weekly*, July 28, 1866, 466, 465.

12 "Relief for the Portland Sufferers: The Great Fire, 1866," https://digitalcommons.portlandlibrary.com; Neal, *Account*, 10; "Portland's Great Fire of 1866," https://www.portlandlandmarks.org.

13 *The New York Times*, July 10, 1866, 2.

14 According to a city directory, Mary and Harriet Gordon lived together at 6 Park Place (S. B. Beckett, *Portland Reference Book and City Directory* [Portland, ME: Thurston, 1866], 94). A later directory indicates that Joshua Gordon's home was destroyed in the fire and that Mary Gordon lived alone at 35½ Danforth Street (S. B. Beckett, *Portland Reference Book and City Directory* [Portland, ME: Thurston, 1869], 323, 113).

15 "The Great Fire," *The New York Times*, July 8, 1866, 5.

16 "Portland's Great Fire of 1866," Portland Landmarks, https://wwwportlandlandmarks.org.

17 *Portland Daily Press*, July 9, 1866, 3.

18 *Portland Daily Press*, July 25, 1866, 3.

19 "Portland's Great Fire of 1866"; "Lincoln Park Fountain," http://www.publicart portland.org.

20 *Portland Daily Press*, October 17, 1867, 2.

21 *Portland Daily Press*, July 18, 1868, 2.

22 The loss from the first fire was covered by insurance (*Portland Daily Press*, June 29, 1868, 2).

23 Auction notice, *Portland Daily Press*, April 19, 1869, 4.

24 Beckett, *Portland Reference Book and City Directory* (1869), 213; *Portland Daily Press*, April 23, 1869, 1.

25 U.S. Census Bureau, censuses for Portland, ME, and Boston (1879), https://www2 .census.gov.

26 *Portland Daily Press*, October 14, 1871, 3.

27 Obituary for William W. Ruby, *Daily Eastern Argus*, March 3, 1906, 16.

28 *Portland Daily Press*, April 8, 1874, 4.

29 For William's October 1874 divorce from Madeline, see Supreme Judicial Court docket 170, vol. 68, 365, Maine Divorce Records, 1798–91, Maine State Archives, Augusta. For his marriage to Sarah Butler, see *Portland Daily Press*, June 11, 1875, 3.

30 "State and City Statistics for '76," *Portland Daily Press*, January 1, 1877, 3.

31 "Sad Accident in the Harbor," *Portland Daily Press*, July 9, 1877, 3.

32 Some exceptions were made for medicinal uses of alcohol.

33 *Portland Daily Press*, September 12, 1877, 3.

34 *Portland Daily Press*, August 25, 1877, 3, and January 30, 1879, 4.

35 For the property settlement against William Ruby, see real property records, June 22, 1877, Cumberland County, bk. 00442, 291, Maine Registry of Deeds. In later years, William Ruby's stepmother, Annie Ruby, was listed as the owner of the house at 9 Hampshire Street, so it likely conveyed directly from Reuben to her.

36 *Portland Daily Press*, July 21, 1885, 1; *Portland Directory and Reference Book for 1885* (Portland, ME: Greenough, 1885), 486.

37 *Daily Eastern Argus*, March 3, 1906, 16.

38 *Portland Daily Press*, December 8, 1885, 4.

39 *Portland Directory and Reference Book for 1886* (Portland, ME: Greenough, 1886), 507; *Portland Directory and Reference Book for 1890* (Portland, ME: Greenough, 1890), 565; *Directory of Portland and Vicinity* (Portland, ME: Thurston, 1896), 739; *Directory of Portland and Vicinity* (Portland, ME: Thurston, 1898), 723; *Daily Eastern Argus*, March 3, 1906, 16.

40 "The Republican Caucuses," *Portland Daily Press*, February 15, 1884, 5, and February 18, 1887, 5; *Daily Eastern Argus*, March 3, 1906, 16.

41 "Brake Her Down, Fire Fighters of Years Ago Man the Machine Again," *Portland Daily Press*, August 26, 1892, 6.

42 "Nominations Made for City Officers," *Portland Daily Press*, March 12, 1888, 5. According to Sean Donaghue and Andrea Donaghue's *Portland Firefighting*, Ruby was "the first African American PFD officer" ([Charleston, SC: Arcadia, 2018], 90).

43 *Philadelphia Inquirer*, July 16, 1884, 2.

44 "Colored Firemen—A Color Line," *Cleveland Gazette*, December 6, 1884, 2.

45 *Cleveland Plain Dealer*, July 17, 1889, 7.

46 "Object to Negro Fireman," *New York Evening Journal*, November 12, 1898, 5.

47 "The Fire Laddies," *Portland Daily Press*, March 29, 1888, 5.

48 *Daily Eastern Argus*, March 3, 1906, 16; Kelley Bouchard, "The Man Who Shouted 'Fire!'" *The Great Fire*, https://specialprojects.pressherald.com.

49 *Portland Daily Press*, July 10, 1891, 5.

50 *Daily Eastern Argus*, March 3, 1906, 16.

CHAPTER II: FAMILY FORTUNES

1 "Immigration to the United States, 1851–1900," https:// www.loc.gov.

2 *Lewiston Evening Journal*, August 25, 1874, 2.

3 "Fire on York Street," *Portland Daily Press*, November 3, 1881, 3.

4 *Portland Daily Press*, August 24, 1874, 4.

5 Portland Home for Aged Women, notes from the Committee on Admissions, collection 2963, 35, Maine Historical Society, Portland.

6 U.S. Census Bureau, census for Portland, ME (1850), https://www2.census.gov.

7 U.S. Department of the Interior, *U.S. Register of Civil, Military, and Naval Service, 1863–1959* (Washington, DC: Government Printing Office, 1903), 1:1229.

8 *Washington Herald* (DC), November 19, 1911, 23.

9 *Evening Star* (Washington, DC), February 22, 1925, 8.

10 Probate record for Sophia L. Manuel, July 7, 1875, real property records, Cumberland County, bk. 00422, 205, Maine Registry of Deeds. Sophia and Christopher Manuel's children were Luther, Calvin, Amos, Edwin, Julia, Henry, Thomas, George, and Christopher. I am indebted to Bob Greene for this information.

11 *Daily Eastern Argus*, September 12, 1868, 1.

12 "Election Results," *Daily Eastern Argus*, March 2, 1869, 2.

13 *Portland Daily Press*, September 2, 1869, 3.

14 *Portland Daily Press*, September 23, 1874, 3; September 24, 1874, 3; and September 25, 1874, 3.

15 *Portland Daily Press*, October 29, 1874, 4.

16 *Bangor Daily Whig and Courier* (ME), October 13, 1870, 3; "City Affairs," *Portland Daily Press*, April 29, 1871, 4.

17 "City Items," *Portland Transcript*, May 6, 1876, 6.

18 "Of the State of Churches in the Cumberland Conference," *Christian Mirror*, June 19, 1845, 3, and June 17, 1847, 2; Randolph P. Dominic, Jr., "Down from the Balcony: The Abyssinian Congregational Church of Portland, Maine" (PhD diss., University of Maine, 1982), 13.

19 "Donation Party," *Christian Mirror*, December 16, 1851, 3.

20 "Rev. Amos N. Freeman," *Christian Mirror*, April 13, 1852, 2.

21 "Abyssinian Church," *Christian Mirror*, January 31, 1854, 2.

22 The 1850 federal census shows Ebenezer Ruby working as a farmer in New Gloucester, Maine. The census for 1860 lists his occupation as "clergyman" (U.S. Census Bureau, censuses for New Gloucester, ME [1850 and 1860], https://www2.census .gov). Also see Mike Cummings, "In the Shadows No More: Divinity School Honors Minister James W. C. Pennington," *Yale News*, September 30, 2016, https:// news.yale.edu.

23 On the dispute between Ruby and the Abyssinian, see entry for October 29, 1875,

Abyssinian Church Records, Congregational Library and Archives, Boston, https://www.congregationallibrary.org.

24 Dominic, "Down from the Balcony," 19–20.

25 "The Steamship *Portland*: The Titanic of New England," Cape Cod Maritime Museum, https://capecodmartimemuseum.org.

26 Stellwagen Bank National Marine Sanctuary, "Steamship *Portland*," https://stellwagen.noaa.gov.

27 "The Portland Sunk," *The New York TImes*, November 30, 1898, 1.

28 "Nearly 200 Ships Are Wrecked," *Buffalo News* (NY), November 29, 1898, 1.

29 "The Portland's Awful Fate," *Boston Daily Advertiser*, November 30, 1898, 1. According to Calvin Mires, the timing of the tragedy was determined by the victims' watches ("The Wreck of the Steamship *Portland*: Rediscovering the *Titanic* of New England," Zoom presentation, November 17, 2021, Maine Historical Society, Portland).

30 Walter V. Hickey, "The Final Voyage of the *Portland*: Reconstructing the List of the Steamer's Crew through NARA Records," *Prologue*, 38, no. 4 (2006), www.archives.gov.

31 *Portland Daily Press*, December 3, 1989, 9 and December 5, 1898, 6.

32 "Abyssinian Church Takes Action," *Portland Daily Press*, June 6, 1900, 7.

33 For decline of Portland's Black population, see U.S. Census Bureau, censuses for Portland, ME (1860 and 1900), https://www2.census.gov.

34 Michael Connolly, "Black Fades to Green: Irish Labor Replaces African-American Labor Along a Major New England Waterfront, Portland, Maine, in the Mid-Nineteenth Century," *Colby Quarterly*, 37, no.4 (2001): 371, 372.

35 See *Bylaws and Rules of Order of the Portland Longshoremen's Benevolent Society of Portland, Maine* (Portland, ME: Berry, 1881 and 1883), sec. 15 in each volume.

36 Connolly, "Black Fades to Green," 363–72; "Peopling Maine," www.mainememory.net.

37 U.S. National Park Service, "Abyssinian Meeting House," National Register of Historic Places, supp. listing record 05001612, February 3, 2006, https://npgallery.nps.gov.

38 On November 11, 1884, Annie Ruby sold one-third of the house (her portion) to a buyer named Wallace King (real property records, Cumberland County, bk. 00453, 45 [probate], bk. 00506, 365 [sale], Maine Registry of Deeds).

39 *Portland Daily Press*, July 4, 1878, 3; *Daily Eastern Argus* July 4, 1878, 3.

40 *Daily Eastern Argus*, February 14, 1870, 2.

41 Application for a headstone for William W. Ruby, Jr., February 7, 1961. Headstone Applications for Military Veterans, 1861–1985, U.S. National Archives; *U.S. Headstone Applications for Military Veterans, 1861–1985*, http://www.ancestry.com.

42 "Nearly a Lynching," *Portland Daily Press*, June 3, 1898, 5.

43 *Portland Daily Press*, June 13, 1898, 7.

44 *Lynching in America: Confronting the Legacy of Racial Terror*, 3rd ed. (Montgomery, AL: Equal Justice Initiative, 2017), https://lynchinginamerica.eji.org. This statistic does not account for the thousands of others who disappeared or were beaten to death or injured as a result of racist violence.

45 *Portland Daily Press*, July 30, 1898, 9.

46 Application for a headstone for William W. Ruby, Jr.

47 For Gordon's birth in Maine, see birth record of Nathaniel E. Gordon, April 28, 1857, Cape Elizabeth, in Maine Birth Records, 1715–1922, Maine State Archives, Augusta. For his supposed birth in Green Bay, Wisconsin, see death record of Nathaniel E. Gordon, July 20, 1922, Portland, Maine Death Records, 1761–1922, Maine State Archives, Augusta. For Gordon's various birthplaces and names, see U.S. Census Bureau, censuses for Portland, ME (1860 and 1910), Queens, NY (1870 and 1880), and South Portland, ME (1900), https://www2.census.gov.

48 "Execution of Captain Gordon," *Chicago Daily Tribune*, February 26, 1862, 3, reprinted from the *New York Herald*.

49 Poem reprinted in Ron Soodalter, *Hanging Captain Gordon: The Life and Trial of an American Slave Trader* (New York: Washington Square, 2006), 198. Nathaniel Gordon's statement was printed in *Constitution* (Middletown, CT), February 26, 1862, 2.

50 U.S. Census Bureau, census for Portland, ME (1860).

51 *Portland Daily Press*, February 4, 1898, 4.

52 "A Yachting Party," *Portland Daily Press*, August 16, 1887, 5; *Portland Daily Press*, December 30, 1897, 8.

53 "Aldermanic Candidate," *Portland Daily Press*, January 1, 1901, 7.

54 The other states were New Hampshire, Vermont, Connecticut, Massachusetts, Ohio, Michigan, and Wisconsin.

55 *Journal of the Assembly of the State of New York, Eightieth Session* (Albany, 1857), 1493–94; *Journal of the Senate of the State of New York, Eightieth Session* (Albany, 1857), 1029.

56 "Repeal of the Rhode Island Personal Liberty Bill," *The New York TImes*, January 26, 1861, 1.

57 Campbell Gibson and Kay Jung, "Maine—Race and Hispanic Origin: 1790–1990," in "Historical Census Statistics on Population Totals by Race, 1790 to 1990, and by Hispanic Origin, 1970 to 1990, for the United States, Regions, Divisions, and States," working paper 56 (Washington, DC: U.S. Census Bureau, September 2002), tab. 34.

EPILOGUE: LOST AND FOUND

1 One publisher's explanation for rejection was that Hurston insisted on writing Lewis's account in dialect. But according to *The New York Times*, other publishers were "unimpressed" with the work (Alexandra Alter, "A Work by Zora Neale Hurston Will Finally Be Published," *The New York TImes*, May 1, 2018).

2 W. E. B. DuBois, *Black Reconstruction in America* (1935; reprint, New York: Free Press, 1992), 347.

3 Martin Luther King, Jr., *The Radical King*, ed. Cornel West (Boston: Beacon, 2014), 116.

4 Rachel Treisman, "Nearly 100 Confederate Monuments Removed in 2020; More than 700 Remain," National Public Radio, February 23, 2021, https://www.npr.org.

5 PEN America Foundation, "Arresting Dissent: Legislative Restrictions on the Right to Protest" (May 2020), https://www.pen.org.

6 Ned Kaufman, "Heritage and the Cultural Politics of Preservation: The African

Burial Ground and the Audubon Ballroom," in *Place, Race, and Story: Essays in the Past and Future of Historic Preservation* (New York: Routledge, 2009), 296–308.

7 Amy Quinton, "Black Burial Sites Paved over in Portsmouth, N.H.," *National Public Radio*, February 22, 2006, https://www.npr.org.

8 Spirits Alive, "Stop 12: Alonzo Stinson Monument, Strangers Ground," in *Eastern Cemetery in 12 Stops*, www.spiritsalive.org.

9 Aspen Pflughoeft, "Sunken Ship of the Only Slave Trader Executed in US May Have Been Found off Brazil," *Miami Herald*, July 13, 2023; Steve Weinman, "Divers Pinpoint Wreck of Last Slave Ship in Brazil," *Divernet*, July 29, 2023, https://www.divernet.com.

10 Roger F. Duncan, *Coastal Maine: A Maritime History* (Woodstock, VT: Countryman, 2002), 286–87.

11 William Willis, *The History of Portland from 1632 to 1864: With a Notice of Previous Settlements, Colonial Grants and Changes of Government in Maine* (Portland, ME: Bailey and Noyes, 1865); William Goold, *Portland in the Past; with Historical Notes of Old Falmouth* (Portland, ME: Thurston, 1886); William Armstrong Fairburn, *Merchant Sail* (Center Lovell, ME: Fairburn Marine Educational Foundation, 1945–55); William Hutchinson Rowe, *The Maritime History of Maine: Three Centuries of Shipbuilding and Seafaring* (1948; reprint, Gardiner, ME: Harpswell, c. 1989).

Index

Note: Page numbers in *italics* indicate figure.

CAROL GARDNER is a native of Portland, Maine with more than 30 years' experience as a writer, researcher, and journalist. She earned a PhD in English from Johns Hopkins University, taught at Johns Hopkins, Wake Forest, and Florida State Universities, and has published pieces in a wide variety of books and periodicals. She is a past winner of a Maryland Individual Artists Award and is the author of a narrative history, *The Involuntary American: A Scottish Prisoner's Journey to the New World* (2019). She lives in Alna, Maine.